BOUNDARIES AND FRONTIERS

BOUNDARIES AND FRONTIERS

J.R.V. PRESCOTT

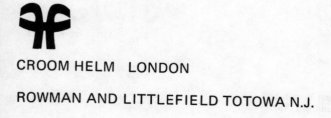

CROOM HELM   LONDON

ROWMAN AND LITTLEFIELD TOTOWA N.J.

© 1978 J.R.V. Prescott
Croom Helm Ltd, 2-10 St John's Road, London SW11

British Library Cataloguing in Publication Data

Prescott, J R V
    Boundaries and frontiers.
    1. Boundaries
    I. Title
    320.1'2   JC323
    ISBN 0-85664-417-X

First published in the United States 1978 by
Rowman and Littlefield
81 Adams Drive, Totowa, New Jersey

ISBN 0-8476-6086-9

Printed in Great Britain by
Biddles Ltd, Guildford, Surrey

CONTENTS

LIST OF FIGURES

This book is dedicated to
Nereda and Michael Hanlon and Bill Wright,
whose friendships have made Australia
a wonderful home for my wife and me.

PREFACE

While this book is based on my earlier study entitled *The Geography of Frontiers and Boundaries,* it represents a complete revision. The following changes are the most important. First, the pronounced African flavour of the previous work has been eliminated by deleting the section on African boundary problems, and by replacing many African examples in the text by examples from Asia and Southeast Asia. This means that there is now a much better continental balance throughout the book. Second, a separate chapter on maritime boundaries has been included in recognition of the growing importance of this subject. Third, the number of maps has been doubled.

Useful new material published since 1965 has been included throughout the book, and in some cases this has reduced my dependence on earlier studies. In response to Professor Rose's plea, all French and German quotations have been translated into English. I gratefully acknowledge my debt to Professor Deryck Nels of the University of the Orange Free State for providing the translations of the quotations from Ratzel's work. My thanks are also due to Mr. R.H.L. Bartlett, of the Geography Department in the University of Melbourne, for drawing the maps so quickly and so well, and to Mrs R. Davis for typing the manuscript in her usual, efficient manner.

J.R.V. Prescott

1 CONCEPTS AND TERMINOLOGY

> The striking feature of the concept of the boundary is its universal acceptance. It is liable to meet with the most diverse interpretations by groups ranging from the man in the street or the peasant to the politician and the scholar. (Lapradelle, 1928, p.9)
>
> The study of boundaries is dangerous for the scholar, because it is thoroughly charged with political passions and entirely encumbered with after-thoughts. The people are too interested in the issues when they speak of boundaries to speak with detachment: the failing is permanent! (Siegfried, in Ancel, 1938, p.vii)

It is impossible to study frontiers and boundaries without being continually aware of the points made by these distinguished authors. First, there is the challenge of studying a subject which has general appeal, and which is of great importance in the fields of political geography and international relations. Second, there is the need to clear the mind of subjective views which will influence the selection of facts and the presentation of cases. The danger of subjectivity is greater in political geography than in any other branch of the subject. Failure to maintain objectivity would be academically embarrassing to a geomorphologist or an historical geographer, but their subjects do not carry the same temptations to be subjective as those considered by political geographers. Questions dealing with raised beaches or the spread of technical innovations do not usually generate strong feelings comparable with those which may be aroused by an examination of a territorial dispute between Israel and Jordan. The present century has seen how subjective studies in political geography can be perverted to serve political arguments. Every effort has been made to preserve the present analysis from prejudice, and the author is grateful that it is written at a time when the passions generated by the Second World War have disappeared and when there is no threatening shadow of war falling across Australia. This advantage was denied to authors such as Holdich, Haushofer and Ancel.

A comprehensive review of the literature in the field of frontier and boundary studies is not possible in this chapter; instead it has been decided to review the works of nine authors, who have written generally on the subject and who span the period 1897-1945. Their works have made the major contribution in helping to fashion the foundations on which subsequent scholars have built. This historical review will be followed by a summary of the main concepts agreed by the authors, an outline of the terminology used in this book, and an indication of the general plan of the remaining chapters.

Ratzel, who was Professor of Geography at Leipzig from 1886 to his death in 1904, expounded a concept of frontiers and boundaries which followed logically from his view of the state as a living organism. The boundary was the skin of the living state and like the epidermis of animals and plants it provided defence and allowed exchanges to occur. This fundamental belief provided the point from which Ratzel sought to define the character of boundaries and the way in which they altered. His main points can be illustrated by translated quotations and brief commentaries.

> The border fringe is the reality and the border line the abstraction thereof. (Ratzel, 1897, p.538)

Ratzel's border fringe, which can be abbreviated to border, consisted of three zones, two of which were the periphery of adjoining states, while the third was a central zone where there was a mingling of the characteristics and authority of the two states. In this view Ratzel was plainly influenced by the nature of divisions in the physical world, such as those which separate land and sea and different plant communities. This was a concept which was accepted and developed by Lapradelle when he considered boundaries in relation to international law. Ratzel described various conditions of the border. He began by considering a state flanked by an unlimited empty space, and showed how the periphery of the state would be distinguishable from the core, where integration was complete. The second stage would see the emergence of another state, which limited the empty space and effectively converted it into a no-man's-land. The third stage witnessed the invasion and incorporation of this no-man's-land by both states to provide the zone of mixing between the two peripheries of the states, and completing Ratzel's concept of the tripartite border. Eventually a precise boundary might be drawn within this central zone, but Ratzel continually insisted that it was unrealistic to attempt to dissect the boundary from the border for individual study. He repeatedly stressed that the fringes of the state were an integral part of the whole and that it was unrealistic to talk of the greater importance of the centre (Ratzel, 1897, pp.605-6 and p.614 ff). This view underlay the second point which was that borders were a factor influencing state power, and at the same time a measure of state power.

> Political balance [between countries] is to a large extent dependent on the [characteristics of] borders between them. (Ratzel, 1897, p.584)
> We have seen how the growth and decline of a region not only find expression in the areal form and protective measures of the border but also in a way prepare and foreshadow themselves therein. (Ratzel, 1897, p.605)

This view that the border was the area within which growth and decline of the state were organised and evidenced was responsible for the emphasis given to territorial adjustment by the geopoliticians thirty years later, and was the precise view attacked consistently, if unsuccessfully, by Ancel. For Ratzel the strongest states showed close ties between the border and state core. Any tendency for the connections to be weakened would weaken the state and result in the loss of the border through its assertion of independence or its incorporation within a neighbouring state. Ratzel regarded borders as dynamic features; when they were fixed they marked the temporary halting of political expansion. This view had been elaborated in one of his earlier studies when he wrote of each state having an idea of the possible limits of its territorial dominion, which he called space conception. He believed that the decay of every state was the result of a declining space conception (Ratzel, 1882, part 1, pp.154-5). His third main point was related to this dynamic quality of borders.

> The law of the evolution of boundaries can be defined as a striving towards simplification and in this simplification is contained a shortening of borders. (Ratzel, 1897, p.555)
> In accordance with the general law of growth of historical spatial phenomena the borders of the larger areas embrace the borders of the smaller one. (Ratzel, 1897, p.557)

Ratzel was describing processes by which Germany had evolved from a large number of small marches, kingdoms and principalities, and by which colonial empires were established in Asia and Africa. He was also concerned with the practical requirements of military strategy and he identified the importance of strong defensive borders such as the transmountain slopes and the further banks of rivers. This concern with strong borders was later echoed by Lord Curzon (1907) and Holdich (1916), but Ratzel's advocacy of borders founded on physical features was not unqualified. He pointed out that not all natural limits made satisfactory borders, and he indicated clearly that the quality of population, the available resources, and the prevailing political situation were also factors worthy of careful consideration (Ratzel, 1897, pp.585-6). Ratzel was convinced that the border would undergo changes as the relationships between states altered, and also pointed out that the functions applied along borders would alter as federal states were formed, using the experience of Germany as an example. The obvious corollary was also noted that if borders were reduced in political status, they might continue to mark variations in the landscape which their existence had previously fostered. These were the relict boundaries which Hartshorne identified in 1936.

While Ratzel did not press his organic concept of the state to the absolute limit, the imperfections of his ideas have been exposed. He has been criticised for providing the concepts which assisted in the development of theories of *Geopolitik,* and because he was too deterministic in according the major role to factors of physical geography. These criticisms are less applicable to his ideas about borders than to his overall theories of states and their growth. When his work became better known in the 1920s the subject would have advanced more quickly if writers had attempted to build on those sound parts of his structure instead of concentrating on those which were transparently faulty. The continued criticism of the concept of natural and artificial boundaries was not justified in view of Ratzel's qualifications about the merits of natural borders when the quality of population and the nature of political circumstances supported alternative zones.

Lord Curzon of Kedleston (1907) brought his experience as Under-Secretary in the Indian and Foreign Offices, and as Governor-General of India, to bear in preparing the Romanes lecture. His interest in boundaries lay in their importance in international relations, and his lecture was delivered close to the end of one of the most intensive periods of boundary construction the countries of Europe had ever known. He was aware, as Mackinder had been three years earlier, that the Columban era, characterised by discovery, annexation, and friction between colonising powers in South America, Asia and Africa, was ended; Curzon expected that the subsequent period would be calmer in terms of international relations, with territorial disputes being settled by international law rather than military forays. The main part of his lecture examined the strength and weakness of the two main types of boundaries — natural and artificial. By these terms Curzon referred to boundaries which were dependent upon, or independent of, physical features of the earth's surface. He considered this classification to enjoy general recognition and possess the most scientific character. These were terms which were used by Holdich but which other writers attacked on the logical ground that all boundaries were artificial because men had to choose a single line, which never corresponded with all the divisions between the patterns of physical and cultural features existing in the borderland. These critics also objected to the implications that natural boundaries were intrinsically more appropriate than boundaries unrelated to the physical landscape. Curzon considered that boundaries located within mountain ranges and deserts were superior to other kinds because they offered better opportunities for defence. None of Lord Curzon's critics seems to have given him credit for distinguishing between two kinds of natural boundaries. The first class was related to some physical feature, and was clearly preferred to the second type:

a class of so-called Natural Frontiers . . . namely those which are claimed by nations as natural on grounds of ambition, or expediency, or more often sentiment. The attempt to realise Frontiers of this type has been responsible for many of the wars, and some of the most tragical vicissitudes in history. (Curzon, 1907, p.54)

This shows that he knew exactly what he meant and that there was no confusion in his mind.

One of the least satisfactory features of his essay was the use of 'frontier' and 'boundary' as interchangeable terms, but since Boggs in 1940 followed the same course although he noted the real difference, one cannot criticise Curzon too much. His essay contained several points which were further developed by later writers. Having carefully followed McMahon in distinguishing between the delimitation and demarcation of boundaries, he put forward three ideas which gained acceptance. First, artificial boundaries were classified into three groups: astronomical, mathematical and referential. The astronomic boundaries followed a parallel of latitude or meridian; the mathematical boundaries connected two specified points; and the referential boundaries were defined with regard to some point or points and included arcs of circles and straight lines. The classification was later used by Fawcett and Lapradelle. Second, Curzon briefly mentioned the idea of distinguishing between frontiers of separation and contact, which was later developed by Fawcett and East. Lastly, in his conclusion, Curzon noted that it was important to study the effects of boundaries upon fortifications, which are aspects of border landscapes, and to revalue continually the suitability of boundaries in the light of technical advances, especially relating to warfare. This was an early hint for geographers to examine the effect of boundaries on landscapes, which was not accepted for a long time.

Curzon gave considerable emphasis to the importance of boundaries in the conduct of foreign affairs. Indeed his most famous statement dealt with this subject: 'Frontiers are indeed the razor's edge on which hang suspended the modern issues of war and peace, the life and death to nations' (Curzon, 1907, p.7). Border conflicts were certain to be in the mind of a Viceroy of India at the beginning of this century, but in even modern times boundary disputes have flared into serious conflict between India and Pakistan, India and China, China and the Soviet Union and Ethiopia and Somalia.

Colonel Sir T.H. Holdich based his study of boundaries in 1916 on his practical experience with many boundary commissions. He deplored the lack of experience of some former authors and singled out Lyde for particularly unfavourable comment. Lyde (1915) had suggested, in a book subtitled *An Aspiration for Europe,* that boundaries should be drawn to give states maximum ethnic homogeneity, through areas where populations would meet and, hopefully, mingle. Holdich criticised these views; his experience had taught him that boundaries should be strong:

> Boundaries must be barriers – if not geographical and natural they must be artificial and strong as military device can make them. (Holdich, 1916, p.46)

He criticised those states in central Europe which were seeking extended ethnographic boundaries rather than selecting strong strategic boundaries, which would leave some minorities outside, but which would offer greater security to the people within the state. Holdich followed Curzon in using the terms 'boundary' and 'frontier' as synonyms, but he did draw attention to the difference between them. He referred to natural frontiers and artificial boundaries, thereby indicating an awareness of the difference which subsequent critics have not always granted. The advantages and disadvantages of these two main categories of divides were examined in terms of defence and the ease of demarcation. This last aspect was important for Holdich and it is characteristic of the man that he was concerned with practical administrative details: 'the escort difficulty is perhaps the most import-ant consideration of any in the arrangements for the successful conduct of the working party' (Holdich, 1916, p.213).

Holdich wrote his book at a time when the military techniques being displayed in Europe called for strong defensive positions regularly buttressed with fortresses. He believed this would remain the general pattern and was thus encouraged in his advocacy of strong boundaries. He had found his perfect boundary in India:

> For at least 1,500 miles does that huge unbroken wall of peak and snowfield shut off India from Tibet or China...this is indeed our ideal of a typical barrier wall, a barrier such as no device of man, no devilish ingenuity of invention, can assail with any hope of successful issue. (Holdich, 1916, p.124)

The successful penetration of the mountains by China in 1962, at the expense of India, is a clear lesson about the dangers of making determi-nist statements. Holdich's predilection for strong defensive boundaries had led him into error in 1896, when he was the British representative on a commission defining the boundary between what were then Persia and British India, immediately south of the tri-junction with Afghani-stan. On the basis of maps in which he had complete confidence Holdich managed to win approval for a line which he described as 'a strongly-marked, and almost impassable natural frontier' (Prescott, 1975, p.216). He then gilded the lily by asserting that 'No more perfect boundary than that afforded by mountains and river combined could be devised' (Prescott, 1975, p.215). Unfortunately the boundary definition contained two serious ambiguities, and the line created three strategic weaknesses which were criticised by McMahon in 1905.

Holdich provided a rich store of anecdotes and boundary case histories, which serve to underline that boundary-making is a practical art. His examples provide the raw material for academic studies, but they also remind the student that the generalisations should not be carried too far. This point was made forcibly and effectively by Jones nearly thirty years later.

Fawcett (1918) was primarily concerned with the geographical facts of frontiers and draws a clear distinction between their zonal character-istics and the linear nature of boundaries. There is an excellent chapter on the nature of frontiers at the physical, cultural and political levels. He concludes that frontiers are distinct regions of transition; while it is admitted that all regions are transitional, it is only when the transitional nature is the dominant characteristic that the region is a true frontier. Fawcett believed that the functions of frontiers were to protect the state and allow the application of restrictions to safeguard security, trade and health, while at the same time allowing approved intercourse between the populations of adjacent countries. He therefore distinguished between frontiers of separation and frontiers of contact, and he considered that generally 'natural barrier frontiers' developed within frontiers of separation while 'artificial boundaries' developed in frontiers of contact. This repeats Holdich's use of these terms, but the generalisation does not apply uniformly because frontiers of separation need not be related to features of the physical landscape; they could be produced in undifferentiated landscapes by the policies of neighbouring states. In classifying artificial boundaries Fawcett used the threefold system proposed by Curzon.

Fawcett concluded by identifying three trends observable at that time. First, he noted a growing precision of boundary definition and demarcation. Second, he identified an increasing coincidence between political boundaries and linguistic limits. This development reflected the attempts being made in Europe to draw boundaries which eliminated minority problems. Third, Fawcett believed there was a distinct tendency to place boundaries within frontiers of separation. Holdich had already showed that the second and third trends were contradictory in Europe, as the Versailles peace arrangements were to prove. In some cases the location of a boundary within a frontier of separation produced minorities as in the cases of Austria and Italy, and Czechoslovakia and Germany. In other cases the selected ethnographic boundary was unrelated to any physical features in the landscape.

Lapradelle was a lawyer and his book published in 1928 dealt with borderlands and international law. This is one of the few studies which does not bear the impress of the period in which it was written. On the other hand the profession of its author is clearly represented in the precise language used, the careful documentation of examples and the simple plan employed.

Boundaries attract the interest of international lawyers because they mark the position where states meet, and where international rights are determined and obligations assumed. While the boundary is a legal reality, Lapradelle agrees with Ratzel that the boundary cannot be considered out of the context of the borderland, and to allow this he distinguishes clearly between frontiers and boundaries. He makes the interesting observation that frontiers exist before and after boundary delimitation as zones having special political, legal and economic regulations. He agrees with Fawcett that the frontier is *un milieu de transformation* — an environment of change — and goes on to suggest a triple division of frontiers based on Ratzel's original concept. Both authors believed that the zone of fusion or mingling in the frontier was bounded on both sides by the extreme peripheral zones of the neighbouring states. The central region is styled *territoire limitrophe* by Lapradelle, and is the area where international law may apply. This is a difficult phrase to translate because *limitrophe* is a technical term for land set aside to support troops in the border; two possible translations are 'neighbouring territory' and 'adjacent territory'. The political flanking areas are called *frontières* and are subject to the internal laws of the states concerned. The total area of these three zones is called *le voisinage* — borderland. Accordingly Lapradelle deals first with the delimitation of boundaries and secondly with the legal organisation of *le voisinage*.

Three stages in the evolution of a boundary are considered: preparation, decision and execution:

> The processes of preparation precede true delimitation. The problem of the boundary's location is debated first at the political level then on the technical level. The question is, in general, of determining, without complete territorial debate, the principal alignment which the boundary will follow ... The decision involves the description of the boundary or delimitation ... The execution consists of marking on the ground the boundary which has been described and adopted, an operation which carries the name demarcation. (Lapradelle, 1928, p.73)

This distinction of the stages of boundary evolution is one which geographers have generally adopted (Jones, 1945). Boundaries were classified by Lapradelle into two groups based on their method of definition. Boundaries which were described by reference to some feature of the physical landscape were called derived artificial limits, mathematical boundaries were named true artificial limits. This latter category was divided according to Curzon's system of astronomic, geometric and referential boundaries. It is strange that boundaries related to cultural features were not considered. It may be that the lawyer was concerned with the terms used in boundary treaties, but many boundaries have been based on ethnic features, even though the definitions might make no reference to them. Certainly any compre-

hensive classification of boundary definition would have to include this
third category as Boggs (1940) showed.

The remainder of the book is concerned with reviewing the legal
aspects of the organisation of the threefold border area, and with
showing how the interests of its citizens in respect of industry and
pastoral farming are protected, and how the states collaborate in
matters of trade, health and police regulations.

In the conclusion the zonal character of the border is emphasised,
and a call is made for an objective study of the legal realities of borders,
rather than the subjective study which believes that the entire state area
is subject to the uniform application of internal laws.

There is no need to consider in detail Haushofer's boundary
concepts outlined in 1927. This retired major-general and honorary
professor of geography in the University of Munich set himself the task
of re-educating the German public and Germany's leaders in matters of
political geography during the period following the First World War. He
accepted Ratzel's view that boundaries were a measure of the state's
power, and considered that it was the duty of the government to
establish the strongest possible boundaries surrounding an ethnically
homogeneous population. The very wide definition of the area
comprising German *Kultur* provided a programme for considerable
German expansion, and it is interesting to recall that Haushofer
proposed a military boundary beyond the cultural limits so that the
homeland could not be bombarded directly by enemy artillery. Like
other students of boundaries, Haushofer attempted their classification,
this time on a basis of state power which produced boundaries classified
under the headings of attack, defence, growth and decay. Haushofer
had little influence upon other workers in different countries, although
he did provoke Ancel, the French political geographer, to publish his
views of boundaries in 1936 and 1938. During the inter-war period
Haushofer had a number of disciples, but the real tragedy of his work
was that it brought political geography into disrepute in Germany, and
discouraged subsequent generations from being deeply committed to its
study. Fortunately, the distinguished work of scholars such as Albrecht
(1974) suggests that this deleterious effect is now passed.

Ancel (1938) wrote his book as an answer to Haushofer's earlier
study, when the immediate troubled future for Europe could be plainly
seen. The book was an amplification of a short study produced in 1936.
He criticised the German view that the boundary determined the
location and territory of the state, which in turn determined the state's
strength. Instead Ancel regarded the boundary as the result of state

power generated by a particular political-social group, rather than its cause. There seems to be little difference between these two views which postulate a close interrelationship between boundaries and a state's strength.

Ancel closely followed the views of Febvre in forming his concept of boundary studies:

> The bound frame or margin, matters little. The inside is the important part, and must receive the chief consideration. (Febvre, 1932, p.309)
> . . . it is not the fame which is important but what is framed. (Ancel, 1938, p.3).

For Ancel the boundary reflects the relationships between neighbouring groups and should be studied to this end rather than as a single element of the landscape. This continues the accepted idea that the boundary is a line within a borderland, and the most useful geographical research results from their joint study. On the other hand, Ancel slightly overstates the case, for there is little chance that research into borderlands will be fruitful until a systematic study of the characteristics of boundaries has been made. This however may well be a point which was assumed by the classical French school of regional geographers.

Ancel's book is organised into three parts and in each case he attempts to consider the boundaries of types of states rather than types of boundaries. In the first part amorphous states are considered under three headings – molecular societies, nomadic states and maritime empires. In dealing with the first two types it seems that Ancel is too concerned with describing the economy and way of life of the citizens rather than the limits of the socio-political group. Even groups in the Congo often clearly distinguished the sovereign limits of the tribe, and many other tribes in Africa marked their limits with fences and ditches and exercised partial control over peripheral zones beyond these defensive lines. Nor is it true to generalise that nomadic tribes do not have boundaries (Ancel, 1938, p.88). It would be more true to say that sovereignty is vested in the nomads over territory which their herds require and which their military strength can control. These limits will fluctuate, but at any particular time they would be understood by neighbouring tribes. The treatment of maritime empires presents some interesting points about their organisation and political geography but fails to demonstrate that the boundaries which limit their overseas possessions form a special class.

In the second and third parts Ancel considers flexible boundaries and mobile boundaries. The concepts of Ratzel are attacked in introducing the consideration of flexible boundaries. Ratzel believed that the boundary was the peripheral organ of the state and that its fluctuations governed the strength or weakness of the state. Ancel maintained that the boundary results from pressures exerted from both sides and considers the line to be an equilibrium between two forces. It is difficult to see the difference between the two views. Surely if Ratzel's statement is applied to neighbouring states it follows that the boundary is the result of forces from each side. After examining the characteristics of medieval and modern boundaries, the latter being divided into physical and human types, Ancel proposes his concept of boundaries as lines of power equilibrium in greater detail. He suggests that boundaries may be likened to political isobars. This point again suggests that Ancel was much closer to the German position than he realised.

Gottman (1952, pp.130-2) and Fischer (1957, p.136) have attacked the climatological metaphor on grounds of implication and accuracy. Isobars do not represent equalisations of two forces; they are lines of equal pressure drawn so that the air pressure is higher on one side and lower on the other. Ancel probably had in mind a line which was maintained in position by equal and opposite forces. This is similar to Spykman's concept (1938), which regarded boundaries as lines where state pressures were neutralised. Gottman also criticised the analogy because of the importance of physical factors at any time in determining the position of isobars. The criticism was softened by reference to other books by Ancel which showed a complete awareness of the importance of human factors. It must also be noted that political boundaries do not have the fluidity of physical frontiers and it is dangerous to postulate that they do. Pressure against a boundary may result in a change in state functions applied at the boundary rather than any change in its location. For example, in 1967 Somali pressure against the Ethiopian boundary was rewarded by Ethiopian concessions regarding the treatment of Somali nationals living in the Ethiopian borderland.

In the final section Ancel examines the manner in which boundaries develop, the means by which they are maintained, and the factors which influence their advance or retreat; again he relates his examples to types of states rather than to types of boundaries. Four definite conclusions follow from Ancel's work. He rejected the idea of natural boundaries based on physical features and historical precedent, and attacked the linear concept of boundaries. He then maintained that boundaries were lines of equilibrium owing their position at any time to the pressures exerted from either side, and again appealed for consideration of boundaries as reflecting the relationship of neighbouring states: 'There are no problems of boundaries. There are only problems of Nations' (Ancel, 1938, p.196).

Ancel's book has received little attention from subsequent workers and this may be due to the fact that he wrote as a Frenchman answering German territorial arguments which were threatening France as well as other European states. It is stated in his introduction that there is no intention of entering into debate with the geopoliticians, but the results might have been more effective, and lasting, if Ancel, with his known ability, had dissected their views as a geographer.

Boggs (1940) wrote his book at a time when the Second World War was imminent and it may well be that the boundary problems associated with the origin of the war and its settlement prompted the book. Boggs began by examining the changing role of boundaries, showing how the self-imposed limits to which Lapradelle had referred had given way to boundary negotiations between adjacent states. The various functions applied at boundaries were listed, and it was noted that they were mainly negative rather than positive. He also measured the international boundaries within each continent and calculated the ratios between total boundary length and total area. He regarded this as a crude index of the interruptive quality of boundaries, which allowed a comparison between continents. For example, Europe excluding the Soviet Union had an index of 7.3 miles of boundary for every 1,000 square miles, while the figure for North America was 1.3. Boggs continued this argument by accepting the concept that pressure against boundaries increases with the number of people living in the country. Therefore he multiplied the first index by the continental population density, and the figures for Europe and North America then became 1,400 and 27. While Boggs admitted that this was a coarse measurement he still did a disservice to political geography by suggesting that generalisations of this kind had any value. This point was strongly criticised by Hinks (1940), who pointed out that the pressure against a boundary was often exerted against specific points rather than uniformly. Whittlesey may also have argued from the premises which he advanced in 1944, that the total continental areas are not effectively subject to national authority. For example, if Boggs made the calculation for Angola in 1977 he would have to discount those areas which were beyond the control of the Angolan government and under the authority of the various rebel movements.

Fortunately, few have tried to develop Boggs' ideas of continental comparisons. Hamdan (1963) quoted Boggs' calculations in reviewing the political map of Africa, without making fresh calculations following the many changes in the status of African boundaries. The figures do not seem to assist Hamdan's argument and it is to be hoped that continental generalisations are avoided in the future. Dorion (1963) attempted to devise formulae to measure the sinuosity of a boundary, but their value is questionable in view of the fact that there are no clear rules about the selection of points between which measurements must be made.

The remainder of Boggs' book is much more satisfactory. After a chapter dealing with the classification and terminology of boundaries he examines the boundary problems associated with each continent. He also has a chapter devoted exclusively to boundaries through rivers, lakes and seas; this is a subject to which Boggs made an original and important contribution (Boggs, 1930, 1937, 1961).

There is one conceptual defect which should be mentioned, and it is revealed in the following quotation: 'one of the principal reasons for making a study of boundaries is the desire to determine what kinds of boundaries have proven to be "good" and which have been found to be "bad" ' (Boggs, 1940, p.21). It is quite unrealistic to generalise about kinds of boundaries being good or bad. Presumably he considered a boundary to be good if it was not the subject of a dispute and bad if it caused friction between the neighbouring states. This view neglects the fact which had been clearly established by Ratzel, Lapradelle and Ancel, that the boundary is the meeting place of autonomous states and that their policies, attitudes and actions determine the extent to which the borderland is peaceful or troubled. While it can be accepted that some physical features, such as rivers with wide meanders, flowing through levees, can create problems if they are selected to define boundaries, the statement by Ancel seems correct: 'There are no "good" or "bad" boundaries; it all depends on circumstances. The boundary of the Pyrenees is today a quiet boundary. . . Formerly it was was a tense boundary.' (Ancel, 1936, p.210).

Bowman's comment in the Foreword that the book by Boggs was a basic text was really only applicable until 1945 when Jones' study filled this role. Boggs' study was useful because it described the general features of the world's principal boundary problems at a time when the English-speaking world needed such a text, but the book did little to advance the study of boundaries by geographers. It fell short of the standards set by Lapradelle in his book and by Hartshorne in his papers on the boundaries of Upper Silesia and boundary terminology. Boggs' book today is most frequently quoted for his exhaustive listing of state functions applied at the boundary, and the means by which boundaries may be defined. It is proper to record that Boggs was once The Geographer of the American State Department. The men filling this office have made important contributions to political geography. Hodgson, the present incumbent, has produced many valuable studies on boundaries and questions related to the law of the sea.

In 1945 Jones published a very important book which dealt with the techniques of boundary making. This book undoubtedly owed its inspiration to the knowledge that after the Second World War many new boundaries would be drawn, but unlike many others which were products of their time, this book has the quality of being timeless in its approach. The comprehensive treatment of the subject will be continuously relevant to all who are connected with boundary construction. The work is carefully documented, and in the two main sections dealing with delimitation and demarcation there are many examples and a clear statement on the techniques for collecting material on which any decisions should be based. It is not only statesmen, treaty editors and boundary commissioners who profit from Jones' book, for the opening sections contain much of interest to the geographer. Perhaps the single most important point made by Jones is that boundaries are unique, that generalisations about them are not very valuable, and that is is not very profitable continually to search for means of classifying them:

> Each boundary is almost unique and therefore many generalisations are of doubtful validity. (Jones, 1945, p.vi).
> It is possible therefore to classify boundaries and their functions in many ways. All share the artificiality of classification. The most real distinction between boundaries is between internal and international. The presence or absence of over-riding sovereignty is the basis. (p.7)
> The process of boundary-making is smoothed by considering each boundary as a special case with individuality more pronounced than resemblance to a theoretical type. (p.11)

This is the most important point which had not been made before, and which was timely, for many studies had aimed at general classifications of boundaries, and had derived from such classifications generalisations about the behaviour of states, and the significance and suitability of boundaries which only applied in a small fraction of cases. It is regrettable that some geographers have persisted in their efforts to classify international boundaries instead of making detailed studies of particular cases. While boundaries are unique they can all be studied by the techniques of field and library investigation which Jones noted.

The stages of boundary evolution examined by Jones were similar to those outlined by Lapradelle. They relate to the allocation of political territory, the delimitation of a specific boundary site, and the demarcation of the boundary on the ground. Jones added a fourth stage which involved the administration of the boundary and the maintenance of the boundary monuments and vistas.

This review suggests four conclusions. First, boundaries are of interest to workers in many fields: lawyers, soldiers and politicians have a practical interest in boundaries. For the lawyer they mark the area of contact between separate sovereignties and judicial systems. McEwen (1971) is one lawyer who has prepared a very useful study of boundary evolution; the area he considers is East Africa. To the soldier they represent the first area which must be defended and the position from which attacks can be launched. To the politician boundaries mark the limits of administrations which should be maintained or extended. The sensitivity of citizens to border questions makes them a vital subject to politicians because they can be used to generate national loyalty, as German, Indonesian and Chinese politicians have all discovered. |The interest of geographers, historians, and political scientists is academic rather than practical although some of their work has been of value to lawyers and administrators. Geographers study boundaries because they are elements of the cultural landscape, and because they represent the limits of political sovereignty which is an important areal quality varying over the earth's surface. Furthermore, geographical factors often play a part in influencing the position and form of boundaries, and the boundaries, once established, may exert some influence upon the landscape which they traverse. Historians study boundaries because they result from different policies in different periods and because they are often the cause of international disputes which have far-reaching effects on political trends. Lamb (1966) produced a masterly study of the McMahon Line which stands as a model for historical boundary studies. The political scientist is interested in boundaries as the legal definition of the state, and in the criteria by which they are established. While political scientists have made much less contribution to boundary studies than scholars from geography and history, those, such as Touval (1972) and Widstrand (1969), who write on this aspect find it a fruitful field of contemporary analysis.

Second, while most of the studies considered carry the imprint of the author's special interest, which is to be expected, many also bear the clear flavour of the period in which the book was written. Holdich's preoccupation with strong defensive boundaries is surely explained by the 1914-18 European war as well as by his extensive imperial experience in India. In similar fashion Haushofer's work owed much to the depressed international position of Germany, and Ancel's answer was partly prompted by the increasing threat to French territory. This fact, together with the divergent interests of the authors, has prevented the systematic advance of the subject and the construction of accepted concepts and a uniform terminology. Unfortunately, progress in more recent times has been occasionally hindered by scholars writing in a partisan style on behalf of a country involved in a major boundary dispute.

Third, one of the concepts which has been generally accepted is that the boundary must be considered in its territorial context. This view started with Ratzel, who saw the boundary as an abstraction and the boundary-zone as the reality, and has been continued. This is in accordance with geographical tradition which views other linear features in connection with surrounding areas. For example, the economic geographer is interested in the traffic generated in the area served by a railway, while the geomorphologist studies rivers in relation to the run-off provided by the catchment and to the structure of the basin drained by the river. Ancel tried to go further by advocating the study of boundaries only to illustrate the relationships of separated states. This is to emphasise a single aspect of boundary analysis and to neglect the boundary as a landscape element.

Fourth, one important concept which is slowly gaining acceptance concerns the originality of international boundaries. Jones was the first writer to state clearly that attempts to generalise about boundaries are fraught with the danger of forming hypothetical concepts which do not accord with any real case. This is a concept which runs counter to the efforts of those contemporary geographers, who, by means of mathematical analysis and other techniques, are searching for useful generalisations. However, there is plenty of scope for such endeavour in the analysis of internal boundaries within a single state. Jones warned against expending too much energy in the attempt to classify boundaries unless the purpose for making the classification is carefully defined.

From this selective review of the literature of frontier and boundary studies the following statement of geographical interest in the matter might be declared. Boundaries and frontiers are elements of the landscape which mark either the legal or actual limits of the state's political sovereignty, which is one quality of areal differentiation. They are therefore objects of interest to both political and regional geographers studying areas within which they occur. There are two aspects of frontier and boundary studies which are of interest to geographers, whether engaged in topical or regional studies. First, the position and character of any boundary or frontier are the result of the interaction of many factors, some of which are geographical, and best studied by geographers. Second, once any frontier or boundary is established it is capable of influencing the landscape of which it is a part and the developments, regulations and policies of the separated states. This aspect is also a legitimate field of geographic enquiry.

There are two qualifications to this view. First, the geographer must be aware that workers from other fields will also be exploring and assessing the non-geographical factors involved in frontier and boundary evolution, and the impact of these features on facets of human life and state organisation which are not part of geography. For example, the geographer looks at the Sino-Indian dispute with a view to isolating the geographic factors of topography, colonisation and settlement which have contributed to its development. The significance of the boundary dispute in respect of the construction of roads and defence works is also of interest, together with the extent to which economic projects in India were adversely affected by the need to transfer development funds to defence purposes. On the other hand historians are likely to trace the boundary policies of the British Raj, the various Chinese administrations and the Indian government, together with the significance of the contribution of persons such as Sir Henry McMahon, the Dalai Llama, Mr Nehru and Mr Chou En-Lai. The political scientists for their part are interested in the interaction of two distinct forms of government, the repercussions of the struggle on the domestic politics of both countries, and the influence of the dispute on international relations in the region and at the United Nations. Therefore the geographer must always be conscious that this is a shared field, and that geographical analysis will rarely provide the complete answer.

The second point is a restatement of Jones' view on the uniqueness of international boundaries and its extension to cover frontiers. Geographers have spent too much time in devising classifications and generalisations about boundaries and frontiers which have led to little or no progress. It would seem more profitable for the geographer to make specific studies and to concentrate on the generalisation of a common body of techniques and concepts for treating such studies. In this of course the geographer must continually be aware of what is being done by other workers in the field, and what is expected of geographers by these other scholars. Lawyers, historians and political scientists have a right to expect that political geographers will have identified the changing locations of a boundary as it passes through the various stages of evolution, and that the political geographer will have described the division of states in administrative units and commented on the principles on which that division is based. This descriptive work has been neglected by geographers, and it has been left to The Geographer of the US State Department to discharge this obligation in a most creditable fashion.

The remainder of this book is organised in the following way. The second chapter considers frontiers and the remaining chapters deal with boundaries. The specific aspects of boundaries which are considered are the evolution of international boundaries on land and the disputes associated with them; maritime boundaries; internal boundaries of states; and the effect of boundaries on the landscape. The separate treatment of internal boundaries is in response to Jones' view that the presence or absence of overriding sovereignty is the crucial basis for classifying boundaries.

An attempt has been made to use correctly such words as have a specific connotation in respect of frontiers and boundaries. A brief indication of these terms follows.

Boundary refers to a line, while *frontier* refers to a zone. The terms *allocation, delimitation* and *demarcation* are used in the sense outlined by Jones (1949). Allocation means the initial political division of territory between two states. Delimitation means the selection of a boundary site and its definition. Demarcation refers to the construction of the boundary in the landscape. Borderland refers to the transition zone within which the boundary lies; it corresponds to Lapradelle's *voisinage*. It has not been found necessary for geographical purposes to distinguish *le territoire limitrophe* from the borderland. Lastly there are the sequential terms proposed forty years ago by Hartshorne (1936). These terms describe the relationship between the boundary and the landscape through which it was drawn. An *antecedent* boundary was drawn before the development of most of the features of the cultural landscape, and if a boundary was drawn through an uninhabited area it was called a *pioneer* boundary. *Subsequent* boundaries were drawn after the development of the cultural landscape. If the boundary coincided with some physical or cultural divide it was described as *consequent*. If however the boundary was not drawn within such a feature it was described as *superimposed*, for which the synonym *discordant* was occasionally used. A *relict* boundary is one which has been abandoned, but is still marked by differences in the landscape which developed during its lifetime.

References

Albrecht, V., 1974, *Der Einfluss der deutsch-französischen Grenze auf die Gestaltung der Kulturlandschaft im Südlichen Oberrheingebiet*, Freiburg

Ancel, J., 1936, 'Les frontières: étude de géographie politique', *Recueil des Cours*, 55, pp.207-97

Ancel, J., 1938, *Les frontières*, Paris

Boggs, S.W., 1930, 'Delimitation of the Territorial Sea', *American J. of International Law*, 24, p.541-55

―――― 1937, 'Problems of Water Boundary Definition: Median Lines and International Boundaries Through Territorial Waters', *Geogr. Rev.*, 27, pp.445-56

―――― 1940, *International Boundaries: a Study of Boundary Functions and Problems*, New York

―――― 1961, 'Delimitation of Seaward Areas Under National Jurisdiction, *American J. of International Law*, 48, pp.240-66

Curzon of Kedleston, Lord, 1907, *Frontiers*, The Romanes Lecture, Oxford

Dorion, H., 1963, *La frontière Quebec-Terreneuve*, Quebec

Fawcett, C.B., 1918, *Frontiers, a Study in Political Geography*, Oxford

Febvre, L., 1932, *A Geographical Introduction to History*, London

Fischer, E., 1957, chapters 4 and 5 in Weigert, H.W. and others, *Principles of Political Geography*, New York

Gottman, J., 1952, *La politique des états et leur géographie*, Paris

Hamdan, G., 1963, 'The Political Map of New Africa', *Geogr. Rev.*, 53, pp.418-39

Hartshorne, R., 1936, 'Suggestions on the Terminology of Political Boundaries', *Annals*, Association of American Geographers, 26, pp.56-7

Haushofer, K., 1927, *Grenzen*, Berlin

Hinks, A.R., 1940, Review, *Geogr. J.*, 96, pp.286-9

Holdich, Colonel Sir T.H., 1916, *Political Frontiers and Boundary Making*, London

Jones, S.B., 1932, 'The Forty-ninth Parallel in the Great Plains: the Historical Geography of a Boundary', *J. of Geography*, 31, pp.357-67

―――― 1945, *Boundary-making, a Handbook for Statesmen*, Washington

Lamb, A., 1966, *The McMahon Line*, 2 vols., London

Lapradelle, P. De, 1928, *La frontière: étude de droit international*, Paris

Lyde, L.W., 1915, *Some Frontiers of Tomorrow: an Aspiration for Europe*, London

McEwen, A.C., 1971, *International Boundaries of East Africa*, Oxford

Prescott, J.R.V., 1975, *Map of Mainland Asia by Treaty*, Melbourne

Ratzel, F., 1882, *Anthropogeographie*, part 1, Stuttgart

―――― 1897, *Politische Geographie*, Berlin

Spykman, J.J., 1938, 'Geography and Foreign Policy', *American Political Science Review*, 32, pp.28-50 and 213-36

Touval, S., 1972, *The Boundary Politics of Independent Africa*, Cambridge, Mass

Widstrand, C.G., 1969, *African Boundary Problems*, Uppsala

2 FRONTIERS

Political geographers use the term 'frontier' in two senses; it can either refer to the political division between two countries or the division between the settled and uninhabited parts of one country. In each sense the frontier is considered to be a zone. There is no excuse for geographers who use the terms 'boundary' and 'frontier' as synonyms although it is not difficult to find geographers making this elementary error.

The remainder of this chapter considers those aspects of frontiers which are of interest to political geographers, and it is divided into three parts. First, there is a consideration of settlement frontiers which exist within a single country. Second, political frontiers, which used to separate neighbouring countries, are examined. The third section contains an account of frontiers in the area occupied today by Nigeria.

Settlement Frontiers

It is necessary to identify two kinds of settlement frontiers. Primary settlement frontiers exist when a state is taking possession of its territory for the first time. The classical example of such a feature occurred during the westward expansion of American sovereignty through its territory in North America. Secondary settlement frontiers are found in many countries today and mark zones which separate settled and uninhabited regions of the state. The two types have different characteristics.

Primary settlement frontiers are historic features, while secondary settlement frontiers are currently found in many countries where an adverse physical environment or inadequate techniques hinder further advances of land-use and settlement. The primary settlement frontier marked the actual limit of the state's political authority, whereas the political authority of modern states extends beyond the secondary settlement frontiers, and can be exerted when necessary. Any country, such as Australia, which includes a large area of desert provides special services which can operate in those uninhabited areas. The range of potential economic activities in a primary frontier is generally greater than in the secondary frontiers. Fur-trapping, timber-felling, semi-subsistence cultivation, grazing, mining and manufacturing and service industries were all found at some point on the American frontier, or developed as it passed. On the other hand, the advance of secondary settlement frontiers is likely to be by the extension of irrigated farming, as in Mali, on the Samanko scheme near Bamako; by extensive ranching as in the Matabeleland regions of Rhodesia; and by the exploitation of new mineral and fuel deposits, as in northern Alaska.

Secondary frontiers normally reflect the limited range of economic activities by a population of low density, while on primary settlement frontiers densities may be moderate to heavy. There are exceptions to this generalisation in some secondary frontiers in Pakistan and Bangladesh. The United States Census Bureau's definition of the frontier, as areas having a population density of two to six persons per square mile, would have excluded many of the early frontiers in Georgia. The development of secondary settlement frontiers is usually carefully planned, and based on a satisfactory communications network, in contrast to the haphazard development of primary frontiers, which were also characterised by 'rudimentary socio-political relations marked by rebelliousness, lawlessness and/or absence of laws' (Kristoff, 1959). Lastly the primary settlement frontiers often advanced rapidly. In 1783, four million acres of the Cumberland Valley were sold in seven months, while in 1795, during only two months, 26,000 migrants crossed the Cumberland River in search of cheap land to the west (Billington, 1960). The advance of secondary settlement frontiers usually involved small areas and comparatively few people.

Much has been written about the primary settlement frontier, but there are only scattered references to secondary settlement frontiers. American historians are largely responsible for the thorough documentation of the American primary frontier, in their efforts to support or refute Turner's frontier hypothesis, that the 'existence of an area of free land, its continuous recession and the advance of American settlement westward explain American development' (Turner, 1953). The small number of contributions by geographers suggest that historians have preempted this field. Whittlesey (East and Moodie, 1956), writing on the expansion and consolidation of the United States, makes only passing reference to the frontier and no reference to the detailed historical studies. Despite this situation, geographers can make a useful contribution beyond the mapping of frontier phenomena, which has been done for the American and Canadian frontiers (Paullin, 1932; Adams, 1943; and Kerr, 1961).

The position of the frontier, which represents the actual zonal limits of political authority, and its width, are of prime interest to geographers. In order to determine the frontier's extent some criteria must be developed to distinguish it from non-frontier areas. A simple basis of population density is unsatisfactory, and a more satisfactory measure is likely to be found in the degree of political and economic organisation. This is a task calling for training in historical and political geography. Information about the position of the frontier at any time will give some indication of the factors which have influenced its rate of advance. Any advance of the frontier probably resulted from a combination of factors, which can be principally divided into forces of attraction based on the nature of the environment, and forces of pressure from the frontier's hinterland, often of a social, economic or political nature. The role of unusually favourable soil groups, such as are found in the Blue Grass country of Kentucky and the cotton lands of the Gulf plains, in promoting the rapid advance of the American frontier, are well known. In a similar fashion, discoveries of precious mineral deposits have caused spectacular frontier advance, as for example in the Transvaal.

Pressures within the frontier hinterland take many forms. Turner (1953) and Billington (1960) have shown how the frontiersmen were seeking to avoid high land prices, heavy taxation, and political and religious disabilities, imposed either by the first, well-established settlers or by the governments of the country of origin. Further, the experience gained on one frontier, in respect of land legislation, mining laws and Indian treaties, were applied at subsequent frontiers and often allowed speedier settlement of these problems. Periods of standstill or retreat along the frontier resulted either from the unfavourable nature of the environment or the inadequacy of techniques for utilising it, the armed resistance of indigenous groups, or the preoccupation of the government with more urgent considerations.

'In these successive frontiers we find natural boundary lines which have served to mark and affect the characteristics of the frontiers, namely: the "fall-line"; the Allegheny Mountains; the Mississippi; the Missouri where its direction approximates north-south; the line of the arid plains, approximately the ninety-ninth meridian; and the Rocky Mountains. The fall line marked the frontier of the seventeenth century; and Alleghenies that of the eighteenth; the Mississippi that of the first quarter of the nineteenth; the Missouri that of the middle of this century (omitting the Californian movement); and the belt of the Rocky Mountains and arid tract, the present frontier. Each was won by a series of Indian wars' (Turner, 1953, p.9).

The maps of Indian battles (Paullin, 1932) show that the fiercest resistance by indigenes often coincided with the most difficult terrain, which offered excellent strategic opportunities for defence. It was in the scrub country of Queensland that Aborigines offered the greatest resistance to the extension of pastoral activities. In Cameroun, during the early years of this century, the Germans faced their greatest problems in pacifying the Chamba and other pagan groups, who were located in the heavily dissected borderland with Nigeria. The stagnation of the American frontier during the twenty years before 1795 resulted from the preoccupation of the colonies with securing independence, establishing a federal constitution and defeating the Indians in the area already settled.

In some cases attempts to halt frontier advance were made by the government or by interested trading organisations. Some of the earliest coastal states in North America tried to restrict the frontier advance, in order to retain political power, and to avoid a further drain on their population. In the hinterland of New York and Pennsylvania, the Iroquois Confederation blocked for a century the route through the Catskill and Berkshire Ranges, by the Mohawk and Hudson valleys, in order that the Indians who supplied the fur trade should not be driven away (Billington, 1960).

Turner maintains that 'each frontier leaves its trace behind it, and when it becomes a settled area the region still partakes of the frontier characteristics' (Turner, 1950, p.4). This suggests a fruitful field for geographical research. Is it possible to attribute any elements of the cultural landscape to the period when the area was a primary frontier? There is probably a connexion between present property boundaries and the original policies of land allocation and appropriation. It seems unlikely that the present economy will reveal many features which can be traced to frontier times, since the earliest economic activities of hunting and grazing will survive only if the land is unsuitable for cultivation, and lacks the resources on which can be built towns with secondary and service industries. It has been noted by Clarke (1959) that when a period of standstill allowed an accumulation of population, as in Georgia and Tennessee, eventual advance was more orderly and complete. Rapid advance, without resistance, resulted in scattered and discontinuous settlement patterns. It would be interesting to know whether settlement analysis reflects this process of development.

Mitchell (1972) has published an excellent analysis of the American primary settlement frontier in the Shenandoah Valley in the eighteenth century. His analysis proceeds along three main themes. First, he considers the movement of migrants into and through the area, for such an investigation provides valuable information regarding the political organisation of the frontier and the distribution of groups with different cultural characteristics. Further, a knowledge of migration routes allows the scholar to understand how the frontier moved and developed differentially. Second, he is concerned with the developments which occurred while the frontier occupied various positions. The processes of land acquisition from the Indians in the first case, and subsequently land subdivision and redistribution by the landowners in the second case, attract Mitchell's attention. The nature of pioneer and post-pioneer economies receives detailed treatment. Third, the changing location of the frontier relative to the settled areas and the uninhabited areas is assessed at intervals throughout the frontier's history. Mitchell concluded that during the frontier phase the Shenandoah Valley was socially more complex and economically more sophisticated than is generally acknowledged. His paper forms a valuable example of useful research which geographers can undertake.

Secondary settlement frontiers are found in all countries which include areas of unfavourable environment, such as tropical or temperate desert, heavily dissected uplands, or thick tropical rain forest, and areas which require the use of advanced and often expensive techniques, if they are to be used for purposes other than mineral extraction. These are the areas which are often bypassed by the primary frontier, when the population is concerned with rapid exploitation and profit. These inferior regions will be attacked later if circumstances require it, and if new techniques or discoveries make it possible to revalue the environment. Burt has recorded the following interesting observation about the Canadian frontier in the mid-nineteenth century: 'the expansion of Canadian settlement ran up against the rocky Pre-Cambrian Shield, with the result that the Canadian frontier movement crossed the [American] border, where it became merged in the greater movement to the northern Middle Western States' (Wyman and Kroeber, 1957). Only when the availability of land in the American West was reduced did the frontier cross the boundary again, allowing the development of western Canada.

In many European states only short secondary settlement frontiers surround small sectors of unfavourable environment. In Australia on the other hand, a long secondary settlement frontier surrounds the central desert. Attempts to thrust forward secondary frontiers usually depend on some incentive, such as shortage of land, shortage of food in times of war, strategic needs, or the discovery of new mineral deposits. Shortage of land in African Reserves in southern Matabeleland led to the cultivation of areas where there is a high risk of drought or rainfall deficiency. In Java, population pressure on available land has caused the cultivation of slopes with a high erosion hazard. In many cases efforts to advance secondary settlement frontiers are guided and controlled by government, because of the large amounts of capital which may be needed, on which there is unlikely to be any rapid return.

Examples of the part played by improved techniques can be found in many countries. The waterless areas of the Kalahari sandveld in South Africa were not settled until after 1903, when the well-drill made it possible to tap underground water reserves, which could be brought to the surface by wind pumps. In Australia the development of heavy machinery and the stump-jump plough allowed more intensive use of the Mallee areas. These areas were covered by species of Eucalypt which forms a tabular mass of hard wood at, or just below, the surface. The foliage was unpalatable to stock, sheep could not be mustered because the vegetation was so dense, and watering points were scarce. In Canada, the development of new strains of wheat has allowed the use of areas with short growing seasons. The spectacular extension of Soviet agriculture in central Asia was stimulated during the 1940s by Germany's capture of areas in eastern Europe.

Nearly a century ago the threat of Russian advance into Hokkaido encouraged the Japanese government to foster the rapid colonisation of that island. The government distinguished between those immigrants who travelled independently, and those who travelled with the aid of a government subsidy. Independent farmers received implements, seed and ten yen for every quarter acre cleared. Subsidised farmers received a rice ration for three years in addition to seed and implements. Their bonus for clearing land was two yen per quarter acre. Independent artisans and merchants received a gift of 150 yen for three years, which eventually had to be repaid (Harrison, 1953). In the decade which followed 1869 nearly 65,000 Japanese migrants entered Hokkaido.

The discovery of new mineral deposits or the change in world trading conditions, which make the mining of known mineral deposits a profitable undertaking, have often caused the advance of secondary settlement frontiers into the Arctic and tropical deserts. Lawless (1974) has described the establishment of a new mining and industrial centre at Arlit in Niger. The French Atomic Energy Commission discovered a major uranium deposit 250 kilometres northwest of Agades which is the nearest town. A town capable of housing 5,000 people has been built and roads leading to the coast have been improved. Production from this site reached 1,500 tonnes in 1975, when Niger was the fifth largest producer of uranium in the world.

Political Frontiers

Geographic interest in political frontiers is mainly concerned with their physical characteristics, their position, the attitudes and policies separated by the frontier, the influence of the frontier on the subsequent development of the cultural landscape, and the way in which boundaries were drawn within the frontier.

Lord Curzon's essay contained the seeds of a classification which was brought to fruition by East. East distinguished between frontiers of contact and frontiers of separation, and observed that 'states have always sought frontiers which foster separation from, rather than assimilation with, their neighbours' (East, 1937). Some frontiers, either by the attraction of their resources, or the ease with which they can be crossed, allowed contact between separated political groups. This contact took the form of trade, the payment of tribute, migration, or conflict. On the other hand the frontier sometimes possessed physical qualities which made it unattractive to exploiters and travellers alike. However, in no case did the geography of the frontier determine the degree of intercourse between states; rather the attitudes and policies of the flanking states were decisive. When Chile achieved its independence its state limits included the Atacama Desert to the north, and the Andes Mountains to the east, both physical barriers which inhibited cultural contacts. Yet during the last century the expansionist policies of the Chilean government carried the country into war with Peru and Bolivia over the Tacna-Arica districts of the Atacama, and into a dispute with Argentina concerning the trans-piedmont slopes of the Andes, which in some cases were settled by Chilean emigrants. The successful northward advance against Peru and Bolivia, made for economic and strategic reasons, delivered to Chile the port of Arica and access to the valuable borax, copper and nitrate deposits (Dennis, 1931).

The effects of a policy of isolation are revealed by considering the case of the Kingdom of Benin west of the Niger Delta. Although the forested frontiers of this state were no more difficult to cross than similar frontiers surrounding other indigenous kingdoms, there was practically no contact between European traders and Benin, because traders were not welcome. Eventually it required an expeditionary force to conquer the country, and to establish relations between the colonial and indigenous authorities.

Political frontiers between states have been replaced by international boundaries throughout the world, therefore research into them must have a strong historical and anthropological basis. Political frontiers generally enjoyed less intensive economic development than the territories they separated. This was because the environment was unfavourable, or because the resources of the existing state area were sufficient, or because it was the policy of the state to neglect the frontier, thereby enhancing its divisive character. Deserts, mountain ranges, rivers, flood plains and woodlands have all formed frontiers at some period in history. It follows from this that frontiers were usually less densely populated than the flanking states and that the inhabitants of the frontier, if there were any, experienced a lower standard of living than the citizens of neighbouring states. Tacitus described the debased condition of the Slavic Venedi, who occupied the woody and mountainous area between the Peucini and Fenni. A more recent example was cited by Tilho (Ministère des Colonies, 1919), namely the wretched Bedde pagans, who lived in the swampy areas between the Kingdoms of Sokoto and Bornu in the western Sudan.

Where there was the threat of invasion or trespass, political frontiers were selected for their defensive advantages, and this point was thoroughly discussed by Curzon and Holdich. Curzon mentioned that deserts formed the best defensive frontiers, but it seems worth remarking that extensive deserts, such as the Sahara, were often the habitat of mobile, warlike tribes, such as the Tuareg, which plagued the surrounding semi-agricultural tribes. Davies made this precise point when he wrote of the northwest frontier of British India: 'So long as hungry tribesmen inhabit barren and almost waterless hills, which command open and fertile plains, so long will they resort to plundering incursions in order to obtain the necessaries of life' (Davies, 1932, p.179). Linear mountain ranges and rivers had the strategic advantage of allowing the defending forces to focus their strength at passes and bridges. The possession of limiting deserts, mountain ranges and major rivers is a matter of geographical good fortune, and it seems likely that many of the original frontiers consisted of woodland and marshes. The swamps and forests surrounding Westphalia played a major part in the defeat of some Roman legions. A more recent example is provided by the forested margins of Kikuyuland in East Africa. This forested zone was about two hours march in width and enabled the Kikuyu to defeat Masai invaders who seemed invincible on the grassy plains of Masailand (Hohnel, 1894, p.1).

Many states tried to mark their frontiers in some way. The famous Roman and Chinese walls are the best examples. The Great Wall of China served not only to exclude nomadic barbarians but also to restrict the number of Chinese who adopted a modified agricultural system which made them more difficult to control from the Chinese capital (Lattimore, 1940). The modern journey from Peking to the restored portion of the Great Wall passes a number of earlier, local walls which show the same disregard for steep gradients exhibited by their famous national equivalent. The walls of the Roman Empire, unlike the Great Wall of China, did not mark a major environmental divide and seemed to be built for the sole purpose of defending the Empire, by permitting some control over if not total exclusion of, the barbarians. Where clear physical features were not available, the Romans constructed walls such as the well known Hadrian's Wall, linking Solway Firth to the Tyne valley. Two others were built across the re-entrant formed by the upper courses of the Rhine and Danube, and east of the Drava-Danube confluence. The barbarians north of the Roman wall also built earthworks to delimit their territory. It is recorded that the Angrivarii constructed a broad earthwork to mark their boundary with the Cherusci. It might be asked whether these walls were not boundaries rather than frontiers, even though they were generally selected in a unilateral manner. The reply would be that the walls formed the first or last line of a system of defence in depth rather than the limit of national sovereignty (Baradez, 1949). The Roman walls were reinforced by establishing farmers on land behind the walls, in a zone called *agri limitanei*. The men of these families were expected to assist in the defence of the wall in time of need, in a way reminiscent of some Israeli Kibbutzim adjacent to Arab territory. However, as an exception to this rule Collingwood (1923) noted that the *vallum* behind Hadrian's wall marked the limits of Rome's civil government.

The counterparts of the Roman and Chinese walls could be found in Africa until quite recently:

The kingdom was surrounded, where there were no natural defences by deep and wide ditches defended by tree trunk palisades and crossed at intervals by narrow bridges. The northern frontier was formed by the Gojeb river, called Godafa by the Kafa. Beiber gives the dimensions of the ditches as 6 metres in width and 3 metres in depth; he describes the gates, *kello* as consisting of circular fenced enclosures entered by drop gates. Customs dues were collected at these gates. Outside the line of fences was a strip of unoccupied land like the *moga* of the Galla states. At points where Galla attacks were expected, the gates were additionally defended by a high rampart and several lines of entrenchment, a form of defence much admired by the neighbours of the Kafa. (Huntingford, 1955, p.116)

The *moga*, or uncultivated strip, of the Galla states of the Horn of Africa was inhabited only by fierce brigands, who were encouraged by the Galla rulers to attack common enemies and recapture escaped slaves.

Fischer maintains that a 'rather extensive literature deals with the development of boundary lines out of such [frontier] zones or related features' (Weigert, 1957). However, the works which he cites do not treat this aspect of boundaries in detail. The general impression is that as states separated by frontiers extend their territory, the unclaimed land diminishes. Eventually property disputes arise, and an attempt is made to resolve these difficulties by delimiting a precise boundary. No doubt this situation has occurred in many cases, but there are some significant variations on this theme, which are examined in the following paragraphs.

We can begin by saying that frontiers normally diminish in width and that frontiers of separation are replaced by frontiers of contact. There have been cases where frontiers have increased in width although this is not usual. An example of a widening frontier was provided by Hashtadan, which is situated on the borderlands of Afghanistan and Iran, southwest of the great northward bend of the Hari Rud at Koshan. This area was investigated by General Maclean in 1888-9 prior to making a boundary award as requested by the Iranian and Afghan governments. He found village ruins, faint field patterns and portions of underground canals which revealed that the area had once been occupied and fairly prosperous. He established that an epidemic throat disease had decimated the valley's population in 1788, and that subsequent raids by Uzbek Hazarah and Turcoman raiders were responsible for the subsequent devastation of the valley.

> But from the appearance of the ruins and abandoned fields it is quite evident that the valley has been deserted for some generations ... Upon the whole, looking to the nature of my present information, it seems to me that neither Persians nor Afghans can produce proofs of recent possession in support of their respective claims, neither having felt inclined to stand the brunt of collisions, in such an exposed locality, with the Turkomans. (Prescott, 1975, p.154)

In the more usual process frontiers diminish in width either by incorporation of parts of the frontier by one or both of the flanking states, or by the creation of subsidiary political units within the frontier.

Annexation of parts of the frontier might take place because of rising land hunger within the state or through the development of new techniques which enable the frontier resources to be revalued. Fifer (1966) has provided a most interesting account of the extension of political control by Bolivia and Brazil over the 'empty, unknown, formerly negative frontiers of separation' which lay between them. She clearly identifies the desire for new lands on which high quality rubber could be produced, during the second half of the nineteenth century. This process was accelerated during the 1880s when a severe drought throughout Brazil's eastern province of Ceara encouraged a mass exodus of labourers in search of work: 'Not until the rubber boom involved the Amazon headwater region, thus probing beyond Brazil's undisputed territorial claims, did old negative frontiers of separation suddenly assume both economic and hence political significance' (Fifer, 1966, p.361).

If the frontier existed because of the internal weakness of the neighbouring states, or their preoccupation with threats from other quarters, the removal of the threat or the resolution of the internal weaknesses might allow the frontier to be appropriated. Alternatively, the frontier may be invaded and annexed for strategic reasons. For example, after the Roman successes in Gaul, the eastern flank of this advance was protected by the annexation of Noricum, Pannonia, Meosia and Dacia in the Danube Basin. This advance also removed the scene of conflict from the Mediterranean centres of the Empire (East, 1950). In some cases annexation for one reason carried additional benefits. The Romans invaded the area between the River Rhine, the River Main and the Taunus ridge to stop the raids by the Chatti. Later they discovered hot springs and iron and silver deposits in the region.

The subsidiary organisations which can be created within the frontier include marches, buffer states, and spheres of interest or of influence. A march is a border territory organised on a semi-permanent military system to defend the frontier. An illustration of the creation of marches was provided by the policies of Charlemagne and Otto:

From these Marks, intended to safeguard the Frontiers of the Empire from Slavonic or alien contact, and ruled by Markgrafs or Markgraves, sprang nearly all the kingdoms and states which afterwards obtained an independent national existence, until they became either the seats of empires themselves, as in the case of the Mark of Brandenburg, or autonomous members of the German

Federation. (Curzon, 1907, p.27)

The German Kingdom was protected from the Slavs and Magyars by a series of marches stretching from the Baltic Sea to the Adriatic Sea. The Markgraves had the responsibility of defending the kingdom and extending the territory subject to it, and the winning of territory led the North Mark and East Mark to become the cores of major states. North Mark, founded in AD 928 by Henry the Fowler, later became known as Altmark, and it acquired Mittelmark, Vormark, Übermark and eventually, Neumark east of the Oder River. This enlarged region was created the Mark of Brandenburg in 1157 and subsequently provided the territorial basis for the unification of Germany. East Mark, after being almost submerged beneath Magyar raids, was recreated by Otto the Great in AD 955. The additions of the Marks of Styria and Carinthia by AD 1282 created the core from which the Austro-Hungarian Empire grew (Figure 2.1).

Buffer states have been constructed in frontiers when two strong neighbours decided to reduce the possibility of conflict between themselves. Britain's prime boundary strategy in the Indian subcontinent involved maintaining a system of small, weak states between British India and the territories of Russia, China and France. In 1895 Britain and Russian fashioned the Wakhan panhandle which extends Afghan territory to the limits of Chinese territory, in order to avoid direct contact between British India and Russian Central Asia. In the Himalayas Britain encouraged the existence of Nepal, Sikkim and Bhutan to separate China and India. Britain would have also welcomed an independent Tibet playing the same role in Sino-British relations as Mongolia played in Sino-Russian relations. In the East Britain tried to persuade Thailand or China to accept the equivalent of the Wakhan panhandle, along the Mekong River, in order to separate British Burma and French Indochina:

> We could not have a conterminous frontier with France in Burmah. That would involve vast expenditure on both sides, and lines of armed posts garrisoned by European troops ... We had proposed the buffer state in the interests of both countries, for it was evident that if our boundaries were contiguous, any fussy, or ill-conditioned frontier officer, whether English or French, would have it in his power to magnify every petty incident into a grave international question, which would be transferred to Europe, and thus grow into a cause of exacerbation between the two Governments. (*British and*

Figure 2.1: The Marches of Eastern Europe

Foreign States Papers, vol.87, 1894-5, p.272 and 379).

Some colonial powers employed neutral zones to serve the same function as buffer states. Britain and Germany separated their spheres of influence in Togoland and the Gold Coast by a neutral zone in 1887; it lay north of the confluence of the Dakka and Volta Rivers. At various times there were also proposals for neutral zones between British and German and between British and Portuguese territories in southern Africa. In 1965 and 1973 Kuwait and Saudi Arabia eliminated a neutral zone which they had jointly controlled. Neutral zones were often convenient solutions to difficult territorial questions, but they were really only short-term remedies. Usually their continued existence proved inconvenient and a greater source of friction than a detailed debate about their division between the two neighbouring states.

The concepts of spheres of interest and influence developed during the last century, when the major European powers were establishing actual and potential claims to parts of Asia and Africa. At no time have the responsibilities assumed under either concept by the claimant powers been defined. Both concepts are means of reserving a portion of territory from the political interference of another state, and it has been assumed that a sphere of interest is a less significant claim than a sphere of influence. Holdich (1916, p.96) suggests that a sphere of interest becomes a sphere of influence when there is the threat of competition by another state, but against this it must be said that the formal definitions of spheres of interest and of influence were found usually in bilateral territorial agreements. An example is provided by the second article of the Anglo-French Agreement of 1890, in respect of African territories:

The Government of Her Britannic Majesty recognises the sphere of influence of France, to the south of her Mediterranean possessions up to a line drawn from Say on the Niger to Barruwa on lake Tchad, drawn in such a way as to comprise in the sphere of action of the Niger Company all that properly belongs to the kingdom of Sokoto. (Hertslet, 1909, vol.2, p.730)

This boundary stretched for 700 miles and the country through which it passed was largely unknown to the two parties. Indeed Lord Salisbury admitted as much when he commented on the results of the treaty.

We have been engaged in drawing lines upon maps where no white man's foot has ever trod; we have been giving away mountains and rivers and lakes to each other, only hindered by the small impediment that we never knew exactly where the mountains and rivers and lakes were. (Kennedy, 1953, p.224)

The degree of interference with the indigenous organisations in the sphere of interest or influence varied in almost every case. At one end of the scale, the European power assumed no responsibility, but claimed the exclusive right of its nationals to trade in the area; at the other end of the scale there was a high degree of political control more appropriate to the condition of a protectorate.

It was noted earlier that one aspect of geographical research connected with settlement frontiers concerned identifying elements in the landscape derived from frontier origins. Such studies are also a proper facet of political frontier studies, although little has been done in this direction by geographers. The best studies are by Cornish (1936) and Wilkinson (1955). Cornish traced the evolution of the language borderlands of Europe, such as Flanders, Lorraine, Friuli, Istria and Macedonia. He found that in each case the language frontier coincided with an earlier political frontier between Christendom and heathen states, which had been static for some time. The growth of polyglot language regions occurred only where the frontier did not coincide with a divisive physical feature. Cornish called such regions link-lands, to emphasise their position between larger state areas. The heathen languages were eventually reduced to writing through contact with Christianity, and their traditions were thus preserved. Cornish points out that only during the nineteenth century, with improved means of mass communication between the larger state areas and the link-lands, did the bonds of language become more important than the regional ties of the link-lands.

Wilkinson shows how the Jugoslav Kosmet, at various times, formed the frontier between the Eastern and Western parts of the Roman Empire, the Bulgar and Byzantine Empires, Christianity and Islam, and Yugoslavia and Albania. This situation has resulted in some neglect of the economic resources of the area and hindered its integrated development. Problems have arisen when boundaries have been drawn through upland areas which provide the summer pastures of a transhumance economy.

The following example of the geographical analysis of frontiers in West Africa is based on fieldwork and the review of an extensive literature, of which the most important works were by Barth (1857), Staudinger (1889), and Hogben (1929).

Frontiers in the Niger-Benue Area

The largest state in West Africa was the Sokoto-Gando Empire, founded by the Fulani Jihad at the beginning of the nineteenth century. This Empire stretched from Libtako in the west to Adamawa in the east, and from Katsina in the north to the latitude of Ilorin in the south. This territory, which was not subject to uniform political authority, was organised into provinces, each having a degree of independence, which varied directly with their distance from Sokoto or Gando. In the provinces of Zaria, Bida, Kontagora, Nassarawa, Kano and Muri, the Fulani subjugated the indigenous tribes. In other areas such as Bauchi and Western Adamawa, enclaves of pagan groups retained their independence on hilltop settlements. Finally, in Libtako and eastern Adamawa, only the main towns on the principal trade routes were subject to Fulani authority. These Fulani towns were exclaves within uncontrolled pagan areas, and might have been described as march-towns (Figure 2.2).

North and west of Sokoto lay the *Habe* states, organised by Hausa chiefs who continued the struggle against the Fulani from new capitals. The westernmost *Habe* state was Kebbi, which had a narrow frontier with Sokoto and Gando, in the neighbourhood of which many raids were carried out and battles fought. The other two *Habe* states, Gober and Maradi, were separated from Sokoto by a frontier of separation, formed from a devastated zone. The towns of Jankuki, Dankama and Madawa were destroyed by Fulani attacks. This depopulated zone became more thickly wooded than the rest of the area, and served as a refuge for robbers. On the northern fringes of this frontier, Maradi established the marches of Gazawa and Tessawa.

Northeast and east of Sokoto lay the Bornu Empire and its vassal states, which included Zinder. The reduced power of Bornu after the Fulani conquest and subsequent Bornu revival had increased the degree of autonomy enjoyed by its traditional northern tributary states, including Zinder. Between Kano Province of the Sokoto-Gando Empire and Zinder, there was a deserted frontier of separation, resulting from the weakness of both states; there were only occasional raids across this frontier.

The frontier of separation dividing Bornu from Sokoto can be divided into three parts. North of the River Gana lived the Bedde pagans, protected by a forested, swampy environment. Armies from

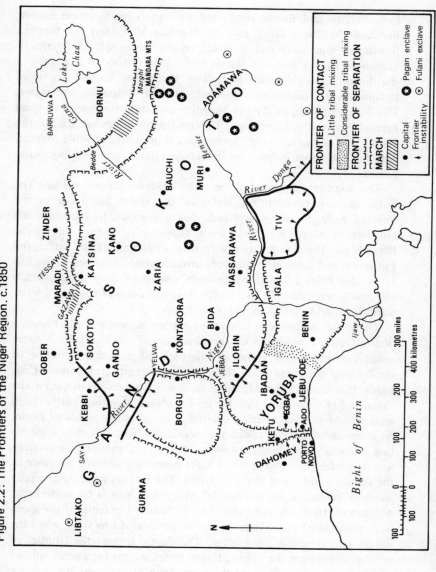

Figure 2.2: The Frontiers of the Niger Region. c.1850

both Sokoto and Bornu conducted slave raids against these people. Between the River Gana and the Mandara Mountains the forested frontier of separation was defended on the Bornu side by a series of quasi-independent marches, which had a long history of resistance to the Fulani. The Mandara Mountains themselves formed the third section of the frontier of separation, between Bornu and Adamawa. This area was occupied by the Marghi pagans, against whom the Fulani exerted intermittent pressure. The continued independence of the Marghi was advantageous to Bornu, since it prevented possible collision with the Adamawa Fulani, and discouraged slaves from escaping southwards.

The southern frontier of the Sokoto-Gando Empire marked the broad division between the states of the Sudan and those of the forested zone. In the west Gando had a common frontier with the kingdom of Borgu. Westwards from Yelwa, on the south side of the River Niger, there was a narrow frontier of contact against which the Fulani exerted continuous pressure unsuccessfully. Between Yelwa and Jebba the River Niger flows through a series of deep gorges, which effectively separated the two states. This frontier was continued westwards from Jebba into a hilly, forested zone.

There was an unstable frontier of contact between Ilorin Province of the Gando Empire and the Yoruba states of the south. Both states maintained permanent armies against each other, and the position of the frontier depended upon their relative strength at any time. Eastwards this frontier broadened into one of separation between the Fulani of Kabba and the Benin Kingdom, resulting partly from weakness of the Fulani and partly from the isolation policy of Benin. At intervals both states raided the frontier for slaves, further fragmenting the small Yoruba groups living there. This frontier of separation was continued east of the River Niger between Nassarawa Province of the Gando Empire and the Igala tribes. The frontier zone lay generally south of the Benue and was flooded with refugees from the north bank, which was effectively conquered by the Fulani. The tribes of the south were protected by the river except at periods of low flow, when the Fulani raiders could easily cross. The Benue formed the frontier of separation between the Tiv and Fulani states, except for a small holding which the Tiv maintained on the north bank of the river. The stability of this frontier resulted partly from the sturdy independence of the Tiv, and partly from their traditional friendship with the Fulani. The other frontiers of the Tiv group were remarkably unstable frontiers of contact, resulting from the outward migration of the Tiv, which involved the absorption of the farmlands of the Igala and Ogoja tribes. This continued migration caused trouble for the colonial authorities. In 1912, after a Tiv raid had dispossessed the Gabu of their land, the authorities built an earth wall, 5 feet high, and 34 miles long, to restrict the Tiv. The plan was not successful and today there are many Tiv south of the wall, which has now fallen into serious disrepair.

It now remains to describe the common frontier of the four recognisable forest-states. The weakness of Borgu, together with the conflicts of the Yoruba Confederation with the Ilorin Fulani, and Dahomey, resulted in Borgu being limited to the south by a wide forested frontier of separation, which was unpopulated except for some brigands. Between Egba, the westernmost Yoruba state, and Dahomey a frontier of separation narrowed towards the coast, which was the target for both states, seeking to dominate trade between the Europeans and the interior. Both armies made frequent raids into the frontier during the dry season when rivers posed no obstacles. The Ewe-speaking refugees from the west and the Egbado refugees from the east formed a complex ethnic mixture in the frontier. The distinction between Yoruba and Benin territory was not a sharp one. The peaceful frontier contained a complex intermixture of both groups, gradually shading to Yoruba dominance in the west and Benin dominance in the east:

> It is impossible, at the present time, to determine the extent of the Benin Empire at any particular period of the past. The frontiers were continually expanding and contracting as new conquests were made and as vassals in the border rebelled and were reconquered. (Bradbury, 1957, p.21)

To the south of Benin the delta tribes, such as the Ijaw, preserved their independence largely as a result of the defensive character of the swamps and creeks. By the middle of the last century the policy of isolation had caused Benin to withdraw its authority from the western bank of the Niger. East of the Niger the political organisation of the Ibo did not rise above the level of the clan or family. While some of these groups must have been surrounded by areas of unclaimed forest, their distribution cannot be reconstructed on the present scale of enquiry.

There seem to be three main results of the former location of past frontiers in the present landscape. First, the colonial boundaries which were superimposed on the indigenous political fabric did coincide to some extent with the indigenous frontiers. The Anglo-French boundary between Dahomey and Lagos was drawn within the frontier between

Dahomey and Egba. The Anglo-French boundary between Niger and Northern Nigeria showed some correspondence with the devastated sections of the frontier between Sokoto and the northern *Habe* states of Maradi and Zinder. The former federal boundary between Western and Northern Nigeria is clearly related to the northern boundary of the former Yoruba and Benin kingdoms. Second, pressure from both flanks of some frontiers of separation has created ethnic shatter zones. The ethnic complexities of the areas between the former Dahomey and Egba kingdoms, between the Kabba and Benin kingdoms, and between Nassarawa and the Igala tribes are revealed in the striking variations over short distances in house types and agricultural methods. Third, these shatter zones, marginal to the cores of the original states and their colonial successors, and lacking unified political control, have remained underdeveloped, and have not shared in the extension of services which have characterised other areas.

References

Adams, J.T., 1943, *Atlas of American History*, New York
Baradez, J., 1949, *Fossatum Africae*, Paris, Arts et métiers graphiques
Barth, H., 1857, *Travels and Discoveries in North and Central Africa*, London
Billington, R.A., 1960, *Westward Expansion*, 2nd edn., New York
Bradbury, R.E., 1957, *The Benin Kingdom*, International African Institute, London
British and Foreign State Papers, 1894-5, 87, HMSO
Clarke, T.D., 1959, *Frontier America*, New York
Collingwood, R.G., 1923, *Roman Britain*, London
Cornish, V., 1936, *Borderlands of Language in Europe and their Relation to the Historic Frontier of Christendom*, London
Curzon of Kedleston, Lord, 1907, *Frontiers*, The Romanes Lecture, Oxford
Davies, C.C., 1932, *The Problem of the Northwest Frontier, 1890-1908*, Cambridge
Dennis, W.J., 1931, *Tacna and Arica*, New Haven
East, W.G., 1937, 'The nature of Political Geography', *Politica*, 2, pp.259-86
────── 1962, *An Historical Geography of Europe*, 4th edn., revised, London
Fifer, J.V., 1966, 'Bolivia's Boundary with Brazil: A Century of Evolution', *Geographical Journal*, 132, pp.360-72
Harrison, J.A., 1953, *Japan's Northern Frontier*, Gainesville, Florida
Hertslet, Sir E., 1909, *Map of Africa by Treaty*, HMSO, London
Hogben, S.J., 1929, *The Muhammedan Emirates of Northern Nigeria*, London
Hohnel, L. von, 1894, *The Discovery of Lakes Rudolph and Stefanie*, London
Holdich, Sir T.H., 1916, *Political Frontiers and Boundary Making*, London
Huntingford, G.W.B., 1955, *The Galla of Ethiopia*, London
Kelly, K., 1969, 'An Explanation of the Great North-south Extent of the Inca Empire in 1532, and of the Position of its Eastern Boundary through Peru and Bolivia, *Journal of Tropical Geography*, 28, pp.57-63
Kennedy, A.L., 1953, *Salisbury 1830-1903: Portrait of a Statesman*, London
Kerr, D.G.G., 1961, *A Historical Atlas of Canada*, Toronto
Kristoff, L.A.D., 1959, 'The Nature of Frontiers and Boundaries', *Annals*, Asso-

ciation of American Geographers, 49, pp.269-82

Lattimore, O., 1940, *Inner Asian Frontiers of China,* New York

Lawless, R.I., 1974, 'Uranium mining at Arlit in the Republic of Niger', *Geography,* 59, pp.45-8.

Ministere des Colonies, 1910, *Documents scientifiques de la mission Tilho,* Paris

Mitchell, R.D., 1972, 'The Shenandoah Valley Frontier', *Annals,* Association of American Geographers, 62, pp.461-86

Paullin, C.O., 1932, *Atlas of the Historical Geography of the United States,* Baltimore

Prescott, J.R.V., 1975, *Map of Mainland Asia by Treaty,* Melbourne

Staudinger, R., 1889, *Im Herzen der Haussaland,* Berlin

Turner, F.J., 1953, *The Frontier in American History,* 3rd impression, New York

Weigert, H., and others, 1957, *Principles of Political Geography,* New York

Whittlesey, D., 1956, chapter 10 in East, W.G. and Moodie, E.A., *The Changing World,* London

Wilkinson, H.R., 1955, 'Jugoslav Kosmet', *Transactions and Papers,* Institute of British Geographers, pp.171-93

Wyman, W.D., and Kroeber, C.B., 1957, *Frontier in Perspective,* Madison

3 THE EVOLUTION OF BOUNDARIES

The missionary, the conqueror, the farmer and, of late the engineer, have followed so closely in the traveller's footsteps that the world, in its remoter borders, has hardly been revealed before one must record its virtually complete political appropriation. (Mackinder, 1904, p.421)

Mackinder was speaking at the close of the most intensive period of boundary construction in the world's history; a period which had created a closed political system enclosing even barren tropical deserts and unexplored equatorial forests. International boundaries have now replaced frontiers in all the continents, including Antarctica. The last chapter showed some of the ways by which frontiers were reduced in width; this chapter examines the ways in which boundaries develop.

Boundary negotiations between states usually originated once a conflict of interest developed or seemed imminent, and they were usually designed to promote peace and better administration. Vattel regarded boundary delimitation and demarcation as a useful cure for international disputes: 'to remove every subject of discord, every occasion for quarrel, one should mark with clarity and precision the limits of territories' (Vattel, 1758, 11, p.137). The conflict of interest sometimes followed direct contact between forces or citizens of the two countries, and in such cases the boundary was determined subsequent to established patterns of occupance, which at the least would involve identification and use of principal routes and the construction of camps or forts. In other cases, however, the conflict of interest would not involve such direct contact, and it would arise because of the territorial basis of national plans or ambitions. For example, many of the boundary negotiations in Africa commenced long before the colonising movements of Britain France or Germany and Portugal came into contact. They were initiated in an effort to realise some grand design, such as France's determination to link her Mediterranean and West African possessions, and Portugal's hope to unite Angola and Mozambique.

When there was direct contact between the citizens of the competing states the boundary often had to be determined within confined limits, because territorial questions were inextricably linked with issues of national pride. While there was greater scope for selecting boundaries through areas which had not been explored or exploited, problems often arose because countries were anxious not to forego any of the valuable resources which might exist in the borderland. In the 1880s Britain and Germany were arguing about the boundary proceeding inland from the coast between Nigeria and Kamerun; a British official recorded that neither side was disposed to make concessions because the disputed area 'might prove to be an Eldorado or a worthless swamp'.

There were three basic situations in terms of the relative power of states under which negotiations might be launched. First, states of comparable strength may decide to enter negotiations in order to solve administrative problems and avoid risks of a serious clash. Second, a stronger state may propose negotiations to a weaker state in order to gain sovereignty over areas not previously held. In 1858 and 1860 Russia was much stronger than China, which was racked by internal rebellion and external threat; by boundary negotiations during that period Russia forced China to cede the trans-Amur and the trans-Ussuri territories. In 1893 France exerted considerable pressure against Thailand and whittled away large areas which today form part of Cambodia. The British Ambassador in Paris described the French tactics in the following terms: 'The Siamese Government were now in possession of an ultimatum a pen-ultimatum and an ante-penultimatum. In fact the world 'ultimatum' had completely lost its meaning, for each new one seemed to procreate a successor' (Prescott, 1975, p.432). The third situation arises when a weaker state proposes negotiations in order to try to protect the sovereignty which it possesses. Mexico in 1848 welcomed boundary negotiations as a device to stop further erosion of its territory by the United States. A quarter of a century later Afghanistan was encouraged by Britain to try to settle a boundary with Russia, in a bid to halt that country's rapid advance across central Asia towards India.

The use of boundary treaties to promote peace is sometimes recorded in the treaty's text. In 1864 Russia and China signed the Protocol of Chuguchak regarding the boundary southwest of modern Mongolia, which recorded that it was for 'the promotion of the good understanding between the two Empires' (Inspector General of Customs, 1917, 1, p.144). Sometimes the treaty was signed after fighting had already commenced. In 1891 a collision occurred between Portuguese forces marching inland from the coast of Mozambique and police of the British South African Company engaged in settling

Rhodesia. There was some confusion over which nationals had valid prospecting treaties with the local rulers of Manica, and on 11 May 1891 the battle of Macequece was fought between 48 police and volunteers on the British side and 359 Portuguese troops, of whom 300 were Africans from Angola. There were no casualties after two hours and the Portuguese withdrew during the night. The British booty consisted of 'nine machine guns [which] were in position on field carriages, thousands of rounds of ammunition of all descriptions, officers and men's baggage, stores of all kinds, and one pair of ladies drawers' (Rhodesian Archives, CT 1/12/1-7, Report by Lt. Col. E.G. Pennefather, 13 May 1891). Exactly one month after this clash Britain and Portugal signed a treaty which defined their respective spheres of influence in the hinterland of the Mozambique coast.

The direct conflict of interests often involved the use of land for grazing and cultivation, mining claims, the use of rivers and passes for travel and trade, and exclusive commercial treaties signed with indigenous chiefs. Governments recognised that apart from the serious risk of military conflict between zealous officers so long as no precise boundary was defined, there was the critical problem of encouraging commercial activities in an uncertain political climate. Rudin (1938) noted that Anglo-German negotiations concerning the boundary between the coast and the Benue River at Yola, separating Nigeria and Kamerun, were finally encouraged because neither administration could persuade firms to develop areas in the disputed zone or near it. Commercial firms regarded such areas as poor investment risks because political expediency might transfer their area of operation from one country to another.

Conflicts of interests which did not involve direct contact were usually of a strategic nature. For example, in 1727 China agreed to further negotiations with Russia about the westward extension of their boundary through the Amur valley, because China wanted to avoid the possibility of any Russian interference amongst tribes in the Chinese borderland. In 1899 Britain proposed various boundaries to China in the area of Hunza and the Aksai Chin, in efforts to secure a good defensive line and to thwart any chance of a Russian advance through the Pamirs. The Chinese neither accepted nor rejected these proposals. Fifteen years later, by some devious diplomacy, Britain attempted to secure a sound defensive boundary in northern Assam through the negotiations which produced the McMahon Line.

The presence of no-man's-land between states facilitated escape by individuals from financial and juridical responsibilities, and sometimes such areas became refuges for brigands. Countries often acted quickly to eliminate such inconvenient areas. In 1899, Britain and Germany agreed to divide the neutral zone, which had separated their colonies of the Gold Coast and Togo, by a river which could be clearly identified by the two administrations.

Three aspects of boundary evolution are appropriate to geographical analysis — evolution in definition, evolution in position, and evolution in the state functions applied at the boundary. Examination of these three aspects will illuminate the two main lines of geographical research into boundaries — the influence of geographical factors on the location of the boundary, and the reciprocal influence of the boundary, once established, on the development of the landscape through which it is drawn.

Geographical knowledge is one of the fundamental factors which influence boundary location, and an indication of that knowledge is often contained in boundary definitions. Geometric boundaries in Africa usually meant that little reliable information was available about topography and drainage. Successive boundary definitions often record advances in exploration and cartography, as geometric boundaries are exchanged for lines coincident with rivers and relief features, or lines of cultural differentiation.

The way in which a boundary influences the development of a border landscape and the lives of its inhabitants is likely to be a function of the accuracy with which that boundary is defined and can be located, and the number and quality of state functions applied at the boundary. Often the most striking influences upon the border landscape and its inhabitants will result from changes in boundary position which transfer areas from one state to another. One example will serve at this point. After the Second World War 2.8 million Germans moved out of former German territory east of the Oder-Neisse line, when it was transferred to Poland. The agricultural activities of the Polish immigrants in the transferred area, on both peasant and communal farms, have produced significant landscape changes (Wiskemann, 1956). In order to measure the geographical significance of the boundary, it is necessary to know the relationship which the original boundary bore to the landscape at the time when the boundary was drawn. This clearly involves the application of the methods of historical geography, in order to discover the original correspondence between the boundary and the cultural patterns, such as the distribution of population groups, the location of economic activities, and the direction and volume of trade.

It is now necessary to consider how these avenues of research can be followed apart from studying secondary sources produced by other scholars. Information about boundaries may be gathered by studying relevant documents and published works, by analysing maps of the area traversed by the line, and by undertaking fieldwork in the borderland.

The documentary material may be classified into three sections. First, there are the copies of correspondence conducted between the negotiating powers and between representatives of the same government. Such records are only rarely published and it is generally necessary to consult them in archives, which will normally restrict access to those files which are more than thirty years old. These sources are invaluable and alone will provide the detailed considerations which led to the selection of a particular boundary. In the letters and minutes and reports can be discovered the geographical, political, economic, ethnic and legal factors which played an important part in producing agreement on the general location and specific site of the boundary. An analysis of the Anglo-French correspondence dealing with the settlement of the inter-Cameroons boundary in 1920 revealed the following points, which could not have been derived in any other way. First, the location of the boundary in Bornu resulted from the incorrect decoding of a British telegram in Lagos, in 1916. France, which benefited from this error, refused to allow the line to be corrected, but this obstinacy permitted Britain to press successfully for the reunification in the British Cameroons of the Holma, Zummu and Higi pagans, who had been divided by the original Anglo-German boundary. Second, France was anxious to secure Garua, a port on the Benue River, and the land route from Douala on the coast to Garua. Meanwhile Britain was anxious to reunite the former Emirate of Yola which had been split between Britain and Germany in the 1880s. Third, the use of inaccurate maps in delimiting the boundary resulted in two disputes. The first, at the southern end of the boundary involved rich plantations, while the other, in the north, related to swamplands which were used for cotton production and winter grazing. Fourth, the negotiations were conducted with regard to boundary arrangements being made in respect of other German colonies (Prescott, 1971, pp.45-62).

The second class of documents and published material consists of the boundary treaties which are eventually agreed between states. Most countries will publish their own treaty series in parliamentary records, and many treaties are recorded in the United Nations Treaty Series. Sir E. Hertslet has published collections of treaties dealing with Africa, Europe and China, while Martens edited a very useful general treaty series. Indeed, the bibliography of publications containing the texts of treaties would be a very long one, and scholars are recommended to consult university and national libraries. The treaties are important because their letter is the final basis on which the boundary is demarcated. If the treaty is not carefully drafted ambiguous phrases may lead to future boundary disputes. Boundary treaties will often include information about the conduct of affairs in the borderland as well as the definition of the line. For example, the fifth clause of the agreement relating to the boundary between Afghanistan and Pakistan, dated 26 February 1895, contains the following provisions:

We have also jointly agreed on the following matters relating to the portion of the boundary line defined in this clause: Firstly, that the rights attaching to the Psein land which is within Afghanistan and close to and to the west of boundary pillars Nos. XVI, XVII, and XVIII of water from the Kakars, who own the right to the water of the Loe Wuchobai nullah above that, will remain as hitherto.
Secondly, that the Kakar Tribe should continue to enjoy the rights of grazing, as hitherto, throughout the country lying between the Kand river, and Loe Wuchobai nullah, and Babakr Chahan and Sam Narai.
Thirdly, that the Pseins should continue to enjoy the right of grazing, as hitherto, in the tract of land commonly known as Psein Dagh, which is situated on the south of the Psein Lora.
Fourthly, that the water of the Psein Lora and Kadanai river belongs jointly to the people residing on both banks of the river.
If any of the subjects of the British or Afghan Government wish to construct a new water channel leading from the Psein Lora or Kadanai river, they must first obtain the permission of the district officers concerned of both Governments. (Prescott, 1975, p.194)

According to the fifth and sixth articles of the Anglo-Tibetan Convention of 1904 Tibet undertook to keep roads between the boundary and Gyantse and Gartok free from obstructions and in a state of repair suited to the needs of trade, and to raze all fortifications along these routes which might impede communications (Inspector General of Customs, 1917, 2, pp.656-7). Lamb (1964) gives a lead to scholars, who may be looking critically at modern treaties, in his analysis of the Sino-Pakistan boundary treaty of 1963.
One of the most fruitful sources of information related to treaties

concerns the decisions of arbitrations. There have been many cases, in the last century and in recent times, when judgements have been made either by a single arbitrator acceptable to both sides, or by a judicial tribunal. For example, in 1875 France ruled in Portugal's favour when Britain disputed Portugal's ownership of Delagoa Bay, immediately south of Maputo. In 1897, Italy adjudicated a compromise boundary between the conflicting claims of Britain and Portugal on Rhodesia's eastern border, and eight years later performed the same service for the same two countries along the border between Angola and Zambia. In 1911, the disputed boundaries of Walvis Bay were settled by Spain, which dismissed the German arguments and found in favour of Britain. In 1962 the International Court of Justice ruled on the alignment of the boundary between Thailand and Cambodia near the temple of Preah Vihear, and in 1968 a judicial tribunal resolved the dispute between India and Pakistan about the boundary through the Great Rann of Kutch. Whenever arbitration or judicial processes are involved the countries submit as much evidence as they possibly can, and the records of these activities contain great stores of useful information on the evolution of the earlier boundaries. In the Rann of Kutch hearings the two sides presented evidence which occupied 10,000 pages of typescript, and illustrated their arguments with 350 maps.

The third class of documents and published works comprise the reports and personal accounts of the individuals who demarcated the boundary or were involved in its creation. Probably because so much of the demarcation work involved travel in remote areas and in some cases primary exploration, many boundary commissioners published accounts in the journals of learned societies, such as the Royal Geographical Society. These accounts often include detailed descriptions of the borderland's physical geography, precise accounts of the nature of indigenous societies near the boundary, and of the attitude of those populations to the presence of the new limit. For example, the papers by Nugent (1914) and von Detzner (1913), who were joint leaders of the Anglo-German demarcation team between Nigeria and Kamerun, give a clearer impression of the problems faced and the dislocation caused by the boundary to the economic and political life of local tribes than any other source. The memoirs of men such as Holdich (1909) and Ryder (1925) who were practically involved in identifying and marking boundaries in the landscape contain much more detail about the boundaries than the memoirs of statesmen such as Sir Mortimer Durand (Sykes, 1926), who, perhaps understandably, were more concerned with the broad questions of international diplomacy rather than the precise alignment of boundaries. Sir Mortimer Durand negotiated the boundary between India and Afghanistan in 1893, which was later known as the Durand Line.

The study of maps by scholars interested in the evolution of boundaries is an essential undertaking for a number of reasons. First, in many cases it will never be possible for the scholar to undertake fieldwork in the borderland, because countries such as China and the Soviet Union, or Iran and Pakistan do not allow such activities. Second, it is important to study the maps available to the negotiators, because these maps will give a good indication of the perception of the area held by them. Many of the decisions of negotiators, which subsequently created problems, are inexplicable if analysed on modern maps, but thoroughly comprehensible when related to the maps available during the negotiations. For example, the Anglo-Russian Convention of 1825 stated that the boundary between Alaska and British Canada should follow 'the summits of the mountains situated parallel to the coast', providing that line shall be no more than 30 miles from the coast (Davidson, 1903, p.81). Commentators have shown that such a boundary cannot be located (Davidson, 1903; Hinks, 1921). This boundary definition was accepted by the negotiators because their work was related to maps based on Vancouver's explorations of 1792-4, which were published in an atlas in 1798. Vancouver represented a range of mountains along the whole length of the Pacific coast of North America, located 10 to 24 miles from the coast. Even in 1867, when Russia transferred Alaska to the United States, the official American charts were still based on Vancouver's maps.

Maps of the period when the boundary was drawn will also be very helpful in identifying places which have changed their names in the subsequent period. Problems connected with place names can be particularly difficult to solve; I recall being uncertain for a number of weeks about the exact location of the Shabina Pass which marked the western terminus of the 1727 Sino-Russian boundary in central Asia; the answer was found after consulting dozens of maps of various ages.

Finally, maps will sometimes provide useful information about the cultural landscape at the time the boundary was established, and will therefore provide a benchmark from which ensuing change in the borderland can be measured. Such maps will often record the patterns of settlement, communication and land ownership, which may not be described in any other form. Obviously, maps on the largest possible scale should be used.

If it is possible fieldwork is a most valuable source of information. Simply by travelling through the borderland it is possible to gain a familiarity with the topography and drainage pattern which will illuminate analysis of the boundary negotiations several decades ago. The techniques of observation and local enquiry do not differ from fieldwork in other branches of geography. It is unlikely that a scholar undertaking such fieldwork would restrict the enquiry only to those aspects useful in understanding the boundary's evolution; while in the region it would be sensible to accumulate information about the current importance of the boundary as a factor influencing the cultural landscape and the lives of people living close to it. For example, it would be useful to acquire information on the state of the boundary's demarcation and whether or not it agreed with the published description. It would also be helpful to identify any significant changes in the cultural landscape near the boundary and the impact of the boundary on the lives of local residents. The major crossing points should be listed and if possible the volume of traffic, at each, over a period of time, should be measured.

During fieldwork on part of the Nigeria-Benin boundary, only three of the twenty monuments marking the section could be found. The three were all found near villages and none was complete, having in each case been used to sharpen cutlasses or axes. There were no significant changes in the cultural landscape within 20 miles of the boundary, and the lives of the people seemed unaffected by the boundary — some Nigerian farms were lying partly in Benin in accordance with the provision of the Anglo-French Agreement of 1906:

> The villages situated in proximity to the boundary shall retain the right to arable and pasture lands, springs and watering places, which they have heretofore used, even in cases where such arable and pasture lands, springs and watering places are situated within the territory of one Power, and the village within the territory of the other. (Hertslet, 1909, 3, p.861)

The two crossing points at Ijoun and Idiroko were 32 miles apart, and most of the border inhabitants crossed the boundary by uncontrolled paths. At times of tax collection, there was some movement across the boundary in order to escape responsibilities. During an interview with the Aleketu, who is a Yoruba chief in Benin, separated from the majority of his tribe in Nigeria, he said, 'We regard the boundary as separating the French and the English, not the Yoruba.' All this information was valuable in understanding the present condition and significance of the boundary, and could be obtained only by fieldwork.

Evolution in Definition

Geographers have propounded several systems of boundary evolution. Brigham (1917) employed a threefold division — tribal, transitional and ideal. The tribal boundaries were primitive and were not defined in any document. Such divisions should be described as frontiers, since they had a zonal quality, however clearly the last lines of defence were marked in the landscape. Brigham envisaged the transitional stage as being one when the boundary was likely to change its position, carrying the implication that the boundaries were finding a position where the forces from either side were neutralised. Finally, in the ideal stage the boundary became permanently fixed, and a gradual diminution of functions applied at the boundary reduced its significance as a landscape element. This altruistic concept of boundary evolution probably owed much to the world situation when it was published, and the ideas have not been further developed by subsequent workers.

Lapradelle (1928) distinguished three stages of boundary evolution — preparation, decision and execution. He emphasised the tentative nature of the first stage compared with those that follow by using *le trace,* which means 'outline' or 'sketch', instead of *la limite* meaning 'boundary'. Jones (1945) follows Lapradelle closely in suggesting four stages of boundary evolution — allocation, delimitation, demarcation and administration. Allocation refers to the political decision on the distribution of territory; delimitation involves the selection of a specific boundary site; demarcation concerns the marking of the boundary on the ground; and administration relates to the provisions for supervising the maintenance of the boundary. Nicholson (1954, p.116) tried to marry the schemes of Jones and Brigham by carrying the process through from the tribal stage to the demarcated boundary. However, he admits that the only correlations between the first frontiers and the final boundaries in Canada were fortuitous, and that there was no continuous development. There seems to be no reason why his ideas should not apply where there is a continuous history of indigenous development. In cases of widespread colonisation, as in America, Africa and Australia, the extent to which colonial boundaries are drawn within indigenous frontiers will depend on the extent to which the colonising state considered existing political structures.

It must not be presumed that all boundaries have passed through the stages of allocation, delimitation and demarcation in an orderly sequence. In some cases the original allocating boundary has been demarcated with no intervening delimitation. In other cases there has been more than one delimitation before demarcation occurred. Finally there are many boundaries in the world which are still undemarcated. In the following discussion of boundary evolution the stages suggested by Lapradelle and Jones are used.

Allocation

When a boundary was created in a frontier where the geographical facts were well known, and where the population density was moderate to heavy, it was sometimes possible to select a boundary site, and in such cases the stage of allocation was omitted. In areas which were less well known, often supporting low population densities, the stage of allocation provided the first formal political division. The boundaries which resulted were often arbitrary and consisted of two main kinds. The first type was made up of straight lines connecting prescribed coordinates or points in the landscape which had been identified, such as a waterfall, or a village. The Portuguese-German Declaration of 1886 described such a line allocating territory to Angola and South West Africa:

> The boundary follows the course of the river Kenene from its mouth to the waterfalls which are formed south of the Hunbe by the Kenene breaking through the Serra Canna. From this point the boundary runs along the parallel of latitude to the river Kulingo [Okavango], then along the course of that river to the village of Andura which is to remain within the German sphere of influence, and from thence in a straight line eastwards to the rapids of Catima on the Zambezi. (Hertslet, 1909, 3, p.703)

The quotation shows how the series of straight lines or stream courses linked up the waterfall, village and rapids which had been identified and approximately located on maps. This boundary has been preserved intact to the present time, because the two sides were unable to agree on any alterations. From time to time there were problems about identifying the exact point where the boundary leaves the Cunene, the location of Andara village, and the exact point where the boundary intersects the Katima Rapids. The problem over the village concerned the fact that the village was moved 3 miles downstream at the turn of the century. In some cases meridians and parallels were selected as boundaries, but of the two lines parallels were more reliable until accurate radio time signals could be sent and received. An official of the Royal Niger Company made this point forcefully in September 1893. 'Meridians move around Africa like mountains. An error of a degree or even half a degree might cost England Kukawa, and therefore all Bornu' (Prescott, 1971. p.34). Kukawa, situated west of Lake Chad, was the capital of Bornu, which Britain claimed by virtue of a treaty. The Company was afraid that if some meridian was accepted which was thought to lie east of Kukawa, it might turn out eventually to be west of that settlement. Accordingly the British government persuaded Germany to define the boundary's terminus as the meridian which intersects the southern shore of Lake Chad 35' east of Kukawa. It was considered by both sides that such a point coincided with the meridian $14°$ east, because the value ascribed to the meridian through Kukawa, by Vogel, in 1853, was $13° 24'$ east. This had been altered to meridian $13° 25'$ east on Kiepert's map in *Deutscher Kolonial Atlas*. In fact the demarcation commission of 1903 found that the meridian passing through Kukawa was $13°$ east, and so the terminus was set on the shore of Lake Chad at $14° 8'$ east.

A straight line connecting known points was often hard for administrative officers to determine when they were some distance from either point. This would be particularly true when the terrain through which the line passed was forested or hilly. It was probably even harder for the local population, in colonial situations, to know exactly where the unmarked straight line traversed their region. Such uncertainties led to serious administrative problems in parts of east Africa, including Rhodesia and Mozambique, where the 1891 Anglo-Portuguese Convention defined meridian $33°$ east as the boundary between the Mazoe River and the parallel $18° 30'$ south. In the three years following that Convention there were several exchanges of letters regarding allegations, by officers of both sides, of trespass and the illegal collection of hut taxes on the wrong side of the boundary.

The second type of boundary defined in principle the division of territory. It has been usual in earlier studies, including the important contribution by Jones (1945), to refer to definition in principle as one of the methods by which boundaries are delimited, but it seems more appropriate to include such definitions in the stage of allocation. Definition in principle means that there is a statement about the basis of territorial division and the result desired. For example, the boundary drawn by Russia and China in 1689 between the Little Gorbitsa River and the coast was defined in the following terms.

> The territories of the two Empires should be divided in such a manner that all land and rivers both great and small which flow from the south side of this range into the River Saghalien Vla [Amur] will come under the sway of the Chinese Emperor, while all lands and rivers which lead in a northerly direction on the other side of the watershed will remain under the control of the Russian Empire. (Prescott, 1975, p.13.)

In short, the boundary had to follow the northern watershed of the Amur River basin. The two countries had a vague idea of the location of that watershed, but in some areas they would not have known to within 20 or 30 miles its exact location. Where there is such uncertainty about the location of the boundary it seems proper to treat it as allocating territory, because delimitation refers to the selection of a specific site. It could be argued that the selection of a watershed or a river implies the selection of specific line, but only in exceptional situations would there be no disagreement possible about the alignment of a watershed or the headwater tributary which represents the source of a particular river.

It is beyond question that definition in principle related to physical features involved considerable uncertainty about the course the boundary would follow. For example, in 1885 Britain and Germany defined their common boundary between Nigeria and Kamerun as following the right bank of the Rio del Rey from its mouth to its source. According to Sir Claude Macdonald it was considered that the river was a long one, as shown on the Admiralty charts of the day (Nugent, 1914, p.647). Unfortunately the chart was wrong as the German Consul Baron von Soden pointed out to his British counterpart in 1888: 'You know as well as I do there is no Rio del Rey, at least no source of such a river. I do not know if the rapids of the Cross river can be more easily found, or whether they have the same mythical existence.' (Prescott, 1971, pp.13-14.) The problem was that the Rio del Rey was only four miles long and it was fed by two main tributaries, the Akpayafe and Ndian Rivers which diverged sharply. Britain regarded the Ndian as the proper continuation of the Rio del Rey, and predictably Germany was equally certain that the Akpayafe River was the correct boundary. At least the Cross River rapids did exist, but instead of being located at 9° 8′ east and 5° 40′ north, as shown on the chart, they occurred at 8° 50′ east and 6° 10′ north.

When the British and Belgian governments concluded an agreement defining their spheres of influence in east and central Africa, in 1894, the boundary between the Sudan and Belgian Congo was stated to follow the watershed between the Nile and Congo Rivers. This watershed is about 400 miles in length and the country is not particularly hilly; it has never been demarcated and it is predictable that any attempt to demarcate the line will provoke debate about its precise alignment.

Definition in principle can also refer to cultural features, which generally are even more likely to cause disagreement than physical features. In September 1885 Britain and Russia defined Afghanistan's northern boundary and east of Hauzi Khan the line had to be 'fixed in a manner which leaves to Russia the land cultivated by the Saryks and also their pastures' (Prescott, 1975, p.124). The demarcation commission which started work within two months of the agreement was unable to agree on the line limiting the Saryk areas and a further set of protocols had to be negotiated at St Petersburg in 1887.

In 1878 the Treaty of Berlin allocated territory between Montenegro and Albania by a line which was defined in principle according to the location of specified tribes:

> It then coincides with the existing boundaries between the tribes of the Kuci-Drekalovici on one side, and the Kucka-Krajna, as well as the tribes of the Klementi and Grudi on the other, to the plain of Podgorica, from whence it proceeds towards Plavnica, leaving the Klementi, Grudi and Hoti tribes to Albania. (Hertslet, 1891, 4, p.2782)

The last boundary treaty between Italy and Ethiopia, in May 1908, which is the most recent negotiated agreement regarding this bitterly disputed boundary between Ethiopia and Somalia, defined the boundary as the line which separated the Rahanwein tribes in the Italian area from all other tribes to the north which remained in Ethiopia. Definition in principle is a clear indication that the exact distribution or location of the physical features or cultural attributes is unknown. Such imprecise lines concern the first stage of boundary definition, and the second stage of delimitation is designed to eliminate this inconvenient uncertainty.

Delimitation

The allocation of territory by arbitrary straight lines or by lines related to the uncertain distribution of physical and cultural features, generally solved immediate territorial conflicts of interest and allowed governments to plan the development of territory with a sense of security, which also extended to some commercial firms. The delimitation of the boundary which requires the selection of a specific boundary site was usually only undertaken when the borderland possessed some intrinsic economic value, or if the interests or antagonisms of the two states required the rigid application of state functions at a specific line.

The retention of the arbitrary straight lines occurred when one or more of the following conditions applied. First, straight lines were preserved if the borders lacked any economic or strategic value, and if the surveying of the boundary would have been an unnecessary and unjustifiable expense. An examination of the political map of the world reveals that many geometric boundaries are located in tropical deserts and Antarctica. Second, straight lines persisted when the two countries concerned were unable to agree on any alteration. This condition explains the continued use of straight sections in the boundary between Angola and South West Africa. It is the inability of the Italians and Ethiopians to reach any modifications after 1908 which underlies the persistent trouble along the Ethiopian-Somali boundary. Third, it was usual for straight lines to be maintained when the same colonial power came into possession of the separated territories. This situation applied between Egypt and the Sudan during the period of British paramountcy, and between Kenya and Tanganyika, and Botswana and South West Africa, when German authority was eliminated after 1918.

Two types of boundary definitions can also be distinguished during the process of delimitation. The first involves complete definition which requires the surveyors to proceed into the field and trace the line which had been so closely described. The second type of definition gives the surveyors power to vary the line, usually by a set distance on either side, in order to make the identification and administration of the boundary easier.

There are three common ways of delimiting boundaries. The first records the alignment of the boundary in the same fashion as the track of a ship by means of bearings and distances. It is important to specify whether the bearings are measured from true or magnetic north and to note precise distances. Further, it is useful to identify by other means some of the most important turning points on the boundary, otherwise any errors made during the demarcation of the line will accumulate. MacLean used this method in delimiting the boundary through Hashtadan when he had to arbitrate between Persia and Afghanistan in 1891. He recorded the forward and back bearings between each pair of consecutive pillars, and as an additional check he also gave bearings from each of the thirty-nine pillars to other prominent features of the landscape, including villages, mills and hills. He was able to specify the distances for twenty-four of the pillars, the remainder would have to be calculated by resection (Prescott, 1975, pp.159-70).

The second method simply records the turning points of the boundary and requires that they be connected by straight lines. The turning points may be physical features, such as the confluence of rivers, a peak, or the head of a ravine, or cultural features, such as crossroads, houses or bridges. There have even been cases where letters of place names shown on a nominated map have been used as turning points. Problems arise when the selected turning point refers to an area rather than a single spot. Physical features, such as hilltops, often possess an area within which the exact turning point must be located, and there is scope for disagreement about the exact confluence of many rivers and their tributaries.

The third method makes the boundary coincide with linear features in the landscape such as roads, rivers, or crests. Once again many of these linear features, especially rivers and crests, possess areas within which a line has to be selected.

It is during the delimitation stage that many of the seeds of future boundary disputes are sown. During the stage of allocation it is recognised that the boundary is arbitrary and likely to be modified to produce a more practical line, but the delimitation of the boundary is expected to produce a definitive line. Disputes of this nature are considered in the next chapter, but it will be useful to indicate here the traps which exist for the unwary boundary architect. Most subsequent difficulties arise because the individuals who define the line have not visited the borderland, instead they rely on descriptions from travellers and especially on maps. It is very easy to draw boundaries on maps because the scale representation of the landscape can be easily comprehended. In addition, because the cartographer has to be selective in the features he records, they are given a prominence which may not be so obvious in the field. Rivers and crests stand out on many maps, especially some of the beautifully hand-coloured maps of the second half of the last century, which can be found in archives illustrating reports of explorers and administrative officers. It may seem sensible when looking at the representation of a river on a map to nominate a bank as the boundary, but different surveyors and geomorphologists would interpret the bank of a river in different ways.

Other problems arise because the treaty draftsmen try to make assurance doubly sure by defining a single point in two ways. This would be helpful if the two ways were always in total agreement, but unfortunately they sometimes contradict each other. For example, the first boundary between Peru and Bolivia included as a turning point the confluence of the Lanza and Tambopata Rivers, which was clear enough apart from the need to select a single point at the confluence. But in an effort to remove any possible doubt the treaty specified that the confluence lay north of the parallel 14° south. In fact the confluence lay south of that parallel and therefore the two administrations argued whether it was the confluence which was important or a location on the river south of parallel 14° south.

It must be noted that some international boundaries are not created by negotiations which produce an allocation of territory followed by the delimitation of a line fitted to the landscape. Some international boundaries are created by the promotion of internal boundaries to international status. The dissolution of the British and French Empires caused internal boundaries to achieve international rank in French West Africa and French Indochina and in British India. Usually internal boundaries are not described with the rigour demanded for international boundaries, and therefore it was not surprising that positional boundary disputes arose between countries such as Benin and Niger, Upper Volta and Mali, Cambodia and Vietnam, India and Pakistan and India and Bangladesh.

Demarcation

Demarcation involves the identification of a delimited line in the field, the construction of monuments or other visible features to mark the line, and the maintenance of the markings. Generally the instrument of delimitation will define the composition of the demarcation commission and the distance by which the final line may vary from the delimited line in the interests of clear marking and good administration. Often demarcation does not follow promptly after delimitation, in fact there are many boundaries which have never been demarcated. Sometimes new boundary agreements render demarcation of the earlier line unnecessary, or matters of greater priority may make it impossible to spare survey teams for the work. The commencement of war in 1914 cut short a number of demarcation agreements which were not renewed after the war. Laws (1932) and Peake (1934) have described how the boundaries separating the former Belgian Congo from Northern Rhodesia and Tanganyika respectively remained undemarcated until copper and tin mining made demarcation essential if major disputes were to be avoided and large companies encouraged to invest further capital.

When many of the world's international boundaries were demarcated the commissioners faced serious problems from hostile tribes, dangerous fevers, slow travel, and adverse climates. Those problems have now almost been eliminated by improved means of travel and communication and the use of aerial photographs and new survey methods. However, modern demarcation commissioners still face the other set of problems which faced their predecessors. These problems concerned the ambiguities and inconsistencies contained in the text delimiting the boundary. Sometimes the delimitation document was so unsatisfactory that the commissioners were unable to reach agreement and had to pass the problem back to the diplomats. Such an event has already been mentioned in connection with the Russo-Afghan boundary in 1887; five years later the British and Portuguese commissioners could not agree on a single interpretation of the text governing the boundary between Rhodesia and Mozambique and the matter was passed to Italian arbitration, which was handed down in 1897.

The classical case of a contradictory definition concerned the boundary between Argentina and Chile which was promulgated in 1881. A section of the boundary was defined as 'the most elevated crests of said Cordillera that may divide the waters' (Hinks, 1921, and Varela, 1899). Unfortunately the process of headward erosion by the rivers flowing eastwards into Argentina has pushed the watershed west of the crest of the Andes, so Chile pressed for the crest and Argentina argued for the water divide.

The boundary may be marked in a variety of ways. In semi-arid areas pillars of stone are often constructed, while in sandy deserts materials had to be imported to construct monuments. At least in deserts there is usually the possibility of long lines of sight between pillars, whereas in forested or scrub areas the clearing of vistas was often a long and difficult undertaking. In addition to erecting pillars along the Sino-Burmese boundary, which was settled in 1960, the demarcation commission also planted flowering trees near the boundary to make its location more obvious.

It is regrettable that many of the boundaries which were demarcated at the beginning of this century in Africa and Asia were not maintained by regular inspections. Various natural processes tend to obliterate boundaries. Vegetation grows up in the cleared lines, plants break down pillars and cover them, large animals may knock them over, and the elements of weather can cause deterioration. There is the added problem that the local population will sometimes move the boundary markers because they do not agree with them, or steal the materials of which the markers are constructed for their own purposes. Clifford (1936) and Ryder (1925), working in Somalia and Turkey respectively, described how nomads destroyed boundary pillars within 24 hours of erection, in the belief that sovereignty was vested in the people rather than in the land. In 1907 a demarcation commission placed 226 beacons along the 270 miles of boundary between Rhodesia and Botswana. Each beacon consisted of an iron pole sunk 3 feet into the ground and surrounded by a pile of rocks. In 1959 a second demarcation commission worked on this line and found only 105 of the original beacons, and some of them were only found after a long search. Lambert (1965) has written an interesting account of the maintenance of the boundary between Canada and the United States.

Evolution in position

Analysis of the evolution of the boundary's position is important for three reasons. First, the operation of state functions at the boundary and of state policies in the borderland can influence the development of landscapes along the boundary. This process may produce recognisable landscape differences along the boundary, and those differences will be a function of the time the process has operated. It is therefore important to know how long the boundary has occupied particular sites. Second, as the boundary changes its position areas will be transferred from one authority to another. Such changes in sovereignty may set in train changes in settlement patterns, the volume of migration, and the orientation of regional economies, and these are all important subjects for consideration. Third, the transfer of territory from one country to another may provide the cause for subsequent irredentist movements within the detached areas, and may underlie territorial claims at a later date by the country which lost the territory.

Before looking at these points in more detail, it is useful to relate the scale of change in boundary position to the stages of evolution in definition. The areas transferred by changes in position usually decrease as the definition proceeds from allocation to demarcation. This point is illustrated by the history of the Anglo-French boundary between the River Niger and Lake Chad. When the second allocating boundary, drawn in 1898, is compared with the first, drawn eight years earlier, it is noticed that the maximum movement of the boundary was 90 miles and that Britain gained 14,800 square miles and lost 4,550 square miles. This situation was reversed by the delimitation of the boundary in 1904, when the maximum movement of the boundary was 70 miles and France gained 19,960 square miles. When this delimited boundary was demarcated in 1907 the commission made only nine small changes, the largest of which involved 17 square miles.

It is proposed to leave consideration of the role of boundaries in landscape construction to the final chapter of this book, but brief reference is made here to the possible effects which the transfer of territory from one country to another may produce.

Several studies of this subject have been made. Pallis (1925) studied national migrations in the Balkans during the period 1912-24, when the boundaries within the area significantly altered. He concluded that the movements were the largest since the break-up of the Roman Empire. The movement of people from territory ceded to neighbouring states formed a significant part of the migrations. For example, in 1913, the total Greek population, numbering 5,000, left the qazas of Jam'a-i-Bala, Melnik, Nevrokop and Stromitsa, when they were ceded to Bulgaria by the Treaty of Bucharest. In 1914, approximately 100,000 Moslems left the portions of central and eastern Macedonia which had been ceded to the Balkan states by the peace treaty with Turkey, and settled in eastern Thrace and Anatolia. This scale of movement was exceeded after the Second World War, when the Polish boundary moved westwards to the Oder-Neisse line, at the expense of Germany. Wiskemann (1956, p.118) estimates that in 1946, 1,460,621 Germans left Polish-occupied territory and settled in British-occupied Germany, and that a further 600,000 moved into the Soviet sector. In the next three years a further 800,000 moved into the Soviet zone. By 1954 the number of Poles living in the Polish-occupied territory had risen from the pre-war figure of one million to seven millions (Wiskemann, 1956, p.213). The changes in population structure in the former German areas were accompanied by alterations in the pattern of agriculture. All holdings over 100 hectares were confiscated and much of this land was redistributed to Polish peasants, as farms having an average size of 12 hectares. Altogether 3.6 million hectares were distributed to 605,000 families. In addition, some collective farms were organised which bore a closer resemblance to some of the former German estimates.

Economic changes resulting from boundary changes have also been studied by geographers, including Schlier (1959) and Weigend (1950). Schlier contrasts the spheres of influence of Berlin before and after the Second World War, in respect of administration, services, food supplies, and employment. His maps show how Berlin's areas of influence in all respects have been truncated by the movement of international boundaries, and how links with the Federal Republic are restricted to a few well-defined roads, railways and air-corridors. Weigend (1950) examined the changes which occurred in that area of the South Tyrol which was transferred from Austria to Italy in 1919. He points to the striking proportional increase of Italians in the population, and makes some interesting comments on the economic changes. The fruit and wine producers of the transferred area continued to export their products to their traditional markets, which now lay across the boundary. Because the Italian producers were now competing on equal tariff terms it was necessary for the producers in South Tyrol to improve the quality of their products. Other farmers in the transferred area adjusted production to the requirements of the population of the Po plain, which had become their obvious market. The constant demand for seed potatoes and Swiss Brown cattle led to their import into, and production in, the transferred areas. Although the tourist trade suffered because of the transfer, this disadvantage was partially offset by the establishment of some industries including hydro-electricity generation and aluminium refining at Bolzano.

A review of the available studies of the effects of boundary changes suggests the general conclusion that the effects will be less severe when one or more of the following situations exists:

1. The altered boundary has existed for only a short time.
2. Few state functions have been applied at the boundary.
3. The groups formerly separated by the boundary have a cultural similarity.
4. The economy of the transferred area was formerly oriented across the boundary.
5. The economy of the transferred area is of a self-contained subsistence nature.

The transfer of the Juba strip to Italian Somaliland from the Protectorate of Kenya after World War I met the second, third and fifth conditions outlined above. Neither the Italian nor British Governments had rigorously applied state functions at the boundary, and the Somali groups from either side were free to cross the boundary to find pastures during their subsistence stock movements. For all these reasons the transfer took place smoothly without any dislocation to the lives of the borderland inhabitants.

The converse of this argument is that boundary changes are likely to be most severe in their effects upon the population and the landscape when the boundary has existed for a long time, when the population of the transferred area is ethnically dissimilar from the state in which they are incorporated, when the states applied many fiscal and security functions at the boundary, and finally when the economy of the transferred area was closely integrated with the core region of the state from which it is removed.

An example of a country reclaiming territory which it lost through the relocation of a boundary is provided by Portugal. In 1886 Germany claimed the Kionga Triangle south of the Rovuma River, and this area was detached from Mozambique and added to Tanganyika. In 1918, after Germany's defeat, Portugal successfully reclaimed the area at the Versailles Peace Conference. A more recent example is provided by the claim of Upper Volta to the narrow strip of territory known as Oudalan, which is held by Mali. This region, which has a plentiful and permanent supply of water and rich pastures, was part of Upper Volta from 1919 to 1932. In 1932 France reorganised the administration of French West Africa, and Upper Volta was divided amongst the neighbouring administrative regions of Mali, Niger and Ivory Coast. The territory was reconstituted in 1947, but the Oudalan was left in Mali, on the grounds that it had been administered from Tombouctou in 1911.

Evolution in Function

The only function of a boundary is to mark the limits of sovereignty. The nature of the boundary's definition and the condition of the demarcated boundary will determine the effectiveness with which the boundary serves this function. In certain areas where international boundaries are located in deserts or tropical forests, it may often be difficult for the traveller to know when he passes from one state to another. This was one of the reasons why the Sino-Indian border situation became difficult in 1961. In most parts of the world, however, it is now difficult for travellers to stray inadvertently across international boundaries and the local residents usually know exactly where the territorial limit lies.

Usually a state will find it convenient to carry out some of its functions at the boundary. At points of entry passports are inspected and customs and health regulations are enforced. These points of entry are likely to be at the boundary on land routes and at airports and seaports for other travellers. In the last two cases the checking is done at the first convenient point after the traveller enters the state's territory, which extends to the outer edge of the territorial waters and to an unspecified height in the atmosphere. Boggs (1940) has listed state functions applied at the boundary although he ascribes them to the boundary itself. There does not appear to be any study of the order in which state functions are applied at the boundary and it is unlikely that one will ever be made. Such a study would have been interesting in the evolution of colonial boundaries in Africa and Asia as administrations played an increasingly important role in the conduct of commercial and strategic relations. Restrictions on the import of weapons and the export of ivory and slaves were often some of the earliest acts of colonial governors. Gradually other regulations were added to control the circulation of people, goods and ideas, until, by the end of the colonial period some of these limits were difficult to cross unless an extensive array of forms had been correctly filled in and certified. Once independence was achieved the new governments acted promptly to ensure that they exercised all necessary functions at the boundary. The supervision of movement across some of these international boundaries was very strictly controlled at times when fighting in neighbouring states produced streams of refugees, as in Zaire in 1960, and when any threat to the established government was detected, as in Benin in 1975. It must also be noted that sometimes countries have closed boundaries in order to register displeasure with neighbouring states. For example, in 1964 twelve boundaries were closed by African states during quarrels with neighbours, and more recently, in 1977 Tanzania closed its boundary with Kenya, and Kenya closed its boundary with Uganda.

Of course there are also cases where there is a reduction in the number of state functions applied at the boundary. The best example in recent years is provided by the greater ease in circulation within the European Economic Community. It seems likely that the most fruitful avenue for research into the evolution of functions will concern the way in which the application of state functions at the boundary influences the development of the border landscape.

To illustrate some of the points made in this chapter it is proposed to consider the evolution of the boundary between Mexico and the United States of America.

Evolution of the Boundary between Mexico and the United States of America since 1847

A state of war legally came into existence between Mexico and the United States on 13 May 1846. In less than a year the American forces had made considerable advances and secured the Mexican Provinces of New Mexico, Upper and Lower California, Coahuila, Tamaulipas, Nuevo Leon and Chihuahua. Accordingly the American Government decided to appoint a Commissioner who would remain with the army and be ready to accept opportunity for negotiating a satisfactory peace (Miller, 1937, p.261). The conditions which the United States Government would find satisfactory were carefully laid down in a draft agreement which was given to the Commissioner; we are concerned here only with the territorial provisions.

At that time the *de jure* boundary between the two states was that promulgated in 1819 and coincident with the Sabine, Red and Arkansas rivers and latitude 42 degrees north. Under Article IV of the draft treaty, the United States sought a southward extension of the boundary to include all Texas, which had joined the Union in 1845, New Mexico, and Upper and Lower California (Figure 3.1).

The boundary line between the two Republics shall commence in the Gulf of Mexico three leagues from land opposite the mouth of the Rio Grande, from then up the middle of that river to the point where it strikes the Southern line of New Mexico, thence westwardly along the Southern boundary of New Mexico, to the South Western corner of the same, thence Northward along the Western line of New Mexico until it intersects the first Branch of the river Gila, or if it should not intersect any branch of that river, then to the point on the line nearest to such branch and thence in a direct line to the same and down the middle of said branch of the said river until it empties into the Rio Colorado, thence down the middle of the Colorado and the middle of the Gulf of California to the Pacific Ocean. (Miller, 1937, p.265)

In addition to this territorial gain the United States sought to secure transit rights for American citizens and other goods across the Tehuantepec peninsula. The draft agreement represents the maximum concessions which America hoped to gain: the government indicated that they would be satisfied with less and outlined a series of payments which could be authorised to Mexico depending upon the territory and rights secured:

Figure 3.1: American Boundary Proposals in 1847

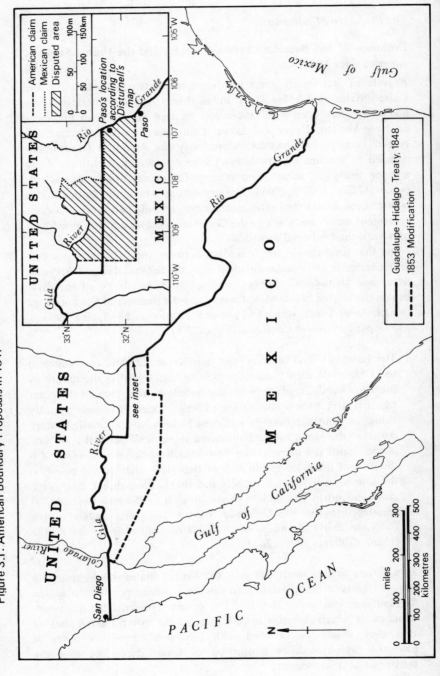

1. Up to $30 millions would be paid for Upper and Lower California and New Mexico, together with transit rights over the Tehuantepec peninsula.

2. Up to $25 millions would be paid either for the three Mexican provinces alone, or Upper California and New Mexico together with transit rights.

3. Up to $20 millions would be paid for Upper California and New Mexico.

If it proved impossible to secure Lower California, the conclusion of the boundary description would be altered to read as follows: 'to a point directly opposite the division line between Upper and Lower California; thence, due West, along the said line which runs north of the parallel of 32° and South of San Miguel to the Pacific Ocean' (Miller, 1937, p.263).

The intention of the boundary definition was clear, but it contained the seeds of disputes. Boggs (1940) has shown the difficulty of identifying 'the middle' of any river. Further, the description assumed that there was no uncertainty about the position of the southern boundary of New Mexico. Lastly, considerable difficult may have been attached to locating the point on the western boundary of New Mexico nearest to any tributary of the River Gila, and the actual situation might have involved a considerable northward extension of the boundary.

Second thoughts by the United States Government resulted in further choices being suggested to the Commissioner. In order to gain the Paso del Norte and the whole of the Gila Valley, which had been identified as a favourable route to the Pacific Ocean, it was suggested that the boundary should follow the Rio Grande to the thirty-second parallel of north latitude and along that latitude to the middle of the Gulf of California. This line could be extended across the Californian peninsula if Lower California could not be obtained, but it was essential that the Americans should have uninterrupted access through the Gulf of California and that San Diego be secured. This course was recommended since it would prevent any dispute about the southern boundary of New Mexico which, so far as America knew, had never been 'authoritatively and specifically determined' (Miller, 1937, p.770).

At the first meetings between American and Mexican Commissioners the latter revealed their Government's proposals. No doubt, like the American draft, there were several possibilities. The most important point which emerged from the first exchange was that the Mexican

Government laid down two conditions as *sine qua non* which prevented even the minimum American demands from providing a basis for discussion. First, the Mexicans required a neutral strip of territory adjacent to the north bank of the Rio Grande, in order to afford military protection against the United States and restrict the incidence of smuggling, which would reduce Mexico's revenue and injure their manufacturing industries. Second, Mexico required a land connexion between Lower California and Sonora around the head of the Gulf of California (Figure 3.2).

Instead of breaking off the negotiations, the American Commissioner exceeded his instructions and submitted a line which met the Mexican conditions to his Government, for their consideration. Historians have undoubtedly judged the Commissioner: geographers can be concerned only with the results of this action. The recommended boundary was defined as follows:

> The boundary line between the two Republics shall commence at a point in the Gulf of Mexico, three leagues from Land, opposite to the middle of the Southernmost inlet into Corpus Christi Bay; thence, through the middle of said inlet, and through the middle of said bay, to the middle of the mouth of the Rio Nueces; thence up the middle of said river to the Southernmost extremity of Yoke Lake, or Oagunda de las Yuntas, where the said river leaves the said Lake, after running through the same; thence by a line due west to the middle of the Rio Puerco, and thence up the middle of said river to the parallel of latitude six geographical miles north of the Fort at the Paso del Norte on the Rio Bravo; thence due west, along the said parallel to the point where it intersects the western boundary of New Mexico; thence northwardly along the said boundary, until it first intersects a branch of the River Gila; (or if it should not intersect any branch of that river, then to the point on said boundary nearest to the first branch thereof, and from that point in a direct line to such branch) thence down the middle of said branch and of the said River Gila, until it empties into the Rio Colorado, and down or up the middle of the Colorado, as the case may require, to the thirty third parallel of latitude; and thence due west along the said parallel, into the Pacific Ocean. And it is hereby agreed and stipulated, that the territory comprehended between the Rio Bravo and the above defined Boundary, from its commencement in the Gulf of Mexico up to the point where it crosses the said Rio Bravo, shall for ever remain a neutral ground between the two

Figure 3.2: Mexican Boundary Proposals in 1847

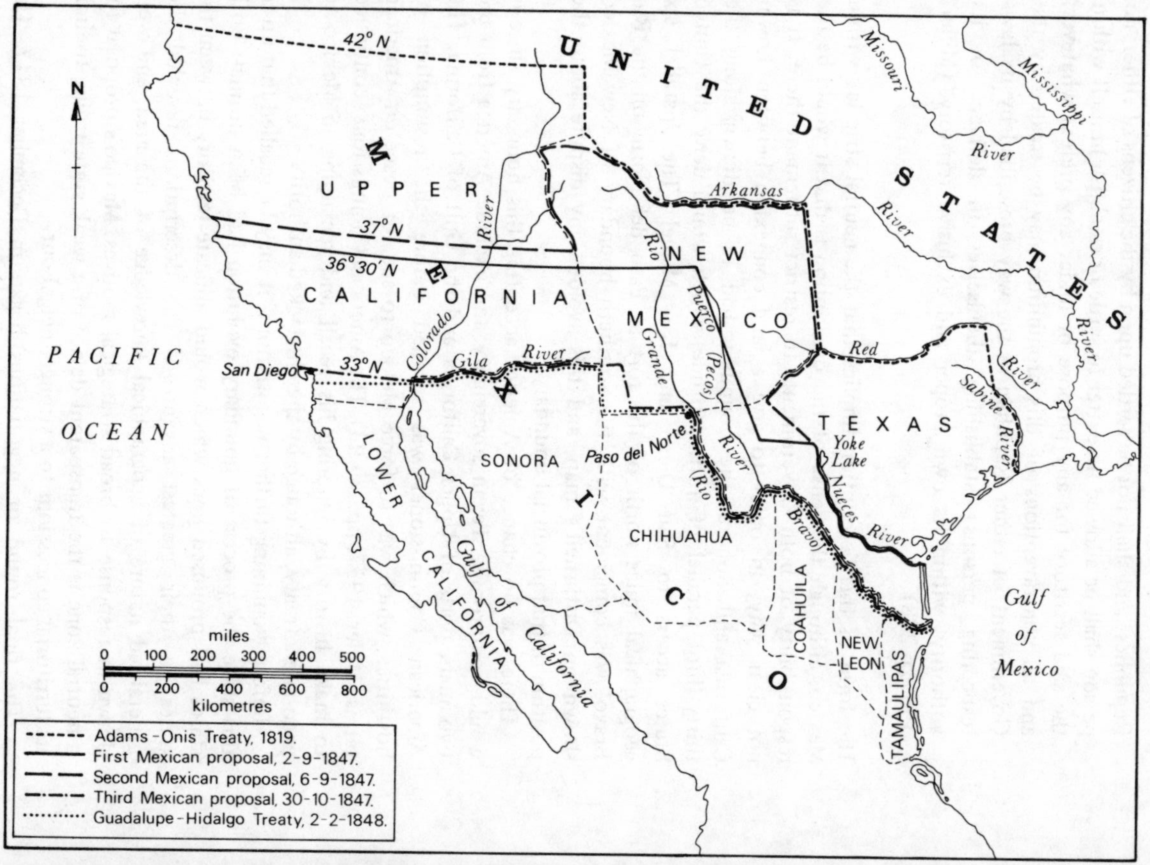

Adams – Onis Treaty, 1819.
First Mexican proposal, 2-9-1847.
Second Mexican proposal, 6-9-1847.
Third Mexican proposal, 30-10-1847.
Guadalupe – Hidalgo Treaty, 2-2-1848.

Republics, and shall not be settled upon by the citizens of either; no person shall be allowed hereafter to settle or establish himself within the said territory for any purpose or under any pretext whatever; and all contraventions of this prohibition may be treated by the Government of either Republic in the way prescribed by its laws respecting persons establishing themselves in defiance of its authority, within its own proper and exclusive territory. (Miller, 1937, p.288)

The form of this description implies that the neutral strip lay within Mexico, although the sense of the description is that it would be the responsibility of both Governments to restrict settlement there. It is not clear why, in order to give a land connexion between Lower California and Sonora, the boundary had to be drawn along the thirty-third parallel of north latitude, which would deny the United States access to San Diego and San Miguel. The 'parallel six geographical miles north of the fort at Paso del Norte on the Rio Bravo' was coincident with the southern boundary of New Mexico shown on Disturnell's map, and this avoided any dispute about the position of that provincial boundary.

There was no chance of America accepting this boundary since it would compromise Texan sovereignty and exclude America from the two main ports of Upper California and the Gulf of California. The American Commissioner was recalled before the resumption of hostilities, which was to force Mexico to sue for peace on American terms (Miller, 1937, pp.289-93). The American Commissioner continued to make history by ignoring his recall and remaining in Mexico to negotiate a treaty, although by then he lacked authority.

Before examining further negotiations, it may be recalled that up to this stage the process of boundary evolution had been normal. Both states had proposed lines which would allocate territory between the states to their greatest advantage. The descriptions revealed the generalised nature of geographical knowledge of the area, and were drawn in response to broad strategical motives. Mexico's proposal for a neutral zone is the transparent device of a weak state trying to limit its territorial concessions to a stronger neighbour.

The final round of negotiations began in December 1847. The Mexicans gave up the idea of a broad neutral zone, and instead sought to draw the boundary parallel to, and one league north of, the river. Further, they introduced a claim calling for part of the boundary to coincide with the summits of the Sierra de los Mimbres, which would have preserved the southwest quadrant of New Mexico. The Mexican Government did not give up its claims for a land connexion between Lower California and Sonora which would include San Diego.

It was only this last point which prevented rapid agreement, for it will be recalled that the American Commissioner had been instructed in the first draft to secure a boundary which was to be defined in the west as follows:

> down the middle of the Colorado river and the Gulf of Mexico to a point opposite the division line between Upper and Lower California; then due west along said line which runs north of the parallel of 32° and south of San Miguel to the Pacific Ocean. (Miller, 1937, p.263)

The American Commissioner found himself in some difficulty for three reasons. First, some cartographic authorities showed San Miguel to be south of latitude 32 degrees north. Second, the Mexican Government, and other authorities, represented the political division between Upper and Lower California as being north of San Diego. Third, it was suspected, correctly, that the mouth of the Colorado River lay south of the thirty-second parallel.

Eventually, after several proposals and counter-proposals, the Commissioners agreed to a boundary which coincided with the original American draft except in the extreme west, where the boundary followed a direct line from the confluence of the Gila and Colorado Rivers to a point on the Pacific coast named Punto de Arena, which was south of San Diego (Miller, 1937, p.325).

This suggestion was transmitted to both Governments, and not surprisingly the American Government decided to accept it although their agent lacked authority in the final negotiations. The treaty was endorsed by the American Senate, with certain amendments which did not relate to the territorial provisions. The fifth article defined the boundary in the following way:

> The Boundary line between the two Republics shall commence in the Gulf of Mexico, three leagues from land, opposite the mouth of its deepest branch, if it should have more than one branch emptying directly into the sea; from thence, up the middle of that river, following the deepest channel, where it has more than one, to the point where it strikes the south boundary of New Mexico; thence, westwardly, along the whole southern boundary of New Mexico

(which runs north of the town called Paso) to its western termination; thence, northward, along the western line of New Mexico, until it intersects the first branch of the river Gila; (or it it should not intersect any branch of that river, then, to the point on the said line nearest to such branch, and thence in a direct line to the same); thence down the middle of the said branch of the said river, until it empties into the Rio Colorado; thence, across the Rio Colorado, following the division line between Upper and Lower California, to the Pacific Ocean.

The southern and western limits of New Mexico, mentioned in this Article, are those laid down in the Map, entitled 'Map of the United Mexican States, as organised and defined by various acts of the Congress of said Republic, and constructed according to the best Authorities. Revised Edition. Published at New York in 1847 by J. Disturnell:' of which Map a Copy is added to this treaty, bearing the signatures and seals of the Undersigned Plenipotentiaries. And, in order to preclude all difficulty in tracing upon the ground the limit shall consist of a straight line, drawn from the middle of the Rio Gila, where it unites with the Colorado, to a point on the coast of the Pacific Ocean, distant one marine league due south of the southernmost point of the Port of San Diego, according to the plan of said port, made in the year 1782 by Don Juan Pantoja, second sailing master of the Spanish fleet, and published at Madrid in the year 1802, in the Atlas of the voyage of the schooners Sutil and Mexicana. (Miller, 1937, pp.213-15)

There are two points to notice. First, the description was similar to that originally proposed by America, and it continued to reflect the generalised topographical knowledge available about the area in question. Second, the definition hoped to avoid the two main points of controversy by specifying the maps which were authorities for fixing the southern and western boundaries of New Mexico and the terminal point on the Pacific Ocean. Subsequent events showed that controversy was not avoided.

In 1849 a Commission tried to determine the Pacific coast terminus of the boundary, which was defined as follows: 'one marine league due south of the southernmost point of the port of San Diego, according to the plan of the said port, made in the year 1782 by Don Juan Pontoja' (Miller, 1937, p.214). The Commission found little correspondence between the map and the actual coastline. They did find one point near the port which appeared to coincide with the present coast.

Accordingly they measured the distance on the map between this point and the southernmost point of the port. This distance was then laid off on the ground, and the marine league measured from there.

In 1852 the United States Government made financial provision for the Commission appointed to demarcate the southern and western boundary of New Mexico. The availability of the money depended upon the following condition being met.

> That no part of this appropriation shall be used or expended until it shall be made satisfactorily to appear . . . that the southern boundary of New Mexico is not established . . . farther north of the town called 'Paso' than the same is laid down in Disturnell's map, which is added to the treaty. (Miller, 1937, p.369)

Now, according to the treaty map the latitude of El Paso was 32° 15′ north, and the boundary intersected the Rio Grande eight miles north of the town, and extended 3½° of longitude west of that river, which was shown to be in longitude 27° 40′ west of Washington. The surveyors quickly found that the correct latitude of El Paso was 31° 45′ north, and the boundary intersected the Rio Grande at longitude 29° 40′ west of Washington. The Mexican members of the Commission pressed for a boundary starting on the Rio Grande at 32° 22′ north and proceeding westwards for 1½° of longitude. This means that they wished to accept the latitude of the boundary shown on the map, but correct the longitudinal error in the river position. For them the position of El Paso was unimportant provided it remained Mexican. However, the American Government insisted on following the map and using the position of El Paso as the datum from which measurements in the field would be made. The area between the two interpretations of the boundary was about 11,000 square miles (Figure 3.3).

Neither side was prepared to concede the area nor to compromise, and therefore new boundary negotiations were started in 1853. After extravagant proposals by both sides a new boundary definition crystallised out of the discussions. The new boundary followed the middle of the Rio Grande to latitude 31° 47′ north, which it followed westwards for one hundred miles before turning due south to the parallel 31° 20′ north. This parallel was followed westwards as far as longitude 111° west of Greenwich. The boundary then followed a straight line to the Colorado River twenty English miles below its confluence with the River Gila, and then upstream along the middle of the Colorado to the line agreed in 1848 (Malloy, 1910, vol.1, p.1122). This line ceded about 24,000 square miles to the United States and

Figure 3.3: American-Mexican Boundary, 1848 and 1853

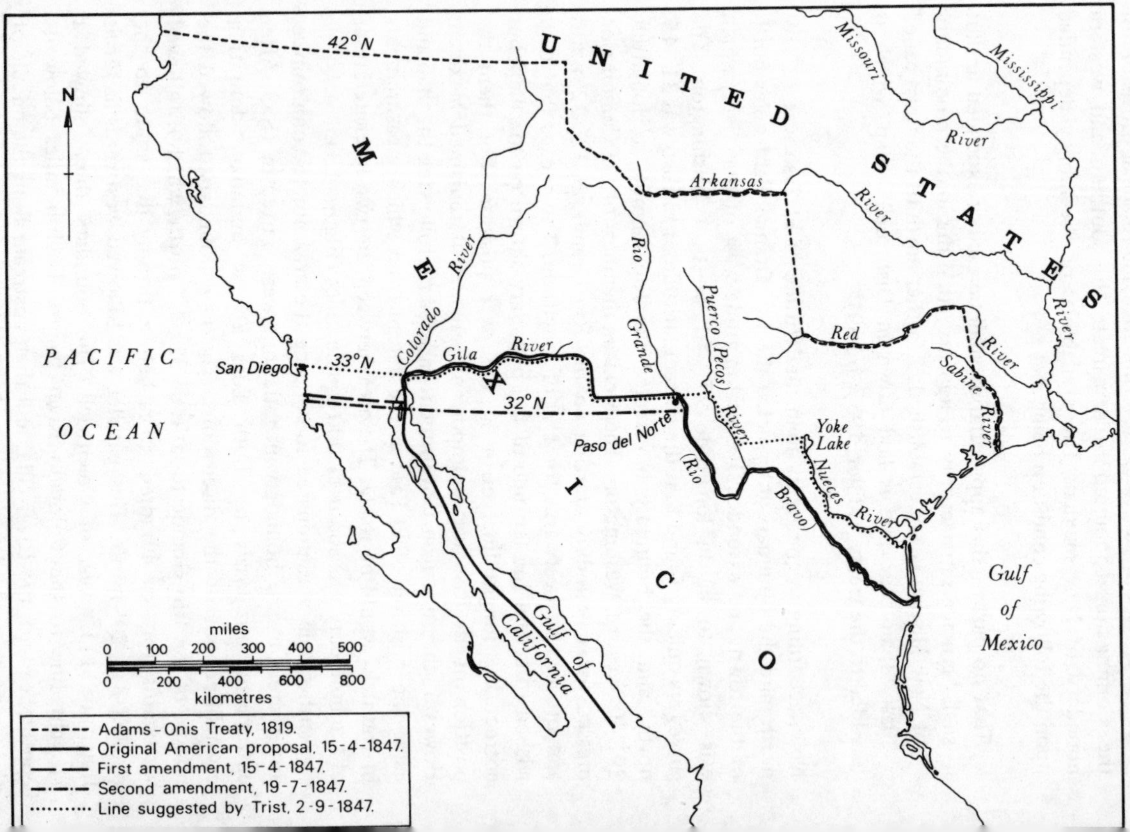

Legend:
- Adams – Onis Treaty, 1819.
- Original American proposal. 15-4-1847.
- First amendment. 15-4-1847.
- Second amendment. 19-7-1847.
- Line suggested by Trist. 2-9-1847.

secured for that state the entire catchment of the River Gila (Figure 3.3).

No problems were experienced in demarcating this second allocating boundary between the Rio Grande and the Colorado River. The only problems associated with the boundary since 1853 have all been concerned with the Rio Grande, which proved to be most unstable in position in the section which marked the boundary. Changes in the river's course occurred gradually by accretion and suddenly by avulsion. The most enduring problem concerned El Chamizal, a tract of 630 acres opposite El Paso on the north bank of the river which forms the boundary. Mexico claimed that this area was south of the boundary in 1853, when the agreement came into force, but was transferred to the north bank of the river, when the course was suddenly changed in the floods of 1864. The two states could not solve the dispute, and arbitration by Canada in 1910 failed to produce an answer. The Canadian decision was that the boundary should follow the course of the river as it existed before the floods of 1864. It did not prove possible to establish this line through this territory to the satisfaction of both sides until 1964, when it was agreed to divide the disputed area. Hill (1965) has written an excellent account of this settlement.

In 1884, the two states agreed that in future the boundary would coincide with the centre of the normal channel of the river and continue to follow changes in the river's course resulting from accretion. The boundary would follow the abandoned river course when changes resulted from avulsion. This meant that the area transferred from one bank to the other, when a meander neck was severed, locally known as *bancos,* would remain under the sovereignty of the original state (Malloy, 1910, vol.1, p.1159). In 1905 the governments agreed to minimise the difficulties resulting from avulsive river changes by exchanging all *bancos* other than those having an area of more than 617 acres or a population of two hundred. A permanent commission was responsible for this mutual exchange, which simplified boundary administration.

Further complications resulted from the fact that the Rio Grande is a valuable resource used by nationals of both states. To regularise the use of the water Mexico and America signed a Convention in 1906 to ensure equitable division. Under the terms of the Convention the United States Government contracted to deliver 60,000 acre feet to the head of a Mexican canal one mile below the point where the river became the internal boundary. The United States would also be responsible for the distribution of water as far as Fort Quitman in

Texas. In order to prevent damaging floods a dam was built in 1916 at Elephant Butte in Texas. This effectively stopped the flood waters derived from above the dam, but the reduction in the flow rate of the river resulted in the deposition of alluvium which had previously been scoured by floods. At El Paso the river bed was 12 feet higher in 1933 than in 1907. To remedy the situation the Governments agreed to construct a rectified canal from El Paso-Juarez to the mouth of the Box Canyon below Fort Quitman. The canal of 88 miles shortened the river course by 67 miles, and the increased gradient prevented alluvial accumulation. The canal was 590 feet wide and was aligned along the boundary axis, requiring both sides to exchange 3,500 acres. In addition to making the adjoining farmlands more secure from flood, the new canal increased the areas of land available for cultivation and simplified boundary maintenance and control.

This account of the evolution of the boundary between the United States and Mexico reveals four points. First, the American motives in concluding the initial boundary agreement were to secure at least the former Mexican territory of New Mexico and Upper California, and to end the war without the need to occupy all Mexico and maintain a military administration. Mexico agreed to negotiate in order to maintain sovereignty over the area south of the ceded portion. Second, at no time was the boundary delimited. The Guadalupe-Hidalgo Treaty laid down a boundary which allocated territory between the two states, and this line was modified by the Gadsen Treaty, when the first boundary definition proved impossible to apply on the ground. In both cases the boundary was defined by imprecise physical features, and straight lines linking known points or coinciding with parallels of latitude or meridians. The descriptions reflected the generalised nature of existing knowledge about the area. Third, the demarcation of these allocating boundaries was hindered by the lack of correspondence between the maps named in the treaty and the actual landscape, and by the nature of the Rio Grande. Fourth, state controls over immigration and trade were applied as soon as the boundary could be identified.

References

Boggs, S.W., 1940, *International Boundaries,* New York
Brigham, A.P., 1917, 'Principles in the Delimitation of Boundaries', *Geogr. Rev.,* 7, pp.201-19
Clifford, E.H.M., 1936, 'The British Somaliland-Ethiopia Boundary', *Geogr. J.,* 87, pp.289-337

Davidson, G., 1903, *The Alaska Boundary*, San Francisco

Detzner, V.H., 1913, 'Die Nigerische Grenze von Kamerun zwischen Yola und dem Cross-Fluss',*Mitteilungen aus den deutschen Schutzgebieten,* 26,pp.317-38

Edwards, H.A., 1913, 'Frontier Work on the Bolivia-Brazil boundary', *Geogr. J.,* 42, pp.113-28

Hertslet, Sir E., 1875-91, *The Map of Europe by Treaty*, 4 vols., London

———., 1909, *Map of Africa by Treaty*, 3 vols., plus atlas, London

Hill, J., 1965, 'El Chamizal: A Century Old Boundary Dispute', *Geogr. Rev.,* 55, pp.510-22

Hinks, A.R., 1921, 'Notes on the Techniques of Boundary Delimitation', *Geogr. J.,* 58, pp.417-43

Holdich, T.H., 1916, *Political Frontiers and Boundary Making,* London

Inspector General of Customs, 1917, *Treaties between China and Foreign States,* 2 vols., Shanghai

Jones, S.B., 1945, *Boundary Making: A Handbook for Statesmen,* Washington

Lamb, A., 1964, 'The Sino-Pakistan Boundary Agreement of 2 March 1963', *Australian Outlook,* 18, pp.299-312

Lambert, A.F., 1965, 'Maintaining the Canada-United States Boundary', *The Cartographer,* 2, pp.67-71

Lapradelle, P. de, 1928, *La frontiére,* Paris

Laws, J.B., 1932, 'A Minor Adjustment in the Boundary between Tanganyika Territory and Ruanda', *Geogr. J.,* 80, pp.244-7

Mackinder, H.J., 1904, 'The Geographical Pivot of History', *Geogr. J.,* 23, pp.421-44

Malloy, W.M., 1910, *Treaties, Conventions, International Acts, Protocols and Agreements between the United States of America and other Powers, 1776-1909,* Washington

Miller, H., 1937, *Treaties and Other Acts of the United States of America,* vol.5, Washington

Moodie, A.E., 1945, *The Italo-Jugoslav Boundary*, London

Nicholson, N.L., 1954, *The Boundaries of Canada, its Provinces and Territories,* Department of Mines and Technical Surveys, Geographical Branch, Memoir 2, Ottawa

Nugent, W.V., 1914, 'The Geographical Results of the Nigeria-Kamerun Boundary Demarcation Commission', *Geogr. J.,* pp.630-51

Pallis, A.A., 1925, 'Racial Migrations in the Balkans during the years 1912-24', *Geogr. J.* 66, pp.315-31

Prescott, J.R.V., 1971, *The Evolution of Nigeria's international and regional boundaries,* Vancouver

———., 1975, *Map of Mainland Asia by Treaty*, Melbourne

Rudin, H.R., 1938, *Germans in the Cameroons,* London

Ryder, C.H.D., 1925, 'The Demarcation of the Turco-Persian Boundary in 1913-14', *Geogr.J.,* 66, pp.227-42

Schlier, O., 1959, 'Berlins Verflechtungen mit der Umwelt fruher und heute', *Geographische Rundschau,* 11, Heft 4, pp.125-51

Sykes, Sir P., 1926, *The Right Honourable Sir Mortimer Durand,* London

Varela, L.V., 1899, *La République Argentine et le Chilli: Histoire de la démarcation de leurs frontières (depuis 1843 jusqu'à 1899),* 2 vols., Buenos Aires

Vattel, E. de, 1758, *Le droit des gens ou principes de la loi naturelle appliqués a la conduite, et aux affaires des nations et des souverains,* Vol.2, London

Weigend, G.G., 1950, 'Effects of Boundary Changes in the South Tyrol', *Geogr. Rev.,* 40, pp.364-75

Wiskemann, E., 1956, *Germany's Eastern Neighbours,* London

4 INTERNATIONAL BOUNDARY DISPUTES

> The relations between modern states reach their most critical stage in the form of problems relating to territory. Boundary disputes, conflicting claims to newly discovered lands, and invasions by expanding nations into the territory of their weaker neighbours have been conspicuous among the causes of war. (Hill, 1976, p.3)

Boundary disputes have long been a popular subject for research amongst political geographers, lawyers, political scientists and historians. These researchers have a refreshing topicality, and often result in governments making available information which would otherwise have remained buried in correspondence files and secret reports. The general term 'boundary dispute' includes four quite different types of disagreements between countries.

The first type of dispute may be described as a *territorial boundary dispute* and this results from some quality of the neighbouring borderland which makes it attractive to the country initiating the dispute. The second type of boundary dispute concerns the actual location of the boundary, and usually involves a controversy over the interpretation of terms used in defining the boundary at the stage of allocation, delimitation or demarcation. This type may be called *positional boundary dispute*. Both territorial and positional disputes can only be solved in favour of the claimant state by altering the position of the boundary; the two remaining types can be solved without altering the boundary's location. The third type arises over state functions applied at the boundary, and they may be described as *functional boundary disputes*. The last type of dispute concerns the use of some trans-boundary resources such as a river or a coalfield. Disputes of this kind usually have as their aim the creation of some organisation which will govern use of the particular resource, and they may be called *disputes over resource development*.

Geographers are not alone in studying boundary disputes, which have also been a profitable field of research for other scholars. For example, Hsu (1965) published a detailed historical account of the boundary dispute between China and Russia in the Ili Valley between 1871 and 1881; Johnson (1966) prepared an interesting account of the legal aspects of the dispute over the Columbia River between the United States and Canada; and Touval (1966) presented a useful study of the boundary dispute between Morocco and Algeria from the viewpoint of a political scientist. However, the facility of geographers with maps and their understanding of regional characteristics have given them an advantage in such studies. There are clearly some aspects of boundary disputes which a geographer is not competent to consider, such as the involved decisions about the legality of treaties, and the role of individual persons in successfully pressing arguments in favour of one or another case. There still remains a great deal which the geographer can study in making a distinct contribution to an understanding of the situation. It is suggested that the analysis of any dispute should be aimed at discovering the initial *cause* of the dispute, the *trigger action* which creates a favourable situation for a claim to be made, and the underlying *aims* of the states concerned. The analysis should then continue to evaluate those *arguments* based in geography, and assess the *results* of the dispute, and its settlement if any, in respect of the borderland and the wider canvas of international relations.

This view may be illustrated by a brief consideration of one territorial dispute between Afghanistan and Pakistan. Afghanistan claims that the Pathan tribesmen in Pakistan should be allowed to form a state with their fellow tribesmen in Afghanistan; Pakistan in reply denies that the Pathans desire the establishment of Pushtunistan, as the proposed state is known. The basic cause of the situation can be found in the Anglo-Afghan Agreement of 1893, which delimited, by means of a map, the boundary between the spheres of influence of Britain and Afghanistan (Sykes, 1940, vol.2, p.353). This agreement was confirmed by further treaties in 1905, 1919, 1921 and 1930 (Qureshi, 1966). This boundary divided the territory occupied by the Pathans in such a way that 2.4 millions remained within British territory. The boundary was the result of a British dilemma. It wanted friendly relations with Afghanistan and a stable boundary behind which British subjects would be safe. There was no obvious boundary and when Britain took action against aggressive hill tribes relations with Afghanistan worsened; if this was avoided by a British retreat sooner or later the hill tribes followed and started to raid British areas.

The trigger action which encouraged Afghanistan to make this claim was the partition of India in 1947, when Pakistan, facing internal difficulties and external pressure from India, replaced Britain as the sovereign neighbour of Afghanistan. After a period when the dispute was dormant, it was revived when the Pakistan authorities were beset with problems of internal revolt in Baluchistan after the secession of Bangladesh, and after the revolution which established a republican government in Afghanistan in July 1973.

The arguments advanced by Afghanistan fall into three categories.

First, it is argued that the 1893 treaty was not legally binding since Afghanistan signed it under duress; that in any case the tribal territories between Afghanistan and the administered territories of the British sphere formed independent territory, and that finally, Pakistan cannot inherit the rights of an 'extinguished person'; namely the British in India (Fraser-Tytler, 1953, p.309). These are legal and moral arguments which the geographer can note, but not evaluate. Second, it is claimed that historically Afghanistan controlled much of India, and certainly the present area of western Pakistan (Taussig, 1961). Recourse to historical political geography shows that the State of Afghanistan was formed in 1747. At the maximum extent of the Durrani Empire in 1797, the area controlled reached eastwards almost to Delhi and Lahore. Lahore was ceded to the Mogul Empire in 1798, and Peshawar was lost in 1823. If territorial control for seventy-six years nearly one hundred and fifty years ago was accepted as a strong argument in favour of territorial reversion, the world map would be liable to dramatic change! Third, it is claimed that the Pathans in Afghanistan and Pakistan form a single ethnic unit, which should be united in one state. This argument is undoubtedly stronger, although Caroe (1961) has shown that the eastern Pathans have enjoyed close economic and political ties with the major states of the Indus valley, and have developed linguistic differences with the western Pathans. Further, the area claimed for Pushtunistan stretches from the Pamirs to the Arabian Sea, and is bounded on the west by Afghanistan and Iran and on the east by the Indus River. This includes large areas where there are few Pathans, such as Chitral, Gilgit, Baltistan and Baluchistan. When the strongest argument is exaggerated so remarkably as to weaken its force, one suspects the altruism of Afghanistan and seeks the real aim of this dispute. The claim to Baluchistan suggests that Afghanistan is hoping to control the proposed state and use it for an outlet to the Arabian Sea. Hasan (1962) has also suggested that the ruling Pathan dynasty in Afghanistan is seeking to bolster its position with regard to the Persian and Turki-speaking Afghans, who form two-thirds of the state's population.

The results of the dispute have been significant on the regional scale, and in international relations. Diplomatic relations were broken off between the two countries in September 1961 and were not resumed until May 1963. During this period the boundary was closed except for a short period in January 1962, when American foreign aid supplies were allowed through from Pakistan. Since Afghanistan's major markets were in India and most of its supplies came from Japan, America and

India, there has been some re-orientation of Afghanistan's trade. The Soviet Union has assumed a more important role in Afghanistan's international commerce than before the dispute. Disturbances and fighting in the area have encouraged Pakistan governments to improve access so that the army and airforce can operate more effectively than in the past. The closing of the boundary also affected the traditional transhumance movements of the Powindas of Afghanistan. Normally, about 100,000 Powindas, with their large herds, migrated to Pakistan's lowlands as winter settled over the Afghan uplands. These people supplemented their incomes in Pakistan by manual labour, especially in harvesting sugar cane, and money lending. After wintering in the lowlands they returned to the new summer pastures in Afghanistan. The Pakistan authorities began to insist on travel documents for the people and certificates of health for the stock, on the grounds that grazing was scarce in Pakistan and the Powindas' herds were suspected of carrying disease. The transhumance movements have not been resumed on the former scale since the boundary was reopened and the Powindas have been resettled in parts of Afghanistan including Sistan.

At the international level, Afghanistan found sympathisers for its cause in the Soviet Union and India; the latter country was presumably comforted by the thought that pressure against Pakistan by Afghanistan would reduce Pakistan's capacity to promote conflict with India. The Soviet Union was able to increase its influence in Afghanistan, which has been a traditional area of Russian concern since colonial days.

It seems likely that this is a dispute which Afghanistan will revive from time to time as it appears suitable. On 31 August 1976 Afghanistan celebrated Pakhtoonistan Day, and eighteen months earlier President Daud had outlined his country's position to the Secretary General of the United Nations:

Afghanistan has, since the time the British divided our land by force of arms and annexed part of our territory to their empire, supported the lawful right of these people [Pathans and Baluchis] living on the borders of Afghanistan and Pakistan, and will continue to do so until they are restored. (*Keesings Contemporary Archives*, 1976, 22, p.27851)

Such sentiments make it difficult to attach much importance to the agreement for Afghanistan's transit trade through Pakistan, which was signed in August 1965.

This brief account indicates the aspects of boundary disputes on which political geographers can most profitably concentrate, and the remainder of the chapter examines the four types of boundary disputes in detail.

Territorial Boundary Disputes

While it must be accepted that if a state feels sufficiently strong it might press territorial claims which have no obvious basis, nevertheless in most cases some arguments, no matter how weak, are raised. Then it will usually be found that the boundary does not correspond with some division of the cultural · or physical landscape. In most borderlands between countries it would be possible to draw a variety of boundaries based on different features, even if the work was done by an impartial commission. For example, the boundary drawn to separate linguistic groups might not coincide with the boundary separating religious factions; neither of these lines might correspond with the boundary which distinguishes areas with particular economic interests; the boundaries of former political entities might provide another set of unique lines, and unfortunately all these cultural divides might follow a different alignment to boundaries which separate the physical regions of the borderland based on morphology, drainage and vegetation. The boundary which is finally selected, after a process of political negotiations, might correspond with none of the lines mentioned, or with different sections of the various lines and therefore lack any uniform characteristic. It will therefore always be possible for a state to make a territorial claim by emphasising some pattern in the borderland which was discounted during the boundary's construction.

It can therefore be expected that most boundaries will be a compromise between the strategic, economic and ethnic requirements of the two states, and will therefore have some degree of unconformity with features in the borderland. In most cases these discrepancies will not be serious enough to provoke a territorial dispute. In those cases where territorial boundary disputes develop it is possible to identify three processes by which the boundary's unconformity might have arisen.

First, the boundary might have been drawn without full knowledge of the distribution of people or topographical features. Many of the boundaries of Africa were drawn through areas for which no precise information was available; this was particularly the case during the stage of allocation, as the last chapter shows. Unfortunately it is also true, in Africa, Asia and South America, that some boundary decisions were based on inaccurate information. Tribal chiefs would frequently exaggerate the extent of their territory in the hope that the colonial powers would establish them firmly over such extended kingdoms. For example, on 4 April 1903, the District Commissioner in Barotseland was instructed to obtain answers in very great detail to sixteen questions regarding the extent of the Barotse kingdom in 1891. This information was necessary because Britain had a disagreement with Portugal about the interpretation of their 1891 treaty regarding the boundary between Angola and Northern Rhodesia. The answers were required within one week! The Commissioner duly replied and reported on the problem and technique for solving it.

It is extremely difficult to collect reliable evidence and to obtain proof of statements as to the distance Lewanika's influence [Lewanika was Paramount Chief of the Barotse] extended in 1891, since practically the only white men who had lived in Lealui at that time were the Revd Mr Arnott and the Revd Mr Coillard, who were both Missionaries and who therefore had no interest in determining the boundaries of the Barotse influence.... it is almost necessary in order to form a correct idea of the position in 1891, to find out the actual truth at some later date, which would permit of no doubt, and then to work back on the most probable assumptions to what the position would have been at the earlier period; here we know to a large extent the position in 1897, and six years earlier in such large areas as these, the position could not evidently have been very different. (File on *Barotse Boundary* in the Archives of Rhodesia)

It was precisely because the colonial authorities were aware of the problems created by boundaries which divided tribes that they made considerable efforts to obtain reliable information. Unfortunately, the task was sometimes beyond them, and in other cases overriding strategic interests caused them to disregard reliable information about tribal distributions. In other cases it proved impossible to reconcile the data regarding tribal distributions which were acquired by both sides.

Second, sometimes at the conclusion of a war new boundaries were forced on the defeated country which did not correspond with established patterns. For example, when the Hapsburg Empire was dismembered in 1919, Italy was awarded the area of Tirol lying south of the Brenner Pass. Nearly 70 per cent of the population in the transferred area spoke German and had strong cultural affinities with the Austrians on the other side of the boundary. Following the surrender of Italy in 1943 and the defeat of Germany in 1945 Austria attempted to reclaim the southern Tirol, but was unsuccessful.

Third, it is possible for new distributions of population to develop after the boundary is drawn and to give rise to territorial claims. This is especially possible following the establishment of an antecedent boundary. After the states of Peru, Chile and Bolivia had been established valuable guano and nitrate deposits were discovered in the coastal areas of all three states, with the richest deposits being located in Bolivia. In Peru the deposits were developed under a government monopoly, while in northern Chile and southern Bolivia the smaller deposits of guano were developed by private contractors, from whom the government derived duty when the material was exported. The manual work was done by Chilean peasants in the entire borderland and their presence in Bolivia, close to Chile, encouraged that country to make a successful claim to the Bolivian littoral, which helped to transform that country to a landlocked state (Dennis, 1931, pp.37 and 73).

Even if a boundary separates a state from a neighbouring area which has certain qualities of attraction, there is no certainty that a dispute will develop. Clearly a definite act is required by the claimant state to initiate the dispute. This action will be taken in the most favourable circumstances, and therefore it will often be noticed that a boundary which has created no problems for a very long time will suddenly become the subject of dispute. Generally the trigger action which creates a favourable situation is related to some change in the government or the relative strengths of the states concerned. It was noted earlier that the Pushtunistan dispute was revived in July 1973 when a republican government replaced the traditional monarchy. The two most common circumstances which have promoted the occurrence of boundary disputes are the conclusion of wars and decolonisation.

At the conclusion of a war it often happens that there is a change in the relative strengths of states, which allows territorial claims to be advanced by the country which has been strengthened. In 1919 and 1945 European boundaries were altered in favour of states such as Poland, Czechoslovakia, and Yugoslavia at the expense of the defeated countries. Civil wars may also promote territorial disputes in two ways. First, while a country is involved in a civil war it is unlikely to engage in territorial claims which might invite attack. However, once that civil war is concluded and the country's strength renewed it may begin actively to prosecute claims to external territory. After

1949 China began to assert itself in the borderlands and demand the renegotiation of treaties which were alleged to have been forced on China during a period of weakness. This development has caused serious disputes with the Soviet Union and India. Once the Cambodian revolution was completed in 1975 it began to press claims against Thailand, and, in the same fashion, the emergence of a communist government in Laos in May 1975, which marked the end of internal strife, was quickly followed by militant policies towards the boundary with Thailand along the Mekong River, which involved artillery duels and the sinking of a Thai patrol vessel. Second, when a country is engaged in a civil war its capacity to resist external aggression is reduced and territorial claims may be pressed against it. The Somali government obviously decided that the serious fighting in the Eritrea Province of Ethiopia in June 1975 provided an excellent opportunity to try to settle the Somali claim to the Haud and Ogaden by force. Libya annexed the northern areas of Chad in 1975 when that government was beset by internal revolt.

The transfer of power to indigenous governments during the process of decolonisation has caused a number of territorial disputes to flare. The new governments have often undertaken a much more diligent surveillance of their boundaries than the colonial administrations. In some cases this has led to a recognition that the boundary does not coincide with tribal distributions or prominent physical features, and boundary issues which were debated and settled by the colonial powers have been revived by the new authorities. Lesotho's claim to much of the Transvaal and the Orange Free State, Uganda's claim to western Kenya, and Tanzania's claim to part of Lake Tanganyika are typical of such territorial disputes. Decolonisation is sometimes the signal for neighbouring states to take advantage of the withdrawal of colonial armies. In November 1971, when Britain withdrew from the Persian Gulf, Iran seized three islands in the Strait of Hormuz which had been controlled by Britain on behalf of the Trucial States. It was noted earlier that Afghanistan's claims to Pushtunistan coincided with Britain's withdrawal from the Indian subcontinent and with fighting between religious groups in Pakistan. In February 1976, when Spain withdrew its forces from Spanish Sahara the territory was annexed by Morocco and Mauritania.

In some cases it is the action of one state which induces another to make a territorial claim. In 1915 and again in 1927 Guatemala made grants of land to the American Fruit Company in the area between the Matagua River and the Meredon Mountains. This immediately prompted Honduras to raise claims which had been dormant for a long time. In a similar fashion, the granting to the United States of a 99-year lease on the Great and Little Corn Islands by Nicaragua, encouraged Colombia to launch a claim that the islands were formerly part of the Province of Veragua and therefore properly part of Colombia under the principle of *uti possidetis*.

When the aims of the state initiating the dispute are considered it is useful to divide them into two classes. First, there are those claims when the state genuinely wants the territory claimed and believes that it has some chance of obtaining it. In such cases the aim involves strengthening the state by the accretion of territory. The increased strength may come from resources found in the area, or from the population which lives there, or from the improved access which the claimed territory gives to the sea or to major lines of communication. For example, the South West African People's Organisation, which is the main nationalist movement in South West Africa, has demanded that the territory of Walvis Bay be transferred from South Africa to the control of authorities in Windhoek. Walvis Bay is the only port on the coastline of South West Africa capable of accommodating large vessels, and it is sought to improve the country's transport facilities. Somalia's latent claim against Djibouti would strengthen Somalia by giving it an economic lever which could be used against Ethiopia, which conducts most of its trade through that Red Sea port. On the other side of the continent it seems certain that Morocco's annexation of the northern part of Spanish Sahara was directly connected with the rich phosphate deposits of Bou Craa. Iraq's claim to Kuwait, six days after that country became independent, was connected with the desire to acquire an area with considerable potential for producing petroleum, and at the same time to extend Iraq's coastline on the Persian Gulf.

The second class of aims applies to those claims which are apparently made without any hope of successful outcome. In such cases it appears that the dispute is initiated to serve some domestic or international policy. For example, it is generally considered that the Philippines claimed north Sabah at the time the Federation of Malaysia was being formed in an effort to postpone or prevent the emergence of that political association. The claim was based on the most flimsy ground and was duly abandoned in June 1977. Some countries have brought forward territorial claims to distract attention from internal difficulties, and it seems likely that the Chinese claims against Russian territory are made less with the hope of regaining territory, and more with the intention of scoring points in the ideological debate, by portraying Russian leaders as latter-day czars, who have precisely the same foreign policy aims and territorial ambitions as their royal predecessors.

It is worth noting that sometimes countries will encourage secessionist movements in neighbouring countries rather than claim territory for themselves. Of course if the secession is successful the new state affords fresh opportunities for diplomatic and commercial influence, and the state from which the territory is detached has been weakened. India's encouragement of secession in Pakistan and Zaire's encouragement of !secessionist forces in Cabinda were not altruistic. India was convinced that Bangladesh would be a better neighbour than East Pakistan and that Pakistan would be made weaker by the loss of its eastern territory. Zaire concluded that its interests would be best served if Cabinda could be detached from Angola, because the small oil-rich state would give opportunities for trade and political influence, and because Angola, from which an invasion of Zaire's Shamba Province was launched in 1977, would be weakened by the loss of a large slice of its export revenue.

It is rarely possible to gain definite confirmation of this second category of aims, except by research in archives long after the event. However, that should not dissuade scholars from making educated guesses about policy aims in contemporary situations.

When the arguments in favour of any territorial claim are considered it is useful to follow the division suggested by Hill (1976, p.26). He distinguishes *legal* arguments relating to a statement that the territory should belong to the claimant state, from all other arguments designed to show that it would be more appropriate if the territory was ceded to the claimant state, but where there is no claim that the territory is illegally held.

While geographers cannot make a major contribution to the analysis of legal arguments in territorial disputes, which remain the proper preserve of the lawyer, it is useful to examine the legal basis of claims to territory; the following discussion of this aspect follows the excellent exposition by Hill (1976, chapter 10). Occupation of territory is one of the soundest bases on which to mount legal claims. Such claims were especially characteristic of the nineteenth century when colonial powers were disputing territory in Africa, Asia and north America. It was generally considered that a statement of intention to occupy territory must be supported by a physical presence in the area. That was certainly the position adopted by the United States in disagreements with Russia over territorial questions in northwest

America. According to the General Act of the Congress of Berlin, legal rights to colonies in Africa could be secured only through effective occupation. Article 35 stated that the claimant state had to demonstrate satisfactorily to other states that the claim should be respected because a sufficient degree of authority was established throughout the area. This article was generally obeyed on the coast, but in the interior it was honoured more often in the breach than in the observance. In 1933, Denmark was able to validate its claim to Greenland against Norway because of its occupation of part of the east coast and the enactment of regulations covering the whole area.

Claims were also made to territory, during the last century, on the grounds of contiguity and territorial propinquity. Such arguments maintain that the closest authority should exercise sovereignty over adjacent unclaimed land. For example, in 1834 Peru claimed the island of Lobos, because although it was 35 miles from the shore it was more distant from other countries. The hinterland doctrine advanced by many colonial powers in Africa was related to these concepts. It was alleged that any country which had occupied a section of coastline was entitled to the hinterland of that shore. It was recourse to this argument which persuaded the British Government not to restrict Germany's claim in South West Africa to a strip 20 miles wide along the coast, when it was urged to do so by the Government of Cape Province in 1884. In a sense various sector claims to Antarctica are also based on concepts of propinquity. Hill (1976, p.153) asserts that such claims have no strength in international law, and in modern times, when the whole land surface of the earth has been politically appropriated, it is difficult to see such arrangements being entertained. However, it is interesting that the concept of propinquity underlies the use of lines of equidistance in settling disputes over claims to areas of the sea and continental shelf. This point is considered in detail in the next chapter.

It is recognised, according to some authorities on international law, that legal claims to fragments of territory could be based on symbolic acts of possession. Such a concept is particularly important in supporting claims to islands in the Pacific and the South China Sea. For example, there is a current dispute between China and Vietnam over ownership of the Paracel Islands, which China occupied with a military force in January 1974. According to Vietnamese sources the Emperor Gia Long had made a symbolic act of acquisition in 1816: 'In 1816, he [Emperor Gia Long] went with solemnity to plant his flag and take formal possession of these rocks, which it is not likely any body will dispute with him' (Taberd, 1837, p.738). Then in 1833, the Emperior Minh Mang ordered trees to be planted on the islands for the benefit of navigators. In 1836 markers were placed on the islands bearing the following inscription:

> In the year Binh Than, 17th Year of the reign of Minh Mang, Navy Commander Pham Huu Nhat, commissioned by the Emperor to Hoang So islands [Paracel islands] to conduct map surveyings, landed at this place and planted this marker so to perpetuate the memory of the event. (Vietnam Foreign Ministry, 1975, p.31)

In 1930 the crew of the French vessel *La Malicieuse* erected 'sovereignty columns' on some of the Paracel Islands. Eight years later further monuments were erected recording French authority and the date 1816, which was the first recorded symbolic act of possession by Vietnam. It is of course entirely possible that the Chinese authorities can produce earlier evidence to support its claim to these islands.

Disputes over islands were common during the search for guano during the last century, and an American statute enacted in 1856 determined that any citizen who discovered a guano island and took possession of it in the name of his government provided grounds for it to be claimed by the President as an American possession.

The legal basis of claims in South America is usually the principle of *uti possidetis* (Ireland, 1938). This principle means that the new states in the post-colonial period accepted the same boundaries as the colonial territories they replaced. This was designed to ensure that the European colonial powers, such as Britain, France and Germany, were prevented from making claims to uncontrolled areas on the borders of the new states. The principle is apparently derived from the same term in Roman law, which applied to an edict which preserved the existing state of possession of an immovable object, such as a house or a vineyard, pending litigation. The principle established in 1810 in fact caused some conflict because of confusion over its interpretation. Some states regarded the rule as applying to the limits legally in force when the act of decolonisation occurred. Others believed that the rule was concerned with the boundaries which were observed for practical administration by the colonial authorities. These two lines did not always coincide and competing states would urge the interpretation which suited themselves best. For example, the Venezuelan Constitution in 1830 proclaimed the state as being coincident with the area previously known as the Captaincy-General of Venezuela. It was then discovered that the Spanish administrators had governed beyond

this legal limit in good faith. Venezuela then espoused the second interpretation. In 1964, the Organisation of Africàn Unity passed a
resolution by which all members solemnly declared that they would
respect the borders existing 'on the achievement of national
independence'. This resolution was not designed to forestall any acts
by the colonial powers; it was aimed at preventing any territorial
disputes between African countries. Unfortunately it has not succeeded
in that intention.

Conquest is another means by which legal title to territory is
acquired. As Hill (1976, p.161) notes, this involves actual possession
based on force, an announcement of the intention to hold the
territory, and an ability to make good that declaration. This is usually a
unilateral action in which no treaty is involved. For example, on 17
December 1961, Indian troops invaded the Portuguese colonies of Goa,
Damao and Diu, and these territories were formally incorporated into
the Indian state on 19 December 1962. It also seems likely that some
territory captured in the Golan Heights and on the West Bank of the
Jordan by Israel, in 1967, will be retained by that country.

Territory is often claimed on the grounds that it was ceded by
treaty. Sometimes the cession may be voluntary, as when Britain ceded
the Wakhan Strip to Afghanistan in 1895, or involuntary. Involuntary
or forced cessions usually occur at the end of a war or after the threat
of force; they are typified by the cession of the south part of Sakhalin
to Japan by Russia in 1905, and the cession of the trans-Ussuri area to
Russia by China in 1860.

The last legal claim mentioned by Hill is based on prescription,
which is defined in the following terms:

> ...the acquisition of sovereignty over territory through continuous and
> undisturbed exercise of sovereignty over it during such a period as is
> necessary to create under the influence of historical development
> the general conviction that the present condition of things is in
> conformity with international order. (Hill, 1976, p.156)

India uses arguments based on prescription as part of its case against
China in the disputed areas of the Himalayas. India maintains that
British authority was exercised for a long, continuous period without
Chinese objection.

A recent example of a territorial dispute argued on purely legal
grounds involved the Philippines and Malaysia. The Philippines, in
1963, began to assert a claim to parts of Sabah on the island of Borneo.

In 1877-8 a British syndicate secured the transfer to themselves of the rights of the Sultan of Sulu over the territories and adjacent islands, in return for the payment of a pension. According to the English translation the treaty stated that the land was ceded and granted forever and in perpetuity. In 1881 the syndicate was taken over by the British North Borneo Company, which received a royal charter in the same year. In 1883 the area was made a British protectorate, and in 1903 a confirmatory deed was signed by the Sultan specifying the islands which had not been individually named in the original treaty. In 1946 the area became a British colony. The Philippine claim rests firstly on the ground that the Sultan was not empowered to sign the treaty since Spain was the sovereign power. That argument did not impress Malaysia because Britain did not recognise the Spanish treaties with the Sultan in 1836, 1851 and 1864, since Spain could not control him. Furthermore, in 1885 Spain renounced its rights in favour of Britain, in return for recognition in the Sulu archipelago. America replaced Spain as the dominant power in the area in 1898, and Britain secured specific American recognition of the British claims in 1930. The second argument used by the Philippines to support its claim questioned the correct interpretation of the Malay word *padak* which is used in the treaty. Britain had interpreted the word to mean 'granted and ceded', while the Philippines insisted that it was more accurately interpreted as 'leased'. In 1977, to demonstrate its goodwill towards Malaysia, the Philippines abandoned its claim at a meeting of the Association of Southeast Asian Nations.

Territorial disputes which are based solely on legal arguments that the territory ought to belong to the claimant state are comparatively rare. It is usual for the legal arguments to be underpinned by other assertions founded in history, geography, strategy and economics. Indeed the largest number of territorial disputes lack any significant legal component, and instead, are based on the view that for a variety of reasons the claimed territory should belong to the claimant state.

In most cases the historical arguments refer to periods that are not well defined and before the period when legal titles may have been gained. In 1919 France claimed the Saar on historical grounds, but its case was weak. Saarlouis alone had been founded by the French (under Louis XIV in 1680), but even this area had not been under French control for more than twenty-three years (Temperley, 1924, vol.2, p.177). Italy's claim to part of the Dalmatian coast at the same conference was based on strategic and historical arguments. The Italian Premier expressed the historical claim in the following sentences:

And can one describe as excessive the Italian aspiration for the Dalmatian coast, this boulevard of Italy throughout the centuries, which Roman genius and Venetian activity have made noble and great, and whose Italianity, defying all manner of implacable persecution throughout an entire century, today shares with the Italian nation the same feelings of patriotism? (Temperley, 1921, vol.5, p.404)

This type of statement seems typical of many historical claims which often appear as padding to the more pertinent arguments. However, a more specific historical argument is provided by assertions that the original colonists of an area have a prior right which takes precedence over claims by subsequent migrants. This was one of the arguments used by the Serbs to Banat, and by Italy to the Julian Venetia.

Geographical arguments are normally designed either to show the desirability of extending a state's territory to make the boundary coincide with some physical feature, or to demonstrate the basic unity of an area which is divided or is threatened with division. The Banat was one such area at the end of the First World War. The territory was contested by Rumania and Yugoslavia and is bounded by the Danube, Tisza and Murec Rivers. As in the Drava valley to the west, the population is of mixed Magyar, Serbo-Croat and Rumanian origin. The Yugoslavs claimed the lower central and western parts, while Rumania claimed the entire area as a geographical unit. This view was based on the 'natural frontiers' which the rivers provide and the complementary nature of the products of the plains and the hills to the east, and the opportunity which the plains afforded to the hill-dwellers for employment. The published reports of the Sino-Indian boundary talks make it clear that India rests much of her case on the 'natural boundary' provided by the main watershed of the Himalayan system:

In the discussions on the location and natural features of alignment, the Indian side demonstrated that the boundary shown by India was the natural dividing line between the two countries. This was not a theoretical deduction based on the rights and wrongs of abstract principles. The fact that this line had received the sanction of tradition and custom was no matter of accident or surprise because it conformed to the general development of human geography and illustrated that social and political institutions are circumscribed by physical environment. It was natural that peoples tended to settle up to and on the sides of mountain ranges; and the limits of societies — and nations — were formed by mountain barriers. The Chinese side recognised this fact that high and unsurmountable mountain barriers provided natural obstacles and suggested that it was appropriate that the boundary should run along such ranges. But if mountains form natural barriers, it was even more logical that the dividing line should be identified with the crest of that range which forms the watershed in that area. Normally where mountains exist, the highest range is also the watershed; but in the few cases where they diverge, the boundary tends to be the watershed range. . .it is now a well-recognised principle of customary international law that when two countries are separated by a mountain range and there are no boundary treaties or specific agreements, the traditional boundary tends to take shape along the crest which divides the major volume of the waters flowing into the two countries. The innate logic of this principle is self-evident. The inhabitants of the two areas not only tend to settle up to the intervening barrier but wish and seek to retain control of the drainage basins. (India, Ministry of External Affairs, 1961, pp.235-6)

Similarly it is manifest that there are passes all along the high mountains and that there are always contacts across the ranges. But this does not invalidate the general conclusion that the watershed range tends to determine the limits of the settlements of the inhabitants on either side and to form the boundary between the two peoples. Neither the flow of rivers through the ranges nor the contacts of peoples across them can undermine the basic fact that a high watershed range tends to develop into the natural, economic, and political limits of the areas on the two sides. (India, Ministry of External Affairs, 1961, p.237)

It is difficult to know where to start challenging this statement, since it contains so many concepts with which a political geographer must disagree. The concept of 'natural boundaries' which is explicit in this statement was once popular in political geography. Simply, it was assumed that the main, linear, physical obstacles in the world set the limits within which nations fashioned their political life. It was the political aspect of determinism which conferred on the environment and the physical landscape the dominant role in shaping man's economic and social characteristics and activities. Pounds (1951, 1954) has published excellent accounts of the origin of the idea of the natural frontiers of France, which were considered to be the sea, the Swiss

Alps, the Pyrenees and the Rhine. But the idea of 'natural boundaries' has been discredited for decades. Writers such as Hartshorne (1936), East (1937), Boggs (1940), and Jones (1945) have clearly shown that all political boundaries are artificial because they require the selection of a specific line within a zone where change in the physical characteristics of the landscape may be more or less rapid. Thus in a mountain range there is not one line along which all physical characteristics change sharply. First, all physical changes occur over a zone which may vary considerably in width, from the very narrow arête which marks a watershed, to the zonal change from one dominant type of vegetation to another. Second, even if the changes in vegetation, climate, drainage, elevation, structure, morphology and altitude could each be reduced to a single line, these lines would not coincide with each other. It must also be added that the response of different human communities to the same environment varies. It is unwise for lowlanders to assume that high mountains mark absolute barriers to highland communities. Kirk (1962) has made the point that there are distinct communities in the Himalayas which follow a complex transhumance economy which carries them over crests and watersheds as they use pastures and camping grounds which to lowlanders appear to be uniformly barren. Kingdon Ward described a similar situation earlier:

> But obviously a pass of 15,000 feet is nothing to a Tibetan who habitually lives at 10,000 or 12,000 feet altitude. The Tibetan is not stopped by physical but climate barriers, and no boundary pillars are needed to make him respect these. His frontier is the verge of the grassland, the fringe of the pine forest, the 50-inch rainfall contour beyond which no salt is (until indeed you come to the sea) or the 75 per cent saturated atmosphere. The barrier may be invisible; but it is a more formidable one to a Tibetan than the Great Himalayan ranges. If he crosses it he must revolutionise his mode of life. (Ward, 1932, p.469)

Ryder (1926) has described the problem of marking a boundary between Turkey and Iran through mountain communities, who removed the pillars as soon as they had been erected because they intersected routes to traditional pastures. In the reports of the men who marked the Durand Line there are dozens of cases where tribal limits did not coincide with obvious watersheds. It is also obvious that communities will occupy both banks of major rivers, and will exist in desert environments, both of which are physical features which the proponents of natural boundaries believed marked the limits of nation-building. Finally, it must be noted that 'natural boundaries' are always the limits to which a state wishes to expand. There is no recorded case of a state wishing to withdraw to 'natural boundaries'.

Turning from a general criticism of 'natural boundaries', it is now necessary to focus on the specific physical limit which provides the basis of the Indian claims. A watershed is the line which separates areas in which the flow of water, after precipitation or the melting of snow and ice, is in different directions. In this situation only surface drainage is considered; the complication of underground drainage, especially in limestone areas, needs not be considered here. Now just as there are first, second and third order rivers, there must be first, second and third order watersheds. For example, in this region, the primary watershed would be between the rivers following into the Bay of Bengal and those which flow intermittently into interior drainage basins of Tibet. The secondary watersheds would separate any two river basins which drain to the Bay of Bengal; thus there would be a secondary watershed between the Tsangpo and the Subansiri rivers. The tertiary watersheds separate the adjacent tributaries of any river; such a watershed would separate the Ange and Tangon tributaries of the Dibang river. This identification of a hierarchy of watersheds can continue until the smallest rivulets are reached. The problem for the Indian government is to justify the selection of one watershed rather than another. Where the watershed and the crest coincide there is no difficulty, but in many parts of the Himalayas the crest and the watershed do not coincide. Rivers, through the process of headward erosion, or because they are antecedent, have cut through the crest displacing the watershed. Unfortunately for the Indian argument the McMahon Line does not consistently follow primary, secondary or tertiary watersheds, or the crests where they form watersheds. It is thus difficult to avoid the conclusion that the alignment of the McMahon Line was the result of a series of *ad hoc* decisions, which the Indian Government has tried to mask by the uniform gloss of the watershed principle. The Indian statement also identifies the watershed by 'the major volume of the waters flowing into the two countries', but it is hard to understand how this can be calculated when a single river basin, such as the Subansiri or Luhit, is divided between the two countries.

Strategic arguments in favour of the transfer of territory usually have one of two aims. In some cases they are designed to deprive a country, with a history of aggressive policies, of territory from which attacks can be easily launched. In other instances the arguments support territory being given to a country which has a history of being attacked, so that its security is increased by the territorial buffer. The Greek and Yugoslav claims against Bulgaria at the Versailles Peace Conference provided examples of the first situation. In each case the territory claimed had been used by German and allied forces to launch rapid and successful attacks. France's claim to the Saar Basin in 1919 was based partly on the desire to move the German boundary farther away from the iron-ore field of Briey and Thionville. These deposits had been quickly overrun in 1914 and their loss had severely handicapped the French production of armaments.

The economic arguments in favour of territorial claims are usually designed to show the economic integration of the claimed area with a zone already held, the need for the area as a routeway or supply of raw materials, or the value of the region as reparations for damage suffered during a war. Czechoslovakia's claim to the Teschen district of Silesia provide examples of the first two types of economic argument. First, the Freistadt area was regarded as being inextricably linked with the industrial complex of Ostrava, where metal foundries depended upon the Karvina coking coal. The coal was also needed to a lesser extent in Bohemia and Moravia. Second, the Czechoslovakian Government claimed that the Olderberg-Jablunka-Sillein railway was of vital importance, since it formed the arterial line connecting Slovakia with Bohemia-Moravia. The railway through the Vlara pass, which Poland claimed could be further developed, was not considered suitable by the Czechs because of the steep gradients and sharp curves. Further, the only other line from Breclava to Bratislava was too far to the south. Poland reversed this economic argument to the east in Zips and Orava, when certain highland areas, occupied by people speaking a dialect transitional between Czechoslovakian and Polish, were claimed on the ground that they were more closely attached with Cracow, because of easy communication, than with Kralovany, the Czech county town.

Economic claims to territory often focus on access to the sea. Bolivia claimed the Gran Chaco from Paraquay because it wanted access to the sea by way of the Paraquay River, and there was fighting over this region in the period 1932-5. The issue was eventually resolved through arbitration which awarded some of the region to Bolivia.

Compensatory claims for property and population losses during the war were made against German colonies. Referring to Belgium's claim to Rwanda-Urundi, Temperley (1924, vol.2, p.243) notes that 'no one wanted to refuse the insistent claim of a state which had suffered so seriously from Germany's aggression in Europe'. The extension of Poland's territory to the Oder-Neisse line was also seen as compensation for losses to Russia, and the need to secure a better strategic boundary. Allied to such arguments are the cases where states secure territorial promises for co-operation with another state. A good example of this is provided by the 1915 Treaty of London between Italy and the Allied Powers, under which Italy agreed to merge her forces in the general war effort. Under this treaty certain territorial promises were made:

In the event of the total or partial partition of Turkey Italy was to obtain a just share of the Mediterranean region adjacent to the province of Adalia.

In the event of France and Great Britain increasing their colonial territories in Africa at the expense of Germany those Powers agree in principle that Italy may claim some equitable compensation, particularly as regards the settlement in her favour of the questions relative to the frontiers of the Italian colonies of Eritrea, Somaliland and Libya. (Temperley, 1924, vol.4, p.290)

A settlement under the terms of this treaty transferred 36,000 square miles of northern Kenya to Italian Somaliland on 15 July 1924. The boundary was shifted west of the Juba River, which had previously formed the boundary, to the present line which was demarcated by a commission in 1930.

Territorial claims based on ethnic arguments refer to the human qualities of nationality, race, language, culture, history and religion. From time to time countries have focused on one of these characteristics as being the definitive guide to the political predilection of a region's population. During the Versailles Peace Conference some delegations laid great emphasis on language as a reliable guide to national aspirations of people and therefore to the proper distribution of territory. Ancel (1936, p.76) noted that if this argument was followed to its logical conclusion linguistic divides would become political boundaries and language would become 'the symbol of the nation'. At that conference efforts were made to draw boundaries which reduced the number of minorities to a minimum. Fisher (1940, chapter 1) praised the settlements because they left only 6 per cent of the population of Europe under alien rule. But the records of the conference show that many of the decisions were inconsistent and that tests of nationality were not uniformly applied. It is difficult to see how any such principles could have been uniformly applied given the complexity of population distributions in Europe. The intermingling of population in the European borderlands often made it impossible to draw boundaries which precisely separated different ethnic groups. In some regions, such as the Western Banat, there was an intricate mixture of Yugoslavs, Rumanians, Magyars and Germans (Bowman, 1923, p.272). In another situation Greece claimed the entire Argyro-Castro area because of the larger Greek rural population which surrounded the towns occupied by Yugoslavs. Yugoslavia used this argument to its own advantage in the Klagenfurt Basin, where the rural population was Yugoslav and surrounded towns occupied by German-speaking people, who formed the basis of Austria's claim to the region.

In Africa territorial claims based on the division of tribes by boundaries drawn during the colonial period are much easier to define because tribal mixing has been on a comparatively small scale. Claims by Somalia to areas of Ethiopia, Kenya and Djibouti, and by Togo to areas of Ghana, have a high degree of precision. It would be much easier over wide areas of Africa to make boundary adjustments without creating new minority problems than it would in Europe.

However, it seems certain that no single characteristic or even group of characteristics can be used with confidence to allocate people to different states. The important criterion must be the wish of the people, and the concept of self-determination, which seemed such an attractive solution to European problems in the 1920s, continues to be resuscitated again and again in modern times. But self-determination is a two-edged sword and the concept has never been applied uniformly, it is invariably subject to decisions of political expediency. For example, the Organisation of African Unity called for the self-determination of Rhodesian citizens, but it condoned the partition of Spanish Sahara between Morocco and Mauritania without any consultation with the local population. The people of Eritrea were not consulted before they were handed over to Ethiopia in 1952, and therefore it is not surprising that the secessionist movement started ten years later, when the Ethiopian government unilaterally abolished Eritrea's federal status.

In an effort to determine the wishes of a group of people regarding alternative nationalities plebiscites have sometimes been held, especially where a solution was being imposed on the area, as in the Klagenfurt Basin. In many cases, however, a plebiscite has not been found satisfactory because the state controlling the area enjoys an important advantage in securing a favourable result. In 1883, the treaty of Ancon, which terminated the war between Chile and Peru, stipulated that the province of Tacna and Arica would be held by Chile for a period of ten years after which a plebiscite would decide by popular vote whether the area should remain as part of Chile or part of Peru (Dennis, 1931, p.297). No attempt was made to hold the plebiscite until 1925, by which time Chile had sufficiently nationalised the area to make a decision in favour of Chile certain. But even so the plebiscite was never held and the commission appointed to conduct it noted that Chile's failure to provide free voting conditions was the major obstacle. It is interesting that at the Versailles Peace Conference ethnic claims were sometimes made not because a particular cultural group formed the majority, but because the actions of a government had prevented them from forming a majority. For example, Italy insisted that it was the policies of the Austrian government which was responsible for the Slav majority on the Dalmatian coast:

> This is the result of the most outrageous violence that the political history of Europe records during the last century. Austria did not recoil before any form of artifice or violence in Dalmatia in order to repress Italian feelings, after 1866 in order to check any movement toward annexation to Italy, and after 1878 and 1882 in order to carry out her Balkan schemes. (Hill, 1976, p.126)

Unfortunately for Italy, the American delegation reversed this argument in respect of Fiume and asserted that it was the policies of the Austro-Hungarian authorities which had allowed an Italian majority rather than a Slav majority to develop in the town.

When the results of territorial boundary disputes are considered it is useful to classify them into two groups. First, there will be the consequences which flow from the dispute being initiated. Second, there will be results which follow any transfer of territory. Claims to the territory of a neighbour will normally cause a deterioration in relations between the two countries concerned and this may be reflected in a reduced level of commercial contact across the disputed boundary. Within the claimed area the authorities in control will probably seek ways to increase their defences. Such measures might include the removal of people who might sympathise with the proposed transfer; the construction of new strategic roads and airfields; the improvement in the services provided in the region to win support from the local people. Both countries are also likely to publish their versions of the compelling reasons why the issue should be decided in their favour. This is a bonus to the interested scholar.

If the matter is settled by the transfer of territory then a wide range of consequences are possible. Some people in the transferred region who opposed the change may cross the new boundary to remain citizens of their original country; new patterns of administrative organisation might be established; the orientation of the region's economy may be altered towards the country which has acquired the land; different forms of production might be encouraged by the new regulations which apply to the area and by access to a different market. It would require careful fieldwork in each case to establish the range of changes which occurred following the alteration of the boundary. In some cases the dispute will enter a dormant phase without any transfer of territory, and this may be encouraged by an agreement between the two countries regarding their border relations. For example, in 1967 Somalia and Ethiopia reached an understanding, which, while not ending the dispute, did encourage better relations between the two countries; promote easier travel across the boundary; and guarantee some safeguards for the civil rights of Somalis living in the Ethiopian borderlands.

Positional Boundary Disputes

While the basic cause of territorial boundary disputes is superimposition of the boundary on the cultural or physical landscape, positional boundary disputes arise because of incomplete boundary evolution. It is not the quality of the borderland but rather the defect of the boundary which is crucial. Positional disputes will usually arise at one of two stages. Most of them will arise during the demarcation of the boundary, because the commission will be faced with the problem of matching the boundary definition to the landscape. However, it is also possible that positional disputes will arise at a much later date if the demarcation commission makes an error. There is probably an important legal distinction between these two situations, because the existence of a demarcated boundary for a considerable period may be used as justification by the satisfied party for maintenance of that location, but essentially they arise from the same causes. These causes are found in the boundary definition and can be grouped into two categories. First, some of the terms will be imprecise, because they will allow more than one interpretation; second, some of the turning points along the boundary will be defined in two ways which are contradictory.

An examination of imprecise terms leading to positional disputes reveals a basic dichotomy between the legal and geographical definitions of phrases in the text. Generally the problems of geographical interpretation are more common. An example of problems over a legal definition is provided by the Anglo-German agreement of 1886 regarding the boundary between Nigeria and Kamerun between the coast and the River Benue. The northern terminus was defined as follows: 'a point on the right bank of the river Benue to the east of and as close as possible to Yola as may be found on examination to be practically suited for the demarcation of the boundary' (Hertslet, 1909, 3, pp.880-1). Leaving aside the error in designating the south bank as the right bank, the real dispute centred on the term 'practically'. When the time came to select the point Britain argued that the term had both economic and political connotations. Politically Britain would find it inexpedient to draw a boundary within sight of the walls of Yola, since the Emir of that important town was losing a considerable slice of his territory to Germany. Economically it was demanded that the boundary should be drawn to allow the free circulation of the people of Yola, which was later clarified to mean that sufficient area would be left to the east to provide satisfactory supplies of firewood and enough pasture. For Germany, of course, the term 'practically' had only a technical meaning in respect of boundary demarcation.

The literature is replete with examples of problems of geographical definitions, and they can generally be divided into three groups. The first group involves the identification of a geographical feature, such as the bank of a river, or the edge of a plateau, or the crest of a range. The second group concerns disagreements about place names, and the third group results from debate over the location of some provincial or tribal boundary which is being elevated to international status. In several cases the problem is complicated because the demarcation is not undertaken until long after the boundary's delimitation, which may make it hard to reconstruct the exact intentions of the people who drafted the boundary's description.

The Anglo-German treaty of 1890 dealing with various African territories provides one good example of an indefinite geographical term which still has not been satisfactorily interpreted. It defined the southern limit of German South West Africa as 'the north bank' of the Orange River. In some sections of the course of the Orange River it was difficult to be certain where the bank was located, especially in view of the fact that the flow exhibited wide seasonal fluctuations. Those variations have now been reduced by the construction of dams in the Orange Free State, but not eliminated. The Germans took the view that the boundary coincided with the river's waterline on the north shore, and as the river level fell or rose, so they increased and reduced their area of control. Britain regarded such a concept as intolerable and wanted a fixed line. Debate between the two sides continued throughout the early years of this century, and by 1909 the Cape Colony Government was prepared to offer Germany the thalweg of the river, provided Britain continued to own all the islands, British subjects had the exclusive authority to operate ferries, and there were safeguards regarding the construction of weirs from the Germany bank. The thalweg of a river is the deepest continuous channel. War intervened before the matter was settled and the question has not been resolved. Hinks (1921) records that a positional dispute arose on the boundary between Peru and Bolivia, north of Lake Titicaca because it proved impossible, before the advent of aerial photography, to identify 'the western source of the River Heath', which was one of the turning points of the boundary.

An interesting positional dispute has arisen between China and the Soviet Union over the location of the boundary at the junction of Amur and Ussuri Rivers (Prescott, Collier and Prescott, 1977, pp.12-13). The treaty in 1860 defined the boundary as following the Amur River to its junction with the River Ussuri, and then turning south along the Ussuri River. Unfortunately, at the junction of the two rivers there is a triangular island with an area of 128 square miles. The triangular island is bounded by three waterways (Figure 4.1). To the north lies the River Amur, or the Hei-lung Chiang according to China; it is a large river with an average width of 1.4 miles. The southwest coast of the island is washed by the Protoka Kazakevicheva (K'o-tsa-k'ai-wei-ch'ai-wo Shui-tao in Chinese), a narrow watercourse which is 18 miles long and 1,000 yards wide. The southeast margin of the island is bounded by a channel which the Chinese regard as the Wu-su-li Chiang (Ussuri in Russian), and which the Russians regard, together with the Protoka Kazakevicheva, as the southern arm of the River Amur. This section of river is 22 miles long with an average width of 1,300 yards. The crux of the problem is to decide the confluence of the Amur and Ussuri Rivers. The Russian authorities place it at Kazakevichevo while their Chinese counterparts are sure it should be at Khabarovsk. In short the Russians believe the island is located between two arms of the River Amur, while the Chinese are equally certain that it is between two arms of the Ussuri River. The Chinese of course still have the added difficulty, even if the Russians accepted that the

Figure 4.1: The Amur-Ussuri Confluence

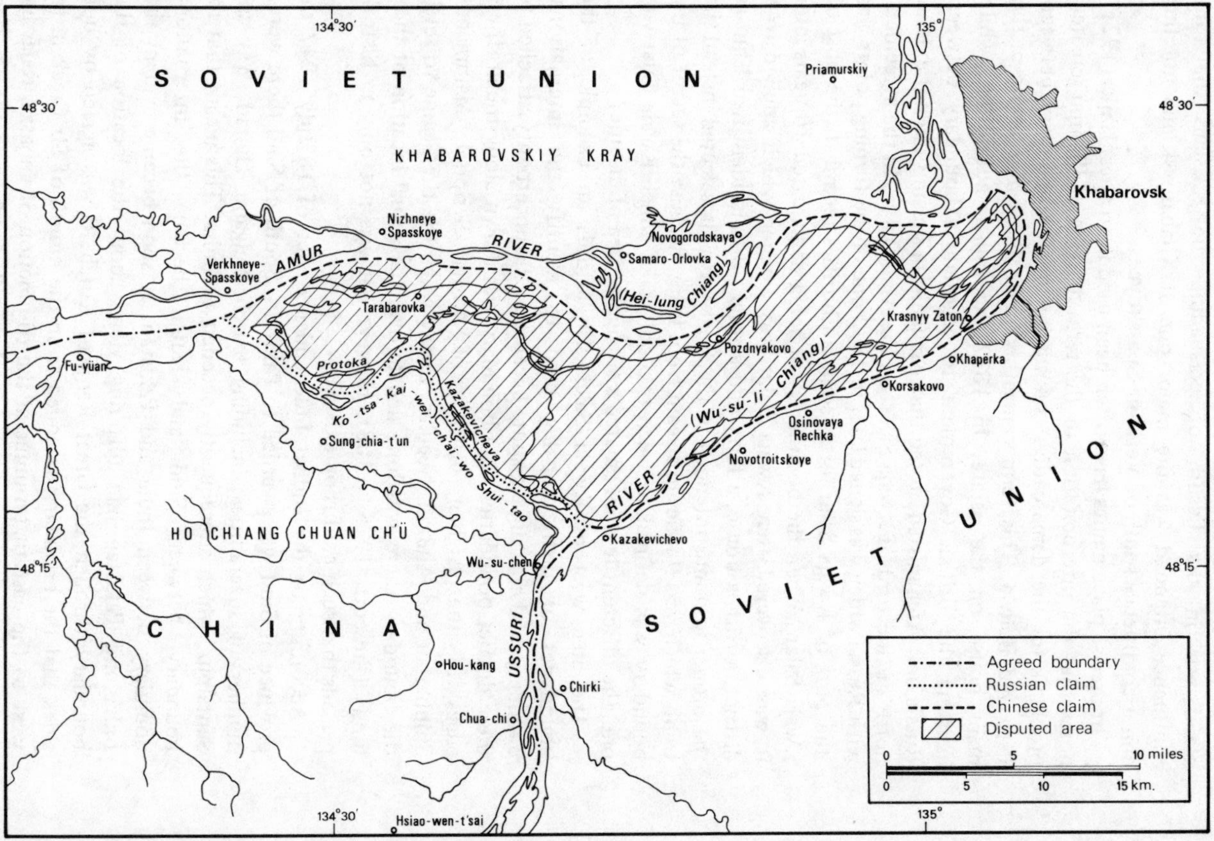

island was in the Ussuri, of persuading the Russians that the confluence intended was the major one at Khabarovsk and not the minor confluence south of Verkhne-Spasskoye.

Imprecise place names have often been used in treaties. Hinks (1921) notes that the interpretation of the term 'barraca of Illampu' created problems for the demarcation commission on the boundary between Peru and Bolivia. This term can either mean the whole estate or the main house on the estate. In 1872 the Indian authorities, while assisting the British Government to negotiate a boundary between Russia and Afghanistan, noted that Afghanistan's claims did not extend north of 'the ford of Kwaja Salar' on the Amu Darya. In the agreement with Russia which was signed later in 1872 one of the turning points was 'the port of Kwaja Salar' or as some authorities record it 'the post of Kwaja Salar'. When the boundary was being demarcated 16 years later it was discovered that Kwaja Salar was a name which applied to a district, a fort, a house, a ferry and a tomb. Britain identified Islim as the proper terminus intended in the treaty; Russia selected instead the tomb which was 9 miles upstream from Islim. Because the sector of the boundary was defined between two points, of which Kwaja Salar was one, the different termini created a triangular area of dispute.

The area west of Kwaja Salar also affords an example of the boundaries of districts being used to identify the international boundary, and creating a dispute because of the uncertainty attached to these district boundaries. The boundary was drawn along the northern edges of the Afghan districts of Aksha, Seripool, Mainmenat, Shibberjau and Andkoi. Needless to say when the time came to settle the boundary there was long debate over the actual location of these limits (Prescott, 1975, p.108). However, it was not only in historic periods that such confusion existed.

According to the Indian Independence Act of 18 July 1947 the province of Sind was awarded to Pakistan. South of Sind there were a number of suzerainties, including Kutch, Sulgam, Tharad, Wav and Santalpur, which subsequently acceded to India. This meant that the boundary between Sind and Kutch became the international boundary between India and Pakistan. It soon became evident that India and Pakistan had differing views about the location of that boundary through the Great Rann of Kutch. It was agreed by both sides that the boundary extended from the mouth of Sir Creek in the west to the eastern terminus at the tri-junction of Gujarat, Rajasthan and Hyderabad. Further they agreed that the western sector had been defined along the Sir Creek to latitude 23° $58'$ north and then

Figure 4.2: The Rann of Kutch

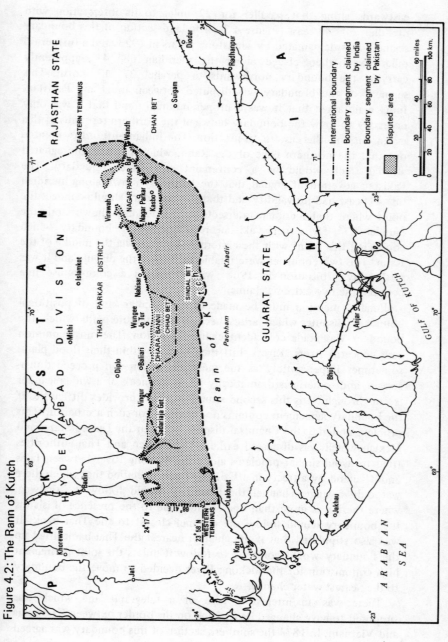

eastwards along that parallel for 22 miles to its intersection with meridian 68° 41′ east (Figure 4.2). The land section of this boundary segment was demarcated by sandstone pillars in 1923, and a further 66 pillars were then placed along the meridian 68° 41′, apparently carrying the boundary northwards to parallel 27° 17′ north. This segment of the boundary was disputed between India and Pakistan. India maintained that it was a proper boundary and that it was only necessary to draw the boundary between the northern terminus of this extension and the eastern tri-junction. The Indian authorities pointed out that the northern edge of the Rann, which is a salt-impregnated alluvial tract, would be a convenient and direct boundary. The Pakistan government argued that the boundary drawn along meridian 68° 41′ east had no validity and that the boundary should connect the point where that meridian intersected the boundary drawn along the parallel 23° 58′ north. Pakistan recommended a boundary which connected this point with the eastern tri-junction via the middle of the Rann. The two countries were unable to resolve the dispute and it was settled by arbitration in 1968, which defined a compromise line between the two extreme claims.

Finally, mention must be made of a particular kind of positional boundary dispute which arises because the feature with which the boundary was made coincident changes position. The most common case concerns rivers. Rivers shift their course within their flood plain, sometimes imperceptibly as the meanders widen and proceed downstream, and sometimes dramatically when the neck of a wide meander is cut through. It is this second situation which provides difficulties if the boundary agreement contains no provision for such a situation. This problem underlay the Chamizal dispute between the United States and Mexico which was discussed earlier. The French and Thai authorities tried to avoid similar problems along the Mekong River between Laos and Thailand by a treaty in 1926. The treaty specified that where there was only a single channel the boundary would follow the thalweg; where there was more than one channel due to the presence of islands the boundary would follow the channel closest to the Thai bank. It was also stipulated that if the channel nearest the Thai bank dried up the boundary would continue to follow it unless the joint permanent high commission for the Mekong River decided to move the boundary to the nearest water channel.

There was an interesting case of a telegraph line which was supposed to have changed its position on the border between Cambodia and Vietnam. In 1873 the southern section of this boundary was agreed between the two authorities and part of the boundary was fixed along the telegraph line between Giang Thanh and Ha Tien. This boundary was demarcated in the period 1873-6. In 1891 the governor of Cochin China shifted the boundary away from the telegraph line which lay close to the Giang Thanh River, and made it coincide with the Mandarin's Way, which transferred 8 square miles of marshy land, occupied by fifty people to Cochin China (Prescott, 1975, pp.471-2). He justified this move on the ground that in 1873 the telegraph line lay along the Mandarin's Way and not along the river road. After complaints from the Cambodian authorities a report was prepared on the matter by the French administrators in the cantons called Ha Thanh and Thanh Gi, which occupied the borderland of Cochin China. This report justified the governor's decision and provided the information that the telegraph line had been moved from the Mandarin's Way to the river road between the definition of the boundary in 1873 and the demarcation of the boundary two years later (Figure 4.3). This alteration was made because the activities of Cambodian rebels had made the Mandarin's Way insecure. The Cambodian complaints continued and a further commission was appointed by the governor-general of Indo-China in 1896. This body included surveyors and administrators from both sides of the boundary. It concluded that the telegraph had been established along the river road in 1870 and had not been moved subsequently. That settled the matter, but it is interesting to record that the authorities in Cochin China used this loss of territory, which had never belonged properly to them, to justify the alteration of the boundary around Ha Tien in 1914, when 3 square miles were transferred from Cambodia to Cochin China.

Positional boundary disputes will usually involve smaller areas than those involved in territorial disputes, although positional disputes in two situations may involve considerable areas. The first will occur when a boundary is only defined by a few points and location of one of those points is disputed. The example of the Russo-Afghan dispute over the proper location of Kwaja Salar was noted earlier. It follows that the relocation of a turning point will affect the alignment of the boundary sectors on both sides; if those sectors are long then large areas may be involved. The second situation occurs when boundaries are defined as following previously existing boundaries, such as the southern boundary of Kutch. In such cases there is sometimes scope for disagreement over major areas. Generally positional disputes create fewer problems for border residents and international relations than territorial boundary disputes.

Figure 4.3: The Southern Sector of the Cambodia-Vietnam Boundary

Functional Boundary Disputes

A functional boundary dispute arises when one country believes that it has been adversely and unfairly affected by the functions of a neighbouring country along the boundary. Unlike territorial and positional disputes it is possible to solve functional disputes to the satisfaction of both sides without any alteration in the boundary's position. House (1959) has described an interesting functional dispute following the adjustment of the boundary between Italy and France in the Alpes Maritimes in 1947. As a result of the boundary change and the state functions applied by both governments problems had arisen for the inhabitants of two communes. The people in a French commune lacked sufficient summer pasture for their stock, while the people in an adjoining Italian settlement lacked sufficient spring and autumn pastures.

Since positional changes in the boundary were not possible the Swiss arbitrator appointed to settle the problem suggested a compromise which allowed the Italian settlements certain grazing rights in France in exchange for the French residents being awarded rights over woodland in Italy. This compromise, which was accepted, was simplified by an earlier convention which permitted the free circulation of people and property within a zone 20 kilometres wide, lying astride the boundary.

Another functional dispute has sometimes caused friction between Iran and Iraq. According to the protocol agreed by Britain, Persia, Russia and Turkey in 1913, the eastern sector of the boundary was drawn along the Persian bank of the Shatt-el-Arab. In 1937 there were small modifications of this line to give Iran an anchorage opposite the port of Abadan. Since Iraq achieved independence it has sometimes used its sovereignty over the Shatt-el-Arab to prevent the passage of Iranian ships between Abadan and the Persian Gulf. Iran has often responded angrily to these obstructions and threatened to abrogate earlier boundary treaties. Iran has now developed an important oil port on an island in the Persian Gulf to reduce its dependence on Abadan, and it has also annexed certain islands in the Strait of Hormuz so that it is in a position to exert counter pressure against Iraq if further obstruction of the Shatt-el-Arab occurs.

Functional boundary disputes are comparatively rare when compared with territorial and positional disputes. In recent years functional disputes have usually been associated either with territorial disputes, or with other international disputes. By imposing new regulations at borders it is possible for states to show their displeasure with a neighbour, as Pakistan did when it effectively blocked the transhumance movements of the Powindas. African states in the post-colonial period have sometimes resorted to closing the border with a neighbour to record displeasure with a neighbour's policies, or to increase national security at a time when civil wars were generating large numbers of refugees. Between 1964 and 1977 there were twenty-four reported cases of African boundaries being closed, and sometimes this produced serious consequences because Africa has the largest number of landlocked states in the world. In some cases the closure of the boundary was designed to force an alteration in a neighbour's policy. For example, in February 1976 Kenya refused to allow the passage of Uganda's trade through Mombasa because President Amin had announced that Uganda had legitimate claims to large areas of western Kenya. These claims were abandoned within a few days of the boycott being imposed. In October 1975 Benin, which was formerly called Dahomey, closed its border with Togo on the ground that this country had been involved in an attempted coup against President Kerekou of Benin. Suspicions were voiced in Ghana and Togo that the closure of the boundary was for another reason. Due to congestion in Lagos harbour many vessels were discharging cargoes for Nigeria at Ghanaian and Togolese ports, and arranging for them to be transferred by lorry to Nigeria. By closing the boundary with Togo and severing this land connection, Benin was serving notice on Nigeria that it would be wiser to unload cargoes in Benin, and avoid the risk of this disruption.

Another interesting case concerned allegations by Lesotho in November 1976, that South Africa had closed three border posts on Lesotho's eastern border, to force that country to recognise the independence of the Transkei. Lesotho alleged in the United Nations Security Council that the closure resulted in 250,000 people being held hostage in the most rugged part of that mountainous state and in interference with Lesotho's major exports, which are livestock and migrant workers. There are thirty-six border crossings along Lesotho's boundary and three of them are with the Transkei; they are Qacha's Nek, Tele Bridge and Ramatsilitshek. The latter is a rough track and mainly used by rustlers. None of the border posts was closed, but at the three posts Transkei officials required purchase of a visa, costing one Rand, which was valid for multiple journeys for a period of three months. In fact several thousand Lesotho citizens were paying this fee and crossing the boundary during the period it was alleged the boundary was closed. The flow of trade between Lesotho and the outside world was unaffected by the border regulations, yet Lesotho was able to persuade the United Nations that it was being severely affected, and in consequence a number of countries and the European Economic Community gave aid to Lesotho to offset the alleged damage suffered by its economy! This successful hoax may have been inspired by the actions of Mozambique which closed the boundary with Rhodesia on 3 March 1976 and then appealed to the international community for aid to make up the loss of revenue.

Resource Development Disputes

The commonest source of such disputes are water bodies which mark or cross any international boundary. Jones (1945) has recorded some disputes connected with minerals, but they are rare. Disputes over maritime resources are considered in the next chapter.

Boundaries were often drawn to coincide with rivers in order to allow easy recognition, and the disadvantages of such features as boundaries have already been considered. In many other cases however, except when the boundary coincided with a watershed, river basins were divided between adjacent states. When the boundary coincided with a watercourse the agreement usually contained a clause providing equal rights for nationals from both sides. Generally the clause did not define the position with regard to the tributaries of boundary waters, nor make provision for the joint control of rivers which crossed the boundary. Often this was because the border areas were under-developed and the use of rivers for hydro-electricity and irrigation had not been envisaged. It was only when the border areas became more closely settled and advances in technology made possible the use of the rivers for purposes other than navigation that disputes about the use of boundary and other waters developed. Many terms are used by different writers in referring to rivers forming and crossing the boundary; it is proposed here to distinguish three types. *Boundary waters* are those features within which the boundary is drawn; this term is preferred to *contiguous waters* used by Griffin (1959). *Tributaries of boundary waters* form the second group. The term is entirely descriptive and it is essential to distinguish the tributaries from the boundary waters. Rivers which cross a boundary are called *successive rivers*. This is a term suggested by Griffin which seems more satisfactory than any other, such as 'divided rivers', since boundary waters are also divided.

Griffin (1959) has shown that customary international law requires that no action should be taken in respect of the boundary waters which will diminish their value and usability to the other state. The Guadalupe-Hidalgo Treaty of 1848 between America and Mexico was explicit on this point, in respect of the Gila and Bravo Rivers: 'neither [state] shall without the consent of the other construct any work that may impede or interrupt, in whole or in part the exercise of this right [free navigation] : not even for the purpose of favouring new methods of navigation' (Miller, 1937, p.217). In fact an American company did interfere with the course of the river and a Mexican complaint to the American federal courts was successful, so that the company had to make restitution to Mexico (*American Journal of International Law*, 1912, pp.478-85).

A dispute involving tributaries of boundary waters developed between Britain and the United States in 1900. The Chicago municipal authority tapped Lake Michigan by means of a canal constructed in the valley of the Chicago River. This resulted in sufficient water to force the diluted sewage of the city through the Des Plaines River and thence to the Illinois and Mississippi Rivers. At that time the canal was carrying 4,167 cubic feet per second away from the lake. Residents of Missouri, through which the Illinois River flowed, complained about Chicago's action, but it was found that the river, as a result of the increased flow, was purer than before! Britain, however, was concerned with the extent to which the lake levels were being lowered, and by 1926, when the flow from the lake through the canal was 8,500 cubic feet per second, it was estimated that the levels of Lakes Michigan and Huron had dropped six inches to a new mean lake level, while Lakes Ontario and Erie had been lowered five inches. Since every inch represented sixty to eighty tons carrying capacity in ships, it was demonstrated that the action of Chicago was impairing the navigability of boundary waters. Britain was successful in her action, and the amounts withdrawn from the lake were diminished in 1927 to 6,500 cubic feet per second, in 1935 to 5,000 cubic feet per second, and in 1938 to 1,500 cubic feet per second, which was within the amount allowed to American concerns under the original agreement (Simsarian, 1938).

Disputes over divided waters are less common than disputes over successive rivers. This is due to two factors. First, most treaties governing boundaries along divided rivers contain clauses guaranteeing both sides equal rights and prohibiting any use which adversely affects the other state. Second, since both states have access to the same parts of the river a unilateral action by one country can be met by retaliation by the other country.

In considering the utilisation of successive rivers it is clear that the lower riparian may be harmed if the flow of water is diminished, while the upper riparian rights may be infringed if the river is dammed downstream to produce flooding beyond the boundary. The classical example of the first situation concerns Egypt's anxiety that the flow of the Nile should not be diminished through irrigation projects in the Sudan. This matter was carefully controlled through the Nile Waters Agreement of 1929, under which Britain undertook not to interfere with the quantity, level or date of the river's regime. The Sudan has continued to respect this agreement, although there is not yet any agreement on how additional supplies of water should be apportioned. When Lake Kariba was formed on the Zambezi between Northern and Southern Rhodesia, Portugal demanded and secured guarantees of a certain minimum flow through Mozambique. The flow of 35,000 cubic feet per second is sufficient to allow navigation of the lower Zambezi throughout the year. At the same time the Rhodesian Governments gained assurances from the Union of South Africa and Angola that they would not draw additional supplies from the Zambezi above the lake.

Glassner (1970) has provided a very interesting and comprehensive account of a dispute between Chile and Bolivia over the Rio Lauca. This successive river rises in swamps on the high semi-arid plateau, called the Altiplano, 75 miles east of the Chilean port of Arica. The first 45 miles of the river's course lies in Chile and there are then 90 miles of the river in Bolivia; it drains into the land-locked Lago de Coipasa, which is set in a salt flat with the same name. In 1939 the Chilean Government announced that it intended to divert water via a tunnel into the valley of the Rio Azapa, in order to allow irrigation of the fertile soils in this arid valley. Bolivia protested against this proposal because it was considered to be contrary to the 1933 Declaration of Montevideo, by which member states agreed that the upper riparian state had the right to use the river provided it did not modify the hydrological conditions and the natural regime of the river. At intervals since 1939 the dispute has flared and died down and there has been no final solution to the question even though Chile is using the scheme. Bolivia argued that the withdrawal of water from the Rio Lauca would increase the rate of salt accumulation in the Bolivian sector of the river and adversely affect the population living there. According to Glassner (1970, p.198) Bolivia has never produced evidence of the damage it alleges has been caused.

A serious dispute developed between India and Bangladesh over the

Farraka Barrage scheme on the River Ganges. In 1951 India began to plan for the diversion of water from the Ganges River into the Hooghly River in order to flush sediment out of the port of Calcutta and improve conditions for navigation. Pakistan objected to the proposals, but India began construction in 1961 and completed the barrage in 1975. Bangladesh had succeeded East Pakistan by this time and was maintaining objections to the scheme. The scheme itself is very old, and there are references to it during the first half of the nineteenth century. Bangladesh is fearful that the withdrawal of water from the River Ganges, 11 miles before it enters Bangladesh, will reduce water levels in the Ganges delta, which comprises much of Bangladesh, to conditions where navigation, fishing and irrigation will be adversely affected. Bangladesh is also concerned that the reduced flow will increase the rate of salt accumulation in parts of the delta. Although there is no reference in literature published by the two governments to the possibility of coastal changes in the delta being caused by the new patterns of water flow and sediment discharge, it should be a consideration. There is plenty of evidence in other parts of the world to demonstrate that alterations to the upper parts of river systems might produce changes in the form and stability of deltas at the rivers' mouths. India argued that the amount of water diverted would not adversely affect Bangladesh and asserted that the supply of water from the Brahmaputra River was most critical to Bangladesh, and that this river was not being efficiently used. After a period of acrimonious debate the two countries initialled an agreement on 30 September 1977 providing for the implementation of short-term dry season sharing arrangements of the Ganges waters, and for the development within five years of a long term solution for augmenting the flow of the Ganges River. By the terms of the agreement Bangladesh was awarded a larger share than India had been prepared to grant earlier in the discussions, and the amount diverted through the Hooghly River was set at about half the volume which officials in West Bengal claimed was essential.

Upstream flooding has often occurred. In 1897 the Canadian Dyking Company made a dam on Boundary Creek in British Columbia which resulted in the flooding of 80,000 acres of Idaho, which of course reduced the rateable value of that State (Simsarian, 1938). A contemporary example is provided by the Aswan High Dam in the United Arab Republic, which has flooded part of the Sudan and caused the resettlement of 35,000 Nubians in the Khashm el Girba area astride the Atbara River.

The Franco-Spanish dispute over the waters of Lake Lanoux provides a convenient example of how technological advances trigger disputes of this kind. Soon after the Second World War France decided to dam the lake, which normally drained towards Spain, and force the water over a drop of 780 metres into the Ariège valley. The water would then be returned by a tunnel to the course of the River Font, which was tributary to the Serge River in Spain. A canal from the French side supplied water to Spanish irrigation schemes. Spain objected to this plan on the grounds that it infringed the Treaty of Bayonne of 1886. The eighth, eleventh and twelfth articles of the *Acte Additionnel* provided that both states had sovereignty over water within their boundaries; that the downstream riparian had a right to the 'natural waters which flow from higher levels without the hand of man having contributed thereto'; that the riparian rights of the upstream state should not be harmed, and that there should be consultation on all new works. Spain requested that France should make the dam less than the planned height to increase the natural flow towards Spain and reduce the electricity production by 10 per cent. France refused this request, and in 1957 the International Court of Justice adjudged that France's plan did not infringe the 1866 agreement.

The Role of Maps in Boundary Disputes

In the previous chapter the importance of using maps to understand the evolution of the boundary was stressed; it is equally important in examining boundary disputes to use maps to understand the basic nature of the problems. Not only are maps used by scholars concerned with objective research, they are also used with increasing frequency, by lawyers trying to prove a particular point, and by governments trying to influence the opinions of citizens and other governments (Murty, 1964). This section examines the characteristics which useful maps will possess and the circumstances under which their use will be most appropriate.

Looking first at the characteristics of the map it is important that the political boundaries under consideration should be marked on them. If the boundaries are not marked there may be an effort to use the fact as evidence that no boundary existed, but such evidence would not be conclusive. Dorion (1964) and Sinnhuber (1964) have both written useful papers on the way in which boundaries are represented on maps. The scale of the map is also very important and maps rapidly decline in usefulness as the scale is reduced. Scales of about 1:50,000 or larger are the most satisfactory; when the scale is reduced to

1:1,000,000 the map is useful only when the boundary follows a pronounced physical feature, such as a watershed or a mountain crest. If it is desired to compare the representation of the same boundary on two maps of different scales it is essential to reduce the large scale map to the smaller scale, since the reverse process cannot be carried out with a sufficient degree of accuracy. For example, the boundary disputed between India and China in Assam is shown in two treaty maps. The first accompanied a secret Anglo-Tibetan treaty and is at a scale of 1:500,000; the tripartite agreement has a map at a scale of 1:3,800,000. It has always been assumed that the two lines are identical, but the scales of the maps make comparison very difficult, and the tragedy for India is that it is only the larger scale map, attached to the secret treaty, which is at a scale sufficient for reasonable identification of the boundary in the landscape. There is of course no reason why China should accept such a document.

The accuracy of the map is also a critical factor, and historic maps which are so often used in connection with boundary disputes, differ much more widely from each other in accuracy than modern maps produced with the benefit of satellite photography and modern photogrammetry. Attention must also be paid to the author of the map, because it is a reasonable inference that boundaries will be shown more accurately on official maps than on unofficial maps, and that certain government departments, such as those concerned with foreign affairs, will be more careful in boundary representation than other departments, such as mining or meteorology. Because maps represent the region at a particular time it is important to match the date of the map to the period of boundary construction or dispute under consideration. For example, it is difficult to fathom the dispute between the United States and Mexico in the 1850s without reference to Disturnell's map of 1847, which was used by the commissioners.

There are five situations in which maps are likely to contribute to the analysis of boundary disputes. First, it is appropriate to concentrate on the map attached to a particular treaty when the map alone defines the boundary or when the attached map is given precedence over the description in the text. For example, the Sino-British treaty of 9 June 1898 defined the extension of Hong Kong on a map at a scale of 1:314,000. The Anglo-Belgian treaty of 1926 regarding the boundary between what are now Tanzania and Burundi specifically noted that if there was any conflict between the text and the map that the map took precedence.

Second, maps are vital when they alone provide the evidence needed to interpret the text. For example, the Anglo-Belgian agreement of 22 November 1934 defined the boundary between what are now Tanzania and Rwanda by reference to a series of pillars built on the headlands of a lake. When the lines between these pillars intersected the shore the line diverged to follow the shore until it intersected the ray joining the next two pillars. Only a map of that period will allow the shoreline of that period to be identified, and the boundary to be defined with accuracy. Similarly, in May 1872, General Goldsmid drew a boundary between Afghanistan and Persia and defined it as following the outer edge of the *naizar*, which is a belt of reeds. Since that feature varies in extent as a result of burning, grazing and collection for thatch, it would have been necessary to have maps showing the *naizar's* extent in 1872 if the boundary had not been redefined in 1905.

The map may be useful in a third situation when evidence is conflicting. Weissberg (1963), in an excellent article, describes how a map was decisive in settling a dispute between Belgium and Holland. A Belgian enclave in Holland was under dispute and the judges were finally very impressed by the fact that a map dated 1841 showed the Belgian enclave quite clearly, in colour, so that its existence was obvious to anyone glancing at the map.

Fourth, maps may be very useful in helping to understand the reasoning by which boundary architects selected a particular line. Reference was made in the last chapter to the role of charts based on Vancouver's explorations in persuading the negotiators to define the Anglo-Russian boundary along the crest of a range parallel to the coast. Finally, maps are very useful in discovering the attitude of governments towards their boundaries. The phrase 'cartographic aggression' is now commonly used to describe the inclusion on a map by one state of territory which is under the control of a neighbouring state. For example Guatemala regularly produces maps showing British Honduras as a Guatemalan province called Belize, and many Tanzanian maps indicate that it owns part of Lake Tanganyika, whereas according to the relevant treaties the boundary follows the shore of the lake.

There was a time when the value of maps as legal evidence in boundary disputes was heavily discounted, as Hyde (1933) and Sandifer (1939) indicated:

It may be doubted whether a series of maps, however numerous, proves that the boundary which they unite in prescribing is necessarily the correct one, to be accepted as the juridical basis of the proper frontier, especially when they are contradicted by trustworthy evidence of title. (Hyde, 1933, p.316)

Maps can seldom, if ever, be taken as conclusive evidence in the determination of disputes which may arise concerning the location of the boundary. (Sandifer, 1939, p.157)

That time seems to have passed and Weissberg, after reviewing a number of recent cases, was able to assert that maps sometimes had an important role: 'Maps may be regarded as strong evidence of what they purport to portray. They may be termed and treated as admissions, considered as binding, and said to possess a force of their own' (Weissberg, 1963, p.803).

References

Ancel, J., 1936, *Géopolitique*, Paris
Boggs, S.W., 1940, *International Boundaries*, New York
Bowman, I., 1923, *The New World*, London
Caroe, Sir O., 1961, 'Pathans at the Crossroads', *Eastern World*, 15, 12, pp.12-13
Dennis, W.J., 1931, *Tacna and Arica*, New Haven
Dorion, H., 1964, 'La représentation géographique des frontières litigieuses: Le cas du Labrador', *Cahiers de géographie de Québec*, 9, pp.77-87
East, W.G., 1937, 'The Nature of Political Geography', *Politica*, 2, pp.259-86
Fisher, H.A.L., 1940, *The Background and Issues of the War*, Oxford
Fraser-Tytler, Sir W.K., 1953, *Afghanistan*, London
Glassner, M.I., 1970, 'The Rio Lauca; Dispute over an international river', *Geogr. Rev.*, 60, pp.192-207
Griffin, W.L., 1959, 'The Use of International Drainage Basins under Customary International Law', *American Journal of International Law*, pp.50-80
Hartshorne, R., 1936, 'Suggestions on the Terminology of Political Boundaries', *Annals*, Association of American Geographers, 26, pp.56-7
Hasan, K., 1962, 'Pakistan-Afghanistan Relations', *Asian Survey*, 11, pp.14-19
Hertslet, Sir E., 1909, *Map of Africa by Treaty*, London
Hill, N.L., 1976, *Claims to Territory in International Law and Relations*, New York
Hinks, A.R., 1921, 'Notes on the Techniques of Boundary Delimitation', *Geogr. J.*, 58, pp.417-43
House, J.W., 1959, 'The Franco-Italian Boundary in the Alpes-Maritimes', *Transactions*, Institute of British Geographers, 26, pp.107-31
Hsu, I.C.Y., 1965, *The Illi Crisis; A Study of Sino-Russian Diplomacy 1871-81*
Hyde, C.C. 1933, 'Maps as Evidence in Boundary Disputes', *American Journal of International Law*, 27, pp.311-16
India, Ministry of External Affairs, 1961, *Report of the Officials of the Governments of India and the People's Republic of China on the Boundary Question*, New Delhi
Ireland, G., 1938, *Boundaries, Possessions and Conflicts in South America*, Cambridge, Mass
Johnson, R.W., 1966, 'The Canada-United States Controversy over the Columbia River', *University of Washington Law Review*, 41, pp.676-763
Jones, S.B., 1945, *Boundary Making: A Handbook for Statesmen*, Washington

Kirk, W., 1962, 'The Inner Asian Frontier of India', *Transactions*, Institute of British Geographers, 31, pp.131-68

Miller, H., 1937, *Treaties and Other International Acts of the United States of America*, 5, Washington

Murty, T.S., 1964, 'Boundaries and Maps', *Indian Journal of International Law*, 4, pp.367-88

Pounds, N.J.G., 1951, 'The Origin of the Idea of Natural Frontiers in France', *Annals,* Association of American Geographers, 41, pp.146-57.

————., 1954, 'France and "les limites Naturelles" from the Seventeenth to Twentieth Centuries', *Annals,* Association of American Geographers, 44, pp.51-62.

Prescott, J.R.V., 1975, *Map of Mainland Asia by Treaty*, Melbourne

————., Collier, J.H., and Prescott, D.F., 1977, *The Frontiers of Asia and Southeast Asia*, Melbourne

Qureshi, S.M.M., 1966, 'Pakhtunistan: The Frontier Dispute between Afghanistan and Pakistan', *Pacific Affairs*, 39, pp.99-114

Ryder, C.H.D., 1926, 'The Demarcation of the Turco-Persian Boundary in 1913-14', *Geogr. J.*, 66, pp.227-42

Sandifer, D.V., 1939, *Evidence before International Tribunals*, Chicago

Simsarian, J., 1938, 'The Division of Waters Affecting the United States and Canada', *American Journal of International Law*, pp.488-518

Sinnhuber, K.A., 1964, 'The Representation of Disputed Political Boundaries in General Atlases', *Cartographic Journal*, 1, pp.20-8

Sykes, Sir P.M., 1940, *History of Afghanistan*, 2 vols., London

Taberd, J.L., 1837, 'Note on the Geography of Cochinchina', *Journal of the Royal Asiatic Society of Bengal*, pp.737-45

Taussig, H.C., 'Afghanistan's Big Step', *Eastern World*, October, p.15.

Temperley, H.W.V., 1920-4, *History of the Peace Conference of Paris*, 4 vols., London

Touval, S., 1966, 'The Moroccan-Algerian Territorial Dispute', *Africa Research Bulletin*, 3, pp.631-3

Vietnam, Foreign Ministry, 1975, *White Paper on the Hoang Sa [Paracel] and Truong Sa [Spratly] Islands*, Saigon

Ward, F.K., 1932, 'Explorations on the Burma-Tibet Frontier', *Geogr. J.*, 80, pp.465-83

Weissberg, G., 1963, 'Maps as Evidence in International Boundary Disputes: A Reappraisal', *American Journal of International Law*, 57, pp.781-803

5 MARITIME BOUNDARIES

The sovereignty of a coastal State extends beyond its land territory and internal waters, and in the case of an archipelagic State, its archipelagic waters, over an adjacent belt of sea described as the territorial sea. (United Nations, 1977, p.21)

Since 1930 there have been four international conferences seeking to establish a comprehensive law of the sea. The conferences held in 1930 and 1960 failed to produce any definite results. The 1958 conference produced four conventions which have been endorsed by a minority of the world's states, and which increasingly have been honoured in the breach rather than the observance. The 1973 conference held its sixth session in the period May-July 1977, and it has been described unkindly, if accurately, as a major growth industry. At the close of that session there were still deep divisions separating the positions of important states and major groups of states on fundamental questions. The competition for exclusive access to the resources of the sea and seabed has been likened to the scramble for colonies by European countries in the eighteenth and nineteenth centuries. Just as those periods witnessed the construction on a grand scale of international boundaries, which today still form the framework of national sovereignty, so this modern period is recording the proliferation of unilateral maritime boundaries and the increasing frequency of disputes over areas of the oceans.

It is for this reason that a separate chapter has been devoted to this subject. After an examination of the origins of maritime claims this chapter describes the various maritime zones which are claimed by states. It then continues by considering the problems associated with defining the critical boundaries, which are the baseline and the edge of the continental margin, and concludes with an investigation of some maritime boundary disputes.

The Origin of National Maritime Claims

The earliest cases of sovereignty being exercised over the oceans are shrouded in antiquity, but there are early records of rulers granting favours to subjects in connection with the adjacent seas. These favours involved exclusive access to shallow fishing grounds, the right to mine salt from saline marshes, exemption from harbour taxes, and unhindered passage through narrow straits. The construction of navies allowed the defence of the state's territory at sea and discouraged unfriendly alien vessels from sailing too close to hostile shores. The development of trade was soon followed by the incidence of smuggling, and this was an activity which could be most easily detected and prevented in coastal waters, rather than after the goods had been landed. The growth of coastal fishing industries promoted claims which excluded alien competition. Some small, weak countries tried to avoid involvement in the squabbles of large neighbours by proclaiming belts of neutral waters around their coasts. For these and other reasons the attention of rulers and lawyers was increasingly directed towwards control over coastal waters.

Fenn (1926), who has written a most detailed account of the origin of the theory of territorial waters, identifies four main contributors during the period before the seventeenth century. The first major contribution was made by the Roman glossators who agreed that the Emperor had the right to punish wrongdoers at sea in exactly the same way as he punished them on land. In the twelfth century Azo successfully argued that the Emperor had the right to limit the communal nature of the oceans by granting privileges based on long and uninterrupted use. In the fourteenth century Bartolus, who taught law at Pisa, asserted that any country owned islands which were within 100 miles of the coast and had authority in the intervening sea. Finally, in the sixteenth century, Gentilis enunciated that coastal waters were a continuation of the territory of the state whose shores they adjoin. It therefore followed that the territorial rights which the sovereign possessed on land extended over the coastal waters. Fenn is certain that 'after Gentilis, it is literally correct to speak of territorial waters in international law' (Fenn, 1926, p.478).

There was of course the related problem of deciding the areal limits which should be applied to these maritime rights. Fenn regarded the delimitation of territorial waters as 'a mere matter of detail' which should be solved by politicians rather than lawyers. It is evident that this detail has stubbornly resisted resolution. It did seem that there was general approval for territorial seas 3 nautical miles wide when Fenn wrote his article, but that illusion has now disappeared. Since that width is the minimum claimed in modern times, it is interesting to record how it developed.

The first claim to a continuous zone of territorial seas measuring 3 nautical miles wide was made by Sweden on 9 October 1756, and this represented the convergence of two different concepts, the first determining that the territorial waters were continuous, and the second that the proper width was 3 nautical miles These two concepts had different origins, the first coming from Scandinavia and the second arising in the Mediterranean. From 1598 Denmark, the most powerful Scandinavian state, had been reserving exclusive fishing grounds around Iceland within 2 leagues of the coast. The Scandinavian league measured 4 nautical miles. During the reign of Christian IV (1588-1648) the reserved zone varied from 2 to 8 leagues in width, and in his successor's reign the width was fixed at 4 leagues. This claim brought Denmark into collision with other more powerful countries including Britain, Holland, France and Russia. For example, in 1743 Russia compelled the Danish governor of Finnmark to allow Russian fishing vessels to operate within 1 league of the coast. If this permission had not been granted the Russians threatened that the land boundary would be closed, effectively stopping trade and the transhumance movement of Lapps. In 1745 Denmark formally reduced its claims to 1 league, but this still did not satisfy the French authorities, who were involved in further diplomatic exchanges with Denmark in 1760, after disagreement over the fate of two English prizes captured by French vessels. France informed the Danish authorities that they would only concede Danish sovereignty over waters measuring 'Three Miles, the Possible Reach of Cannon Shot from Land' (Prescott, 1975, p.39). This was the limit generally accepted in areas of the Mediterranean and southern Europe.

In 1610 Holland referred to the cannon shot rule during a dispute with Britain, and Walker (1945, pp.211-18) has shown that this concept was common amongst such countries as France and Holland in the seventeenth century. Bynkershoek is usually credited with formulating this generalisation into international law in 1703, in an effort to avoid the imprecision associated with claims to areas of sea within sight of land.

> Therefore it evidently seems more just that the power of the land [over the sea] be extended to that point where missiles are exploded ... [the power of the land] is bounded where the strength of arms is bounded; for this as we have said guards possession. (Balch, 1912, p.414)

There was still some debate about the exact application of this rule because it was unclear whether it applied to guns actually in position, or to an imaginary line of guns placed around the entire coast. The narrow interpretation operated in favour of the strong, well-armed states, while the general interpretation placed all countries on an equal footing. It was probably this consideration which led Galiani, in 1782, to propose that instead of waiting to see where a neutral country mounted its coastal pieces, each country be awarded a belt of coastal waters 1 league wide. This southern Mediterranean league measured 3 nautical miles, and the new proposition, which had already been successfully employed by Sweden since 1756, received general acceptance. Baty (1928, pp.517-32) has provided a comprehensive list of cases where states accepted 3 nautical miles as the limit of territorial waters in the first half of the nineteenth century. While some Russian, Austrian, Prussian and Italian regulations still referred to 'the range of guns' or 'the distance of a cannon shot from the shore', in the period 1848 to 1866, use of this formula was declining rapidly. It is impossible to disagree with the American diplomat who informed the French Government in 1864 that 'no other rule than the three mile rule was known or recognised as a principle of international law' (Crocker, 1919, pp.659-60).

That was certainly the position maintained by most unilateral declarations and bilateral agreements in the period leading to the 1920s. This situation existed mainly because the powerful maritime countries, such as the United States, Britain, Germany and Japan, refused to recognise any wider claims. Italy, Russia, Spain and Uruguay tried to claim wider seas but without much success. However, the international conference at the Hague in 1930, which was attended by 47 countries, demonstrated that it was impossible to secure agreement on the maximum width of territorial seas. As the number of countries attending subsequent conferences has increased from 86 in 1958 to 150 in 1977, agreement has proved harder to achieve. Further, the maximum width of territorial seas is now only one of the problems to be resolved; there are other equally important questions concerned with the zones claimed by countries for particular purposes. In the past there were only territorial waters and in some cases fishing grounds to be considered; the contemporary conferences are dealing with claims to six maritime zones.

National and International Maritime Zones

There are six maritime zones which are or will be subject to national or international authority (Figure 5.1). The zone closest to the shore consists of *internal waters*. The zone is not necessarily continuous because internal waters lie on the landward side of the baseline from which the next three maritime zones are measured. Thus internal waters would not exist where the baseline was considered to be the low water mark of the shore; they would only exist where straight baselines had been drawn along indented coasts or across the mouths of bays, rivers or harbours. With a single exception, internal waters are legally indistinguishable from the land territory of the country. The single exception occurs in respect of those internal waters created by the construction of new straight baselines along indented coasts; if such waters had not previously been considered internal waters alien vessels continue to enjoy the right of innocent passage through them. The right of innocent passage means navigation through territorial seas for the purpose either of traversing those waters or proceeding to a port, in a manner which is not prejudicial to the peace, good order or security of the coastal state. Submarines are required to navigate at the surface while exercising the right of innocent passage.

Proceeding seawards from internal waters the next zone consists of the *territorial sea*. This zone is measured seawards from a baseline which must be defined according to certain agreed rules, which are considered later. According to the Informal Composite Negotiating Text (ICNT) every state has the right to establish a territorial sea not exceeding 12 nautical miles in breadth. As the title of this text suggests it does not represent international law, but it does represent the culmination of four years work by the conference, and if the final treaty is significantly different from the ICNT then it is safe to predict that the conclusion of the treaty lies in the distant future.

At the end of 1977 twelve different widths of territorial seas were claimed by 123 countries. Some generalisations can be made about the most important groups. The twenty-eight countries which claim 3 nautical miles include several developed maritime countries with a major concern with trade and fishing, such as West Germany, the United States, the United Kingdom, Australia, and Japan. It also includes a number of island countries such as Cuba, Singapore, Grenada, Fiji, Taiwan and New Zealand. Finally, four of the countries are located in the Middle East — Jordan, Bahrain, Qatar and the United Arab Emirates. The claim to 4 nautical miles is made by three Scandinavian states and Iceland; the distance of course represents one Scandinavian league. By contrast, claims to 6 nautical miles seem to be associated with Mediterranean countries. Nine of the eleven countries are either located in the Mediterranean or are former colonies of Mediterranean states. In 1958 the Israeli delegate to the conference on

Figure 5.1: Maritime Zones

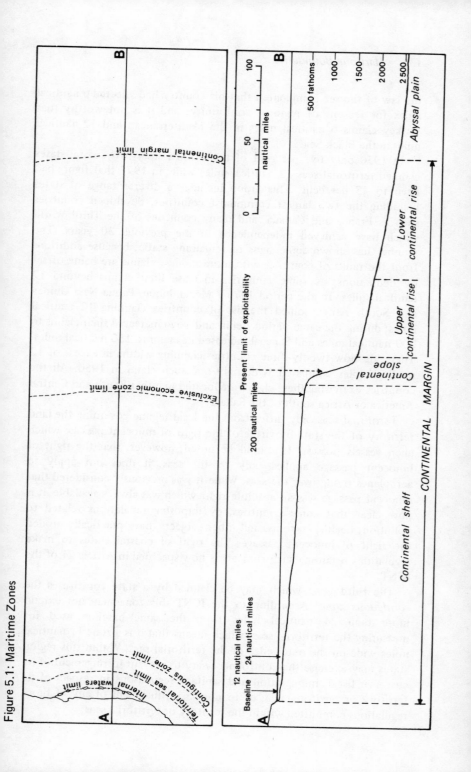

the law of the sea commented that his country had selected 6 nautical miles for reasons of regional conformity, and it is noteworthy that Turkey claims 6 nautical miles in the Mediterranean and 12 nautical miles in the Black Sea.

In 1950 only five per cent of the world's sixty-two coastal states claimed territorial seas 12 nautical miles wide; in 1977 that figure had risen to 45 per cent. This group includes a diverse range of states including the two largest communist countries, developed countries such as France and Canada, and many countries of the Third World which have achieved independence in the previous 30 years. The number has shown some signs of remaining static, because additions from the ranks of countries with more modest claims are being offset by deductions, as some countries increase their claims beyond 12 nautical miles. In the period 1976-7 Mozambique, Papua New Guinea and South Africa joined the list of countries claiming 12 nautical miles; during the same period Benin and Togo increased their claims to 200 nautical miles and Senegal increased its claim to 150 nautical miles. There are now twenty-three countries claiming widths in excess of 12 nautical miles compared with only one such claim in 1950. All the countries exercising these claims are located in either South and Central America or Africa south of the Sahara.

Territorial seas only differ from the legal regime governing the land territory of the state by virtue of the right of innocent passage which alien vessels possess. It should be noted, however, that the right of innocent passage applies only to the seas, it does not apply to aeroplanes flying over the seas. While it was previously considered that innocent passage was an absolute right which was always available, it is now clear that some countries, by imposing regulations related to pollution, health, customs, and other subjects, have practically eroded the right of innocent passage. The right of coastal states to make regulations regarding such subjects is now specified in Article 21 of the ICNT.

The third zone which may be claimed by a state constitutes the *contiguous zone*. According to the ICNT this zone may not extend more than 24 nautical miles from the same baseline used for measuring the territorial seas, which means that it is a zone 12 nautical miles wide on the outer edge of the territorial seas. Within this region states may exercise the control necessary to prevent infringement of its customs, fiscal, immigration and sanitary regulations in respect of its territory or territorial sea, or to punish infringement of any of those regulations committed within the territory or territorial seas.

The fourth zone, which may extend for 200 nautical miles beyond the baseline from which the territorial seas are measured, is called the *exclusive economic zone*. In the exclusive economic zone the coastal state has sovereign rights for the purpose of exploring and exploiting, conserving and managing natural resources, whether living or non-living, of the seabed and subsoil and the superjacent waters, and using the seas and winds for the production of energy. This means that no alien can conduct any economic enterprise, such as fishing or mining, without the permission of the coastal state. However, aliens do have the right to navigate vessels through the exclusive economic zone, to lay submarine cables on the seabed and to overfly. In addition to the sovereign rights the coastal state may also exercise jurisdiction in respect of the establishment and use of artificial islands, marine research, and the preservation of the marine environment. One of the fears of many developed countries is that some states will not distinguish between exclusive economic zones and territorial seas in the exercise of authority.

If countries are bordered by continental margins which are wider than 200 nautical miles, they are entitled to claim the *continental shelf* as the fifth zone. According to Article 76 of the ICNT, states are permitted to claim the seabed and subsoil of submarine areas which extend beyond its territorial sea throughout the natural prolongation of its land territory to the outer edge of the continental margin. Plainly the rights in respect of the exclusive economic zone already comprehend the continental margin out to a distance of 200 nautical miles seaward of the baseline from which the territorial sea is measured. The claim to the shelf beyond 200 nautical miles is restricted to the mineral and other non-living resources of the seabed and subsoil together with living organisms belonging to sedentary species, which at the harvestable stage are either immobile on or under the seabed or are unable to move except in constant physical contact with it. Thus the state has no exclusive claims to fish in the waters above the continental shelf more than 200 nautical miles from the coast. Indeed the waters lying outside the exclusive economic zones of states constitute the high seas. Within the high seas all states have equal rights to navigate, to overfly, to lay submarine cables, to construct artificial islands, to fish and to conduct scientific research.

The sixth zone, which is considered to be the common heritage of mankind, consists of the *deep seabed and subsoil beyond the limits of national jurisdiction*. This means that the line where states cease to claim areas of the continental shelf marks the beginning of the deep seabed which is jointly owned by all the countries of the world. This zone is referred to in the ICNT as 'The Area'. International control over this area does not affect the rights of states in the high seas.

It is now necessary to explore the problems of defining the boundaries of these six zones. The discussion can be divided into three parts. First, it is necessary to examine the baseline from which the territorial sea is measured. This line limits the seaward edge of internal waters, and is the datum from which the outer edges of the territorial sea, contiguous zone and exclusive economic zone are measured in a completely mechanical way. Second, it is important to consider how the edge of the continental margin is defined. This limit is quite independent of the baseline and marks the division between the seabed under national sovereignty and the deep seabed which forms the common heritage of mankind. Third, it is essential to consider the question of how countries will draw common boundaries when seas and seabeds separating them are narrower than their total maritime claims. For example, the Florida Strait between the United States and Cuba is only 82 nautical miles wide and it will therefore be necessary for these two countries to agree on a boundary separating their exclusive economic zones. The passage known as the Dragon's Mouth between Trinidad and Tobago is only 6 nautical miles wide and these countries must agree on a boundary which will separate their territorial seas. It follows that in this case there will be no contiguous zones, or exclusive economic zones, or continental shelf claims for either of these states in the vicinity of the Dragon's Mouth. In the case of the Florida Strait the United States and Cuba will each be able to claim their full entitlement of territorial seas and contiguous zones, but they will only be able to claim truncated exclusive economic zones and they will not be able to claim any continental shelf outside the exclusive economic zone.

The Definition of the Baseline

The current rules for drawing baselines from which the territorial seas, contiguous zones and exclusive economic zones are measured and which marks the outer limit of internal waters were established in 1958 at the First United Nations Conference on the Law of the Sea. Those rules have all been incorporated in the ICNT and certain additions have been made. Normally the low-water line would mark the baseline around the coasts of any country, including the coasts of any islands which the country might own. Plainly the low-water line will lie further seaward than any other tidal limit and will thus allow states to claim the maximum area of territorial seas. The ICNT does not specify which low-water line should be selected, and coastal geomorphologists and sailors will be aware that the low-water line varies throughout the year along most coasts. It is up to the individual country to select one low-water line and to mark it on a large scale chart so that other governments can be aware of the baseline's location. The low-water line is a difficult line to survey on coasts with waves of high energy, and in such cases it is possible that surveys based on aerial photographs taken on relatively calm days at the time of low tide will provide the simplest and most accurate method.

Two sets of deviations are permitted from the low-water line under special circumstances. The first set of deviations occur along short sections of the coast and they link up longer sections where the low-water line is used. For example, deviations are allowed by drawing straight lines across the mouths of rivers and the entrances to harbours. It is also permissible to draw straight lines across the mouths of bays owned by a single country providing they meet two conditions. First, the sea width of the mouth of the bay must not exceed 24 nautical miles. This means that if there are islands in the mouth of the bay only the sea entrances between the islands and the flanking headlands are measured. If the mouth of the bay exceeds 24 nautical miles the country may select points within the bay which are less than 24 nautical miles apart, and which enclose the maximum area of water. The second condition relates to the surface area of the bay, which must be larger than a semicircle constructed with a diameter equal to the measured entrance to the bay. For purposes of measurement islands within the bay are included in the area of the bay.

States may also close bays which are wider than 24 nautical miles if they do so on historical grounds. Historic bays are not defined in the ICNT, indeed they are only mentioned as bays to which the normal rules do not apply. It is generally considered that historic bays must satisfy three conditions. They must have been used exclusively for a long time by the claimant state; a formal claim to sovereignty must be made; and that claim must be accepted by other countries. Thus Hudson Bay is an historic bay since it satisfies all the conditions. However, the Gulf of Carpentaria could not be claimed by Australia on historic grounds because it has been used in recent times as fishing grounds by Russian and Japanese trawlers.

Two other features may also be used to justify deviations from the low-water line of islands or the mainland. First, states are entitled to include within their baseline any roadsteads which are normally used for the unloading, loading and anchorage of ships, and which would otherwise be situated wholly or partly outside the outer limit of the territorial sea. Second, countries are entitled to measure their maritime claims from low-tide elevations which lie less than the width claimed for the territorial sea from the shore of the mainland or an island. A low-tide elevation stands above the sea at low tide but is submerged at high tide.

The second set of deviations involves the construction of straight baselines along comparatively long sections of coast which are deeply indented or cut into or where there is a fringe of islands in the immediate vicinity. Norway's fjord coast and the Dalmatian coast of Yugoslavia provide excellent illustrations of these two situations. In fact the Norwegians have been measuring their territorial waters from straight lines linking the outer line of the headlands at the entrance to fjords and islands off the coast since 1869. The islands along Yugoslavia's coast were formed when mountains created during the folding of the Tertiary period were drowned by the Quaternary rise in sea level. The linear islands aligned northwest-southeast represent the remnants of the outer ranges of the Dinaric Alps.

The ICNT has made three additions to these rules. First, in the case of islands with fringing reefs the baseline will be the seaward low-water line of the reef. Second, long segments of straight baselines may be constructed around the outer edge of unstable coasts and maintained in their original position even though the coast behind them is eroded. This rule will be useful to countries with large deltas which are currently being eroded. For example, Egypt's claim to territorial sea need vary no longer as the Nile delta retreats. Third, the ICNT allows archipelagic states to draw straight baselines around the outermost points of the outermost islands and drying reefs subject to four conditions. First, the system of straight baselines must not depart to any appreciable extent from the configuration of the archipelago. Second, the ratio of water to land within the baselines must not exceed nine to one. Third, no segment of the straight baseline should exceed 125 nautical miles. And fourth, no more than 3 per cent of the segments may measure between 100 and 125 nautical miles in length.

The establishment of archipelagic baselines creates a separate maritime zone known as *archipelagic waters*. Such waters bear a stronger similarity to territorial waters than to internal waters, but the archipelagic state must respect the traditional fishing rights of countries within waters enclosed by baselines, and must allow countries which have laid submarine cables through the area when it consisted of high seas to repair those cables. The right of innocent passage still applies through archipelagic waters but the archipelagic state may designate shipping lanes through them, and these must be followed by alien vessels.

The use of these short and long deviations from the low-water mark are designed to simplify the identification of the outer edge of the territorial sea along coasts with a complex plan, and at the same time eliminate unnecessary and inconvenient enclaves of high seas in the territorial waters of coastal states. If these rules had been applied in this spirit by all the countries concerned there would be no need for the following discussion. Unfortunately, in many cases countries have ignored the spirit of the rules by totally distorting the interpretation of terms used in the 1958 convention and in the ICNT. While it is true that many countries are not signatories to the 1958 convention it is equally true that all countries have been party to the discussions which produced the ICNT. It would be possible to prepare an academic examination of the range of meanings which could be given to every term used in the rules, but this would be a major undertaking without any real practical value. It seems more useful to consider the baselines which have been proclaimed and to indicate the way in which some of them have contravened both the spirit and the letter of the rules. This will give a clearer indication of the latitude which countries can hope to obtain in the construction of new baselines.

A survey of 128 coastal countries shows that 70 have proclaimed deviations along short and long straight lines. In 19 cases the information provided is insufficient to determine whether the baseline observes the rules which have been outlined. In most of these cases the principles on which the baseline is constructed are stated but there is no indication of the sections of coast where these principles have been applied. However, in some cases, including those of Saudi Arabia, Egypt, the Sudan, Syria and Oman, the definitions used in the proclamation clearly do not correspond with the rules laid down in the ICNT. For example, the decree governing the baseline of Saudi Arabia which was issued on 21 February 1958, defines an island as any islet, reef, rock or permanent artificial structure not submerged at lowest low tide, and places no restriction on the width of bays claimed as internal waters.

In 23 cases the baselines conform exactly to the spirit and letter of the 1958 convention and the ICNT. Seven of the countries included in this group could be classed as under-developed countries, but Angola, Guinea Bissau and Mozambique are still using the baselines which were proclaimed by Portugal when it was the colonial authority.

There are 20 cases where the letter or the spirit of the present and proposed rules have been breached. Three of the countries could be described as developed; they are Sweden, Spain and Portugal. The other 17 countries would all be classified as developing. In a few cases the baselines lie so close to smooth coasts that there is very little improper erosion of the area of high seas. For example, on 1 March 1960 Albania proclaimed a baseline 88 nautical miles long between the mouth of the Bojana River and Cape Gjuhezes. The line encloses six bays of which only two, Pellg i Drinit and Gji i Vlones satisfy the semicircular test. The grain of the Albanian topography is transverse to the coast, in direct contrast with Yugoslavia's Dalmatian coast where the Dinaric grain is aligned along the coast. The headlands are composed of low limestone spurs, covered with garrigue, and they define smooth bays possessing alluvial coasts laid down by the discharge of rivers such as the Drin and Shkumbin. Since these bays do not penetrate deeply into the coastline the baselines do not significantly increase Albania's territorial sea.

On 21 January 1967 Mauritania proclaimed a straight baseline measuring 90 nautical miles between Capes Blanc and Timiris enclosing the Banc D'Arguin, which is generally less than 8 fathoms deep and provides good inshore fishing grounds. Because the baseline in some parts is| 30 nautical miles from the shore it causes significant erosion of the high seas. If Mauritania claimed 12 nautical miles of territorial waters the baseline reduces the area of high seas by 1,325 square nautical miles; the present claim of 30 nautical miles improperly annexes 773 square nautical miles of the high seas. It is likely that part of the explanation for Mauritania's action is found in the trouble it has experienced with vessels from the distant fishing fleets of other countries poaching fish in its territorial waters. In the first half of 1976 Mauritania arrested several Spanish fishing vessels.

Unfortunately there are more serious cases involving baselines which have eroded the high seas in a totally unacceptable way. The longest segment of baseline was proclaimed by Burma on 15 November 1968. It closes the Gulf of Martaban which measures 222 nautical miles at the mouth, between Alguada Reef and Long Island. This line is justified because of the 'geographical conditions prevailing' on the coasts, and the need to safeguard the vital economic interests of the inhabitants of the coastal region. The effect of the baseline is to annex about 11,660 square nautical miles of the high seas, assuming that Burma continues to claim 12 nautical miles of territorial seas.

On 28 June 1971 Ecuador proclaimed a straight baseline with four segments totalling 345 nautical miles; the shortest was 56 nautical miles in length. This baseline contravenes the ICNT in four ways. First, the line does not conform to the general direction of the coast. Second, the coast is not deeply indented nor cut into, nor does it have a fringe of islands in the vicinity of the coast. The third contravention involves the use of La Plata Island as a point on the baseline though it is an isolated feature. The fourth is caused by fixing the terminus of the line at a point in the ocean. There is no provision in the ICNT or the 1958 convention for baselines which are not related to areas of land. Use of the baseline by Ecuador would erode 4,485 square nautical miles of the high seas if the calculations were based on a territorial sea 12 nautical miles wide; because Ecuador claims territorial seas 200 nautical miles wide the baseline only increases its claim by 1,569 square nautical miles.

Uruguay and Argentina have interpreted the article which permits river mouths to be closed in a remarkable way. On 30 January 1961 they agreed to close the mouth of La Plata estuary by a straight line measuring 120 nautical miles between Punta Rosa in Argentina and Punta del Este in Uruguay. No geomorphologist would fix the mouth of the river at the location selected by the two countries, and such an interpretation is quite contrary to the spirit of the rule about river mouths.

Burma, Cambodia, Mexico and Thailand have all drawn straight baselines around the outer edges of islands which cannot be properly considered to fringe the coast. On 30 August 1968 Mexico established a system of straight baselines in the Gulf of California connecting scattered, isolated islands along smooth stretches of coast. There are seventeen segments along the west coast of the gulf totalling 267.4 nautical miles and 5 segments on the east coast totalling 90 nautical miles; the two sections meet at San Estaban Island which is 175 nautical miles from the head of the gulf. The system effectively converts one third of the high seas which used to lie in the gulf into internal or territorial waters of Mexico (Figure 5.2).

There are several cases of bays being closed even though they do not satisfy the semicircular test specified in the 1958 convention and the ICNT. For example, on 6 September 1967 the Dominican Republic announced straight baselines, and segments of the system closed the bays called Yuma, Andres, Ocoa and Esenada de los Agullas. Each of these bays has a mouth narrower than 24 nautical miles but none satisfies the semicircular test. On 29 December 1966 the government of

Figure 5.2: Mexico's Straight Baselines

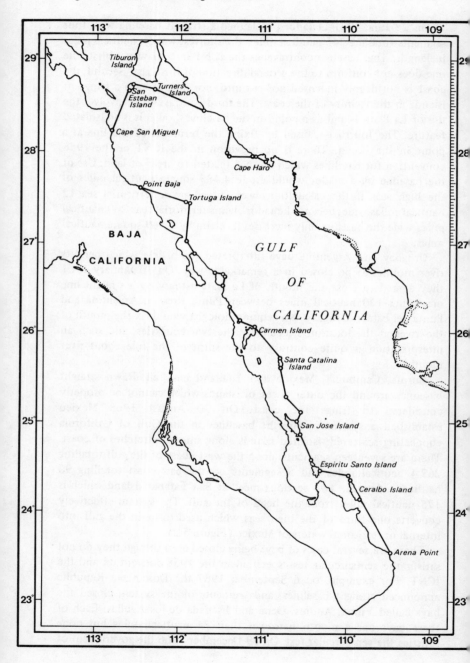

Argentina proclaimed baselines across the mouths of San Matias Gulf and the Gulf of San Jorge, which measured 65 and 58 nautical miles respectively.

Eleven countries have proclaimed straight baselines around archipelagos: they are Indonesia, the Philippines, Fiji, Papua New Guinea; the Maldives, Tonga, Ethiopia, China, Denmark, Ecuador and Spain. The last five countries seem to be disqualified from proclaiming baselines around archipelagos since they are not formed entirely from archipelagos, but consist of mainlands with attached island groups. However, where the islands are closely grouped, as with the Paracel Islands of China, or the Faroes of Denmark, the baselines will have a negligible effect on the extent of territorial waters claimed.

The other six countries are truly archipelagic states but they do not all satisfy each of the four conditions laid down in the ICNT for the construction of archipelagic baselines. The Indonesian system satisfies all the conditions; indeed it almost appears that two of the conditions were designed with the Indonesian case in mind. Two of the Indonesian segments measure 124 nautical miles, and the maximum permitted length is 125 nautical miles. Further, 2.6 per cent of the segments measure between 100 and 125 nautical miles, and the maximum permitted proportion is 3 per cent. However, the ratio of water to land in the Indonesian system is about 1:1, which is well below the maximum ratio of 9:1. The Philippines system has one segment measuring 140 nautical miles, and this will have to be modified if the system is to conform with the rules. At present the offending segment closes the Moro Gulf south of Mindanao; it could be easily modified to satisfy the distance requirement and at the same time correspond more closely to the shape of the archipelago. The present ratio of water to land within the Tongan system is 25:1 which is well in excess of the suggested maximum ratio.

There are two main lessons to be learned from this survey of baselines proclaimed by states throughout the world. First, there are no major rules which have not been breached in both the spirit and the letter. The qualification of 'major' rule is necessary because there is no evidence that any country has wrongly interpreted the regulations regarding the use of harbour installations as baselines. Second, the majority of baselines which contravene the existing and proposed rules have been drawn by countries which could be classed as developing countries.

There seem to be three aims which may be pursued by the creation of straight baselines. The first seeks to push the baseline seawards in order to increase the area of sea to which national claims may be made. Due to the irregularity of coastlines and the increasing width of the territorial sea, the contiguous zone and the exclusive economic zone, it is usual for the greatest increase in area to occur in the zones closest to the coast. For example, measurements were made of the difference in the area of the various zones along the coast between King Sound and Napier Broome Bay, in Australia, using first the low-water line and then a straight baseline joining the outer islands. The area of internal waters was increased by 7,666 square nautical miles; the outer limit of the territorial sea eroded 876 square nautical miles which had previously been part of the contiguous zone; the new contiguous zone eroded 228 square nautical miles which had previously been high seas; and no change could be detected in the outer limit of the exclusive economic zone drawn from the different baselines. This result is quite typical and it is possible to predict that the chief result of drawing baselines, in terms of changes in the area of maritime zones, will be a dramatic increase in the area of internal waters and a smaller though significant increase in the area of territorial waters. It therefore follows that the construction of baselines within the rules laid down in the 1958 convention of the ICNT will not significantly increase the area of seabed and overlying waters available for exclusive economic use. It should be noted that the baseline has no effect on the claim to continental shelves wider than 200 nautical miles. Clearly then decisions regarding baselines are administrative rather than economic decisions. If the authorities prefer the smallest possible area of internal waters they will restrict the use of baselines, and will follow the same course if they prefer to keep to a minimum the area of territorial waters which have to be supervised.

The second aim seeks to use baselines to gain an advantage vis-à-vis another country in the construction of a common maritime boundary. This seems to be a vain ambition because an inspection of thirty-three bilateral treaties dealing with international boundaries separating territorial seas, or fishing zones, or continental shelves has not produced any case where a country benefited by having straight baselines. The reason seems to be that if one country seeks the advantage of straight baselines then the other country quickly acquires the same advantage with its own set of baselines.

The third aim is the easy identification of the seaward limits of the territorial sea and the contiguous zone. If these zones are measured from each fringing island and cape rather than a straight baseline, their outer limits can sometimes follow convoluted courses which create deep embayments of contiguous zones or high seas. Such irregularities cause problems for navigators trying to avoid territorial waters and contiguous zones, and for patrol vessels trying to enforce regulations within those areas. At the very first conference on the law of the sea at the Hague in 1930 this problem and solution were stressed, so that if deep indentations did occur in the seaward limits of these zones they could be smoothed out (Prescott, 1975, pp.54-6). The post-war conferences have never returned to the question, perhaps in the belief that the use of straight baselines would avoid the difficulty.

The Definition of the Edge of the Continental Margin

The ICNT defines the continental shelf over which the state may exercise sovereign rights for the purposes of exploring and exploiting its natural resources in the following terms:

> The continental shelf of a coastal State comprises the sea-bed and subsoil of the submarine areas that extend beyond its territorial sea throughout the natural prolongation of its land territory to the outer edge of the continental margin, or to a distance of 200 nautical miles from the baselines from which the breadth of the territorial sea is measured where the outer edge of the continental margin does not extend up to that distance. (United Nations, 1977, p.52)

It is only necessary to consider the first part of this definition, since it is plain that where the margin is narrower than 200 nautical miles the claims to the shelf and the exclusive economic zone are indistinguishable. The first part of the definition was obviously settled by lawyers rather than geographers, or geomorphologists, or marine scientists!

First, it must be noted that the continental shelf and continental margin are equated, although the geomorphologist would consider the shelf to be only one part of the continental margin, which also includes the continental slope and the continental rise. This is a small problem which would disappear if the claim was made in respect of the continental margin alone. The term 'natural prolongation' is not defined and is probably incapable of definition in a way which will satisfy all parties to the conference on the law of the sea. It was probably derived from the judgement of the International Court of Justice in 1969 when Germany successfully petitioned for access to areas in the middle of the North Sea which are closer to Denmark and Holland than they are to Germany. In a judgement which has been criticised the court concluded that the delimitation of boundaries between adjacent states should be by agreement, in accordance with equitable principles so as to leave to each state as much as possible of the seabed which forms 'a natural prolongation of its land territory into and under the sea'. Brown (1971, pp.43-71) and Friedmann (1970) have criticised the judgement because it tries to establish a measure of distributive justice which will open the doors to litigation without setting precise guidelines on all the relevant factors which should be taken into account.

The most critical defect of the term 'natural prolongation' is that it does not provide guidance on the disposal of submarine plateaus which may lie close to coasts but be separated from the margin by a deep trough. The use of this term in the ICNT is typical of the rather general language which is being increasingly used to achieve compromise. The effect is that such terms as 'natural prolongation' mean different things to different states and there is a serious risk of disagreement between states which both approve of the ICNT. The variety of interpretations regarding the baseline rules provide irrefutable evidence of this danger. South Korea's claims to the natural prolongation of its continental margin south of the Korean peninsula, which disregarded the Japanese islands of Torishima and Danjo gunto, created a difficult dispute with Japan which was only resolved in 1974 when the two countries agreed to an area of joint control.

The phrase 'outer edge of the continental margin' is another imprecise concept which is likely to be interpreted by different countries in different ways. On the basis of the thousands of measurements of continental margins made around the world it is possible to describe precisely the average continental margin. It consists of a shelf 40 nautical miles wide which descends at a gradient of $0°\ 7'$ to a water depth of 72 fathoms at the junction with the continental slope. The slope occupies a horizontal distance of 12 nautical miles and descends at an angle of $4°\ 17'$ to a water depth of 1,600 fathoms, where it joins the rise. The average continental rise, which consists of an apron of debris masking the junction of the continental slope and the abyssal plain, stretches for about 100 nautical miles, with gradients varying from $1°\ 26'$ at its landward edge to $0°\ 4'$ at the junction with the abyssal plain. Unfortunately this average continental margin is a statistical abstract and the actual margins reveal a very wide range of characteristics. For example, in some cases, such as the Barents Sea, the continental shelf is 700 nautical miles wide, in other cases the rise extends for 400 nautical miles from the foot of the slope, as it does off

Dakar in West Africa. Unless a more precise definition is given to the outer edge of the continental margin there is considerable scope for international disagreements.

The delegates to the conference on the law of the sea are aware of the problem, and at the end of the sixth session in 1977 it was decided to explore four possible definitions, with a view to adopting one of them. It was impossible to return to the definitions of the 1958 convention which permitted the use of the 200 metre isobath or the depth at which resources could be exploited. The set distance was too constricting and the limit based on exploitability allowed creeping claims to sovereignty as techniques improved. The four limits which were nominated for investigation were the 500 metre isobath, 200 nautical miles, the Hedberg zone and the Irish zone. Each of these must be considered in turn so that their particular advantages and disadvantages as submarine boundaries are discovered.

The 500 metre isobath (273 fathoms) would generally be the most restrictive of the four proposals and would force a number of countries, including the Soviet Union, the United States, Argentina, Canada, Australia and China, to yield potentially valuable areas of continental margin. It is also likely that the uneven surface of the continental margin would produce a number of exclaves shallower than 500 metres which would lie at varying distances from the main area of margin adjacent to the coast. Such a patchwork of seabed sovereignty would unnecessarily complicate the administration of the deep seabed outside national sovereignty by the international authority. Further there is no reason to suppose that a completely arbitrary line would produce a satisfactory boundary, especially when the configuration of the isobath is highly irregular. The transference of such an irregular isobath to the surface of the sea as an international limit would increase the problems of navigation for companies interested in deep sea mining. It is of course possible that the restrictive nature of this limit would be an attractive feature to the landlocked and geographically disadvantaged states which form one of the pressure groups at the conference. The greater restriction of national claims will leave a larger area of seabed available for exploitation by international authorities which are pledged to distribute the profits in a manner which favours this group of states.

A line fixed 200 nautical miles from the baseline used to measure the other maritime zones would have two principal defects, and no obvious advantages. First, a number of countries, including Australia, Argentina, Canada, the United States, the Soviet Union and

Madagascar, will have to yield potentially useful areas which lie on margins wider than 200 nautical miles. The countries involved are sufficiently numerous and important to make it very unlikely that such a sacrifice would be made obligatory. There is also the converse situation that the 200 nautical mile limit will deliver to some countries, such as Fiji, with narrow shelves, areas of the deep seabed which they have no chance of exploiting under their present circumstances of capital and technology. Further, if such countries invite international companies with the necessary capital and skills to undertake the mining, those countries will be acting in competition with the international authority administering the exploitation of the deep seabed outside national jurisdiction. The second disadvantage arises from the fact that any decision to measure the margin's extent from baselines exposes countries to the temptation to draw those baselines in order to claim the largest possible area. Once again it is possible that the landlocked and shelf-locked countries will approve of a concept which will leave certain areas of the accessible margin for the international authority, but such states do not seem to form a group strong enough to force its views on other states.

The third boundary introduces the concept of the Hedberg zone. Hedberg, an American geologist, published his ideas in a paper in 1976. After a general survey of the processes by which hydrocarbon resources formed under the sea, Hedberg (1976) advocated that a boundary should be designed which would allow each country to claim the area within which there was a reasonable chance of finding such deposits off its shores. He decided that the continental slope was the world's most impressive geomorphological feature and recommended that the boundary should be linked to it. He proposed that countries should identify the line which marks the junction between the continental slope and rise and use it as the baseline of a zone within which the outer edge of the continental margin should be set. The width of the zone would be settled by international agreement, depending on whether it was desired to restrict the claim or make it as wide as possible.

The advantages of this scheme mean that every country will secure all the margin which they will be able to exploit in the foreseeable future. Exploration companies are now exploring in deeper and deeper waters as they recognise that there are chances of finding fields of petroleum and natural gas on the slope. Such deposits might exist in submarine fans, slope troughs and slope basins. The fans are submarine deltas nourished by rich supplies of sediment from adjacent coasts; they may contain layered, lobate sand reservoirs. Some of the rich fields discovered in the world represent ancient submarine fans. These structures are known to exist off the coast of southern California. Slope trough reservoirs are found where the structure of the slope creates a series of sedimentary traps in a regular arrangement. For example, a series of parallel folds aligned on the same azimuth as the coastline will provide submarine valleys within which sediment will accumulate. Such features are usually thicker and more extensive than the slope basins; a good example of slope troughs is found off the mouth of the Magdalena River on the north coast of Colombia. The slope basins result from irregularities in the surface of the slope which encourage the accumulation of sediment. These depressions are irregular in shape and size, which explains why they are usually less attractive prospects than the slope troughs, although occasionally they are very deep. They are often formed by the upwelling of salt and shale diapirs which form the edges of the basins.

There is a very clear trend for exploration wells to be sunk in waters deeper than 100 fathoms. The first well of this type was sunk by Humble Oil in 1965, when exploring the seabed off southern California. By the end of 1976 the drilling rig *Discoverer* had sunk a well for Esso, off Thailand, in 439 fathoms of water, and vessels now have the capacity to drill in 830 fathoms of water. In the decade ended in 1976, 124 wells were sunk in water deeper than 100 fathoms, and exactly half of this total was drilled in 1975-6.

Hedberg's plan also means that the country has some choice in the line which it finally selects and that the boundary will consist of a series of straight lines, drawn within the zone, which will be easily marked on charts and readily identified by navigators. It is considered an essential part of the scheme that the selected boundaries should be approved by an international commission appointed for that purpose. Of course, Hedberg's proposal still requires the discovery of the junction between the continental slope and rise. In some cases that will be a simple undertaking, in others it will be much harder, and in every case it will require careful submarine surveys; it will not be possible to infer the location of that junction from the inspection of most existing charts.

There seem to be three general situations regarding the nature of the continental rise. Where the coastline has been continually arid throughout the Quaternary period there will be only a small rise. Where the coastline has experienced fluctuating humid and arid cycles there will probably be fossil rises. Finally, where the coastline has been persistently humid throughout the Quaternary the pronounced rise will probably still be growing. Indeed, it is possible off some deltas for the delta to merge into the rise, the slope having been entirely buried. There will be some coasts where the continental slope leads directly to deep submarine trenches where there is no rise. However, the problems of locating the contact between the slope and rise in common situations and of developing rules to deal with the situations where the slope has been entirely buried, or where a trench replaces the rise, do not seem to be insuperable. It seems likely that the majority of countries with wide margins would approve of this system which allows an element of choice and guarantees that all the potentially valuable hydrocarbon reservoirs will fall under the sovereignty of the coastal state. For exactly the opposite reasons the Hedberg zone may not be an attractive concept to the shelf-locked and landlocked countries.

The Irish representatives at the Law of the Sea Conference in 1977 suggested that coastal states should have a choice of drawing boundaries along the outer edge of the continental margin according to two formulae. The first coincides exactly with the Hedberg zone, which would measure not more than 60 nautical miles from the junction between the slope and the rise. The second permits the line to be drawn through a series of points at each of which the thickness of sedimentary rocks is at least 1 per cent of the shortest distance from the point to the foot of the continental slope. The proposal defines the foot of the slope as the point of maximum change in the gradient at its base. The second formula would be much more difficult to apply and much more difficult for any supervisory body to verify.

It seems certain that countries with margins wider than 200 nautical miles will press for the Hedberg zone or some similar concept. Each will argue for the system which provides access to the potentially valuable zones which might contain hydrocarbon fields. To test the possible relationship of the proposed boundaries other than the Irish alternative, charts of two sections of the Australian coast were inspected. The first section stretched along the Great Australian Bight from Albany in Western Australia to Kangaroo Island in South Australia; the second occupied Australia's northwest coast north of Shark Bay.

The section in the Bight presented a simple picture. The 500 metre isobath enclosed the smallest area, although this line lay close to the inner edge of the Hedberg zone south of Albany and Kangaroo Island. In each of these localities the existence of submarine canyons ensured that the isobath followed a convoluted course, which would have been inconvenient if used directly as a boundary. Apart from a very small area of the continental rise southwest of the submarine Ceduna Plateau, a boundary drawn in accordance with the Hedberg zone would have enclosed a much smaller area than one delimited 200 nautical miles from the Australian baseline. In fact the 200 nautical mile boundary south of Esperance lay 100 nautical miles seaward of the outer limit of the Hedberg zone. Of course it is entirely possible that the small area of rise southwest of the Ceduna Plateau, more than 200 nautical miles from the coast, would turn out to be economically more valuable than the much larger area of the abyssal plain enclosed by that limit.

The pattern off the northwest coast of Australia reveals a different relationship between the boundaries (Figure 5.3). While the 500 metre isobath still encloses the smallest area it follows a smooth course which would be suitable for use as a boundary. The Hedberg zone would give Australia sovereignty to a much larger area in this locality than the 200 nautical mile limit. The boundary based on distance would forfeit the western part of the Exmouth Plateau. It is interesting that the Hedberg zone and the 200 nautical mile limit will both enclose areas of the Argo abyssal plain and Cuvier abyssal plain, yet neither will contain the submarine Wallaby Plateau which is separated from the Dirk Hartog Shelf by a trough. There is every reason to expect that the coasts of other countries will show variations and that countries which are neither shelf-locked nor landlocked will prefer a formula which allows claims based on the Hedberg zone when the shelf is wider than 200 nautical miles.

The Division of Maritime Zones between Adjacent and Opposite Countries

There are two situations in which it is necessary for countries to draw maritime boundaries to separate the areas over which each exercises sovereignty. The first situation involves countries which share the same shore line, such as India and Pakistan, Belgium and France, and Chile and Peru. In these cases the sea boundary is a continuation of the land boundary. Under normal circumstances this projection of the land boundary will separate, in turn, adjacent areas of territorial waters, adjacent contiguous zones, adjacent exclusive economic zones and adjacent continental margins. If the countries claim different widths for these zones they will not be perfectly matched on each side of the boundary.

The second situation concerns first those countries which are separated by an arm of the sea which is narrower than 400 nautical miles, and second, where the arm of the sea, being wider than 400 nautical miles, is underlain by a continuous continental shelf. In the second case the two countries will have to agree on a boundary

Figure 5.3: The Continental Margin's Boundaries off North West Australia

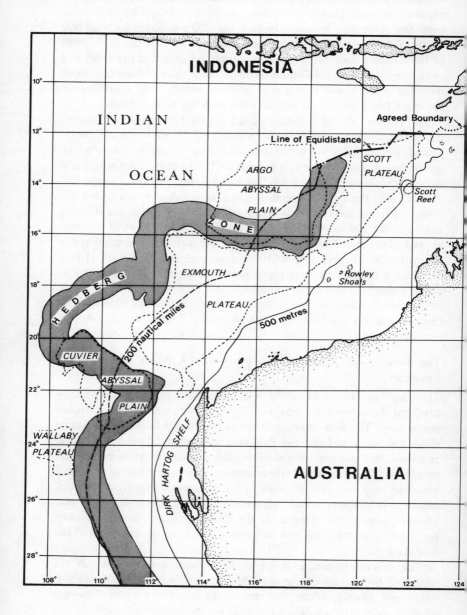

separating their areas of the continental margin. In the first case, if the width is between 48 and 400 nautical miles, the countries will select a boundary to divide their exclusive economic zones. If the width is between 24 and 48 nautical miles the boundary will separate their contiguous zones, and if the width is less than 24 nautical miles the common boundary will separate territorial seas. Boundaries between countries separated by the sea need not be attached to land; for example, the boundary agreed between India and Indonesia on 8 August 1974 extends for 48 nautical miles in the centre of the Great Channel between Sumatra and the Nicobar Islands.

The ICNT lays down formulae by which boundaries should be drawn between territorial seas, exclusive economic zones and continental margins, and they are the same for adjacent and opposite countries:

Where the coasts of two States are opposite or adjacent to each other, neither of the two States is entitled, failing agreement between them to the contrary, to extend its territorial sea beyond the median line every point of which is equidistant from the nearest points on the baseline from which the breadth of the territorial seas of each of them is measured. This article does not apply, however, where it is necessary by reason of historic title or other special circumstances to delimit the territorial seas of the two States in a way which is at variance with this provision. (United Nations, 1977, pp.24-5)

The formulae for delimiting the exclusive economic zones and the continental margins are identical:

The delimitation of the exclusive economic zone between adjacent or opposite States shall be effected by agreement in accordance with equitable principles, employing, where appropriate the median or equidistance line, and taking account of all the relevant circumstances. (United Nations, 1977, see p.55 for the definition of the continental shelf)

While lawyers could probably argue for a long time about the semantic differences between these two definitions, for practical purposes they cannot be distinguished. In both formulae states must agree on the boundary after taking into account 'special circumstances' or 'relevant circumstances', and one of the options available is to use a line of equidistance.

A line of equidistance is the geometric answer to the problem of dividing shared seas. The line, being equidistant at all points from the nearest points of the opposite or adjacent coasts, ensures that countries secure the seas and seabed which are closer to their territory than to the territory of any other country. Such a line is unique and each cartographer working on the same chart would produce exactly the same line provided there was agreement about the location of the baseline. This last caveat is important because the ownership of a small island at some distance offshore can cause the line of equidistance to be significantly displaced, and can provide a claim to a quite disproportionate area of the sea and seabed at the expense of an adjacent or opposite state. Countries which have been placed at a disadvantage in this way often claim that detached islands provide the 'special circumstances' which make it proper to construct some line other than the line of equidistance. Before looking at the problems of interpretation which beset the construction of common maritime boundaries it will be useful to examine the agreements which have been reached by countries.

Looking first at recent agreements concerning the division of territorial waters between adjacent states it is evident that there is a tendency to select simple lines which will make the task of navigation less difficult. For example, on 30 September 1976, Brazil and Uruguay agreed on a boundary following a bearing of 128° from true North, from the terminus of their land boundary on the Atlantic shore. This line was described as being 'nearly perpendicular to the general line of the coast'. In March 1976 Guinea Bissau and Senegal had drawn their common boundary along a bearing of 240° from true North, and on 9 October 1974, the Soviet Union and Turkey had selected bearing 290° from true North as the appropriate boundary. In December 1975 Colombia and Ecuador chose parallel 1° 24′ 27″ north as their sea boundary, and for good measure they defined a buffer zone 20 nautical miles wide astride the boundary. Within this zone the accidental intrusion of fishermen on the wrong side of the boundary is not considered as a violation of the agreement. The boundary between Mexico and the United States of America off the mouth of the Rio Grande was agreed on 23 November 1970, and contains a novel feature. Because the mouth of the Rio Grande tends to occupy different positions on the coast, one fixed point has been settled 2,000 feet off the coast to act as a hinge between the seaward boundary section, which is permanent, and the short landward boundary section which will move as the mouth of the Rio Grande moves. In fact the single, permanent section lies very close to the course of the line of equidistance; it was considered by the two parties that such a straight line had administrative benefits over the exact line of equidistance. The agreement between East and West Germany on 5 October 1976 also deviated from the line of equidistance in favour of West Germany. The reason was to allow free access for that country to its port of Travemunde. The line of equidistance would have intersected the navigable channel which has been used for a very long time. However, Poland's common boundaries with the Soviet Union and East Germany, concluded on 19 October 1973 and 28 November 1975 respectively, both follow lines of equidistance.

At the end of 1977 there were thirty-one agreements concerning maritime boundaries between opposite states. Five applied to territorial waters in narrow straits and the remainder dealt with the seabed. The earliest agreement on territorial water was between Denmark and Norway which delimited a boundary through The Sound on 30 January 1932. The other agreements involve Indonesia and Malaysia, Indonesia and Singapore, France and Canada, and Finland and the Soviet Union. The Franco-Canadian boundary concerns the islands of St Pierre and Miquelon which are located 10 nautical miles off the coast of Newfoundland. In March 1972 the two countries fixed a common boundary measuring 54 nautical miles by nine points. Five of the points are equidistant and the other four are all closer to the Canadian mainland than the French islands. Of the other agreements only that between Indonesia and Malaysia draws a line of equidistance between the sets of straight baselines fringing the Strait of Malacca. All the others use some equidistant points and others where the existence of small islands has been discounted.

Of the twenty-six agreements dealing with seabed boundaries only two make no use of equidistant points. One of these, between Britain and West Germany, obviously could not have any equidistant points because Germany was only able to extend its control to the centre of the North Sea because of concessions by Denmark and the Netherlands, following the judgement of the International Court of Justice in Germany's favour. The other treaty which eschews equidistant points lies between Iran and Dubai. This boundary, which was settled in September 1975, discounts the Iranian island of Sirri, for the purposes of dividing the seabed; the boundary follows the limit of the island's territorial waters. Ten of the bilateral agreements used lines of equidistance throughout; they are Bahrain and Iran, Norway and Britain, Denmark and Norway, Denmark and Britain, Netherlands and Britain, Finland and the Soviet Union, Norway and Sweden, Canada and Denmark, India and Indonesia, and Japan and Korea. The boundaries between these pairs of countries took accounts of all islands and rocks, no matter how small.

The remaining fourteen argreements drew lines which included sections of equidistant boundaries and sections where the existence of islands had been discounted. These agreements were concluded between Argentina and Uruguay, Denmark and West Germany, the Netherlands and West Germany, Iran and Qatar, Iran and Oman, Iran and Saudi Arabia, Bahrain and Saudi Arabia, Abu-Dhabi and Qatar, Trinidad and Tobago and Venezuela, Norway and the Soviet Union, Italy and Yugoslavia, Australia and Indonesia, Indonesia and Malaysia, and India and Sri Lanka. An interesting point about the boundary between Venezuela and Trinidad and Tobago is that there is heavy deposition along the Venezuelan coast which is advancing seawards.

Of the thirty-one agreements delimiting boundaries between opposite states only one leaves an island belonging to one country on the continental shelf awarded to another country. The case concerns the island of Martin Garcia which belongs to Argentina. The island is small and has been left 0.4 nautical miles on the Uruguayan side of the boundary. According to the treaty the island will be devoted exclusively to a natural reserve for the conservation and preservation of native flora and fauna.

There are two sets of problems which may cause disputes over the delimitation of maritime boundaries between opposite or adjacent countries. The first set involves islands; the second concerns depressions in the seabed. The problems associated with islands can be divided into two classes. First, there are disputes over the ownership of islands, and second, there are disputes over the extent to which certain islands should be taken into account in drawing maritime boundaries. Disputes over the ownership of islands are exactly the same as territorial or positional boundary disputes; for example, Cambodia's claim to the Vietnamese island of Phu Quoc is a simple territorial dispute, while the dispute between Equatorial Guinea and Gabon over islands in Corisco Bay is a positional dispute.

There were five islands in dispute between Cambodia and South Vietnam at the time those countries came under the influence of communist governments in 1975. There have been no reports that the dispute has been resolved since that date. The five islands are called Panjang, Wai, Phu Du, Tian Moi and Phu Quoc. The latter is the only large island and the only one with any intrinsic value, but together the islands support claims to 14,580 square nautical miles of the seabed, where there are strong possibilities of finding oil and natural gas.

According to the evidence of Chhak (1966, pp.154-5), who was once the Cambodian Foreign Minister, and who was reported to have shared Prince Sihanouk's exile in Peking, the dispute over Phu Quoc is of long standing, but it is unnecessary to pursue the question before 1913. In that year the French Administrators of Hatien in what is now Vietnam, and the French Resident in Kompot, in what is now Cambodia, received applications for mining concessions on some of the offshore islands. The two authorities were unable to resolve the matter and it was referred to the Governor General of Indochina. A decision was issued from the Governor General's office in January 1939! The Governor General noted that the close proximity of some of the islands to the Cambodian coast called 'logically and geographically' for them to be placed under the administration of Cambodia, and that this arrangement would avoid the need for citizens to make long journeys to settle matters with the authorities in Saigon. The division of islands between the two administrations was made by a boundary drawn at right angles to the coast at the point where the land boundary reached the shore. The line was defined as making an angle of 140 G (126°) with the appropriate meridian. This line divides Phu Quoc but the Governor General assigned the whole island to Cochinchina. In doing so he recorded that he had only concerned himself with questions of convenient administration and policing of the island, and not with *la dépendance territoriale*, which remained unresolved.

It will be interesting to see whether the communist governments of these two countries have more success in solving this dispute than their predecessors. The matter has greatest importance for Cambodia since most of its available continental shelf is in dispute with either Vietnam or Thailand, whereas those countries have large areas of continental shelf where their sovereignty is unchallenged (Prescott, 1976, pp.2-3). There are many other disputes over islands in the seas around mainland Asia (Prescott, 1976). The most serious concern the Spratly Islands, some of which are occupied by military units from Taiwan, Vietnam and the Philippines. China also claims sovereignty over the Spratly Islands; its case is founded on precisely the same arguments which justified China's reoccupation of the Paracel Islands in January 1974.

The positional dispute between Gabon and Equatorial Guinea flared on 23 August 1972 over the ownership of some islands in Corisco Bay. The Franco-Spanish treaty of 27 June 1900 awarded the islands of Elobey and Corisco to Spain, and the government of

Equatorial Guinea is convinced that this award implied Spanish sovereignty over all the islands. Gabon, however, insists that the islands of Mbane and Cocobeach were not named in the treaty because they were beyond Spanish control. Gabon occupied these two islands, and a very serious situation was apparently only avoided after the intervention of the Presidents of Congo and Zaire. There have been unconfirmed reports of oil strikes by American companies in the vicinity, and further unconfirmed reports that the dispute was settled in July 1974, when a positional dispute was settled over the land boundary between the two countries in the vicinity of the town of Bitam in Gabon and Ebebiyin in Equatorial Guinea.

Disputes over the extent to which particular islands should be taken into account in drawing a maritime boundary generally involve islands which are distant from the mainland or from other islands. The agreements between Italy and Yugoslavia and between Iran and Saudi Arabia involved disputes over the discounting of Italian and Iranian islands as points for calculating the common boundary.

Hodgson (1973) has prepared a very interesting analysis of special circumstances associated with islands, and in that study he considered the weight which should be given to islands of different sizes from rocks at one extreme to very large islands at the other. He concluded that rocks should not be taken into account when drawing lines of equidistance between territorial seas, but that all other islands should be considered. When his attention was focused on seabed boundaries he classified islands into three categories: they were those which should be given full effect, those which should be entirely discounted and those which were intermediate to those two categories. Amongst the islands which he thinks should be given full effect he includes large islands, islands which are geographically related very closely to the mainland, independent island states, and islands which are mutually accepted by both negotiating parties. The islands which should be totally discounted include islands in dispute, islands in the middle of restricted water bodies, small uninhabited islands beyond the contiguous zone of the mainland and main islands, and islands which states agree to discount. The intermediate category which is partially discounted include remote islands with large populations, and islands which it is agreed should be partially discounted. Article 121 of the ICNT stipulates that rocks which cannot sustain human habitation or an economic life of their own shall not support claims to exclusive economic zones or continental shelves.

Very often the state which feels disadvantaged by the existence of islands belonging to an opposite or adjacent state raises issues of justice, and this is not surprising given the reference in the ICNT to 'equitable principles'. Papua New Guinea has made claims that the northernmost Australian islands in Torres Strait should be discounted, and the agreement which the two countries reached on 5 June 1976 recognised the force of this argument. By the agreement Australia accepted that the seabed boundary would lie north of all inhabited Australian islands except Boigu, Dauan and Saibai; these islands are located close to the Papuan coast. It was further agreed that a zone will be established in Torres Strait to protect and preserve the traditional way of life and the livelihood of the Torres Strait islanders and the residents of the adjacent coast of Papua New Guinea. Griffin (1976) has edited a series of seminar papers on the Torres Strait dispute and there is also a very interesting and comprehensive parliamentary report (Joint Committee of Foreign Affairs and Defence, 1976). Political difficulties within both countries have made it impossible to complete a final agreement.

The second kind of problem, involving depressions on the seabed, only affects the construction of seabed boundaries. The general case is illustrated very well by a dispute which once existed between Australia and Indonesia. West of longitude 133° 23′ east in the Arafura Sea there is a deep depression known as the Timor Trough, which divides the continental margins into two unequal parts. The trough, which descends to a depth of 1,700 fathoms, has its long axis parallel to the south coast of the island of Timor; to the north of the trough there is a narrow margin only about 30 nautical miles wide, while to the south the margin adjoining the Australian coast is about 200 nautical miles wide. Australia argued that the proper boundary should be located along the axis of the Timor Trough; Indonesia argued that this was just an incidental depression in a continuous continental shelf, and that it should be ignored in constructing a median boundary between Timor and the Australian mainland. Australia by agreements with Indonesia in May 1971 and October 1972 made concessions (Prescott, Collier and Prescott, 1977, pp.78-9). The boundary was drawn on the southern slope of the trough, and Australia conceded about 3,000 square nautical miles of the disputed area, which amounted to nearly 20,000 square nautical miles.

The Anglo-Norwegian agreement in the North Sea ignored the comparatively shallow Norwegian Trench and the Canadian-Norwegian agreement between Baffin Island and Greenland similarly ignored a major depression. It appears likely that such depressions will tend to be ignored in the future, unless there are wide discrepancies between the strength of the states concerned or if there are very unfriendly relations between them.

Conclusion

By the end of 1977 the Law of the Sea Conference had lasted four years and was evidently still a long way from producing a final treaty which all members could support. There seem to be two risks, which are mutually exclusive, but which might produce the same dangers. The first risk is that no treaty will be produced in the foreseeable future. This would mean that coastal countries would be able to make unilateral claims to areas of the oceans, and that disagreements would arise in confined areas, such as the Mediterranean Sea, the Caribbean Sea, and the South China Sea, and off coasts where there are rich fishing grounds, such as Peru and South West Africa. The second risk is that agreement on the form of the treaty will only be secured by making its terms so vague that they can be interpreted in different ways by countries with different interests. In this case some countries would use the imprecise language of the text as a licence for encroaching into areas of the sea considered by other countries to be part of the high seas. Once again friction would result.

The best hope for the peaceful and orderly exploitation and conservation of the oceans' resources lies in an unambiguous text setting out precise rules for the conversion of coastal waters to areas subject to national sovereignty, and which also contains enforceable procedures for settling disputes.

References

Balch, T.W., 1912, 'Is Hudson Bay a Closed or an Open Sea?', *American Journal of International Law*, 6, pp.402-15.

Baty, T., 1928, 'The Three Mile Limit', *American Journal of International Law*, 22, pp.503-37

Brown, E.D., 1971, *The Legal Regime of Hydrospace*, London

Chhak, S., 1966, *Les frontières du Cambodge*, Paris

Crocker, H.G., 1919, *The extent of the Marginal Sea*, Washington

Fenn, P.T., 1926, 'Origins of the Theory of Territorial Waters', *American Journal of International Law*, 20, pp.465-82

Friedmann, W., 1970, 'The North Sea Continental Shelf Cases: A Critique', *American Journal of International Law*, 64, pp.229-40

Griffin, J., 1976, *The Torres Strait Border Issue: Consolidation, Conflict or Compromise*, Townsville College of Advanced Education

Hedberg, H.D., 1976, 'Ocean Boundaries and Petroleum Resources', *Science*, 191, pp.1009-18

Hodgson, R., 1973, *Islands: Normal and Special Circumstances*, US Department of State, Washington

Joint Committee of Foreign Affairs and Defence, 1976, *The Torres Strait Boundary*, Canberra

Prescott, J.R.V., 1975, *The Political Geography of the Oceans*, Plymouth

————., 1976, 'Asia's Maritime Boundary Problems', *Dyason House Papers*, 2, no.4, pp.1-4

————., Collier, H.J., and Prescott, D.F., 1977, *Frontiers of Asia and Southeast Asia*, Melbourne

United Nations, 1977, *Informal Composite Negotiating Text of the Third Conference on the Law of the Sea*, A/CONF. 62/WP 10, New York

Walker, W.L., 1945, 'Territorial Waters: The Cannon Shot Rule', *The British Yearbook of International Law*, 22, pp.210-31

6 THE INTRA-NATIONAL BOUNDARIES OF STATES

> The most striking feature of local administration in Bizen [Japan] of 1200 is that, despite successive changes in the organisation of power, the boundaries within which local administration was exercised tended to conform to the familiar shapes which had existed from the Nara period. (Hall, 1966, p.158)
> Many scholars have tended to overlook the importance and significance of internal administrative changes in the development of nations. (McColl, 1963, p.53)

McColl's observation is reinforced by a survey of the literature dealing with the intra-national boundaries of states; the number of studies in this field is much smaller than the studies which deal with international boundaries. There are obvious reasons why this situation exists. International boundaries are often the subject of dramatic conflicts between countries and attract much public attention; the history of international boundaries is fully documented in national archives, and is usually readily available. By contrast intra-national boundaries rarely attract public attention, and research into their evolution is often a difficult task because sometimes the records are widely scattered and incomplete. However, it is probably true that the pattern of intra-national boundaries within a country impinges more directly on the lives of the majority of citizens than the country's international limits. For many citizens such boundaries determine the electorate in which their votes are cast; the method by which the rateable value of their property is assessed; the availability of schools for their children; the type of use to which land may be put; the hours during which alcohol may be consumed in public houses; and the frequency with which refuse is collected. In short, the pattern of local and regional government fixes various codes of rules which affect social and economic activity to a greater or lesser extent. Further in some countries, such as Canada, Nigeria and Uganda, intra-national boundaries have marked out the areas within which the ferment of regional consciousness has threatened the stability of the whole country. In other countries, such as South Africa and Rhodesia, intra-national boundaries may define the areas within which different ethnic groups live and work.

There are two main types of intra-national boundaries — federal and internal. Federal boundaries separate states within a federation, while internal boundaries mark the limits of administrative units within the individual federal states or unitary states. If this classification is accepted it means that there is a threefold hierarchy of boundaries — international, federal and internal. A fourth category — extra-national — could refer to the boundaries of international organisations, such as the North Atlantic Treaty Organisation, but they would usually be sections of existing international boundaries. A federal state would possess all three categories, while a unitary state would possess only international and internal boundaries. Clearly all these categories can then be further subdivided according to the well-known sequential, functional and morphological classifications. International and federal boundaries are normally delimited through bilateral or multilateral negotiation, whereas internal boundaries are based on unilateral decisions of a single sovereign power. This means that international and federal boundaries are less susceptible to change than internal boundaries, which can be varied according to the needs of the state. Of course this generalisation would not apply to those quasi-federal countries such as the Soviet Union and South Africa; it would apply to federations such as the United States, Canada and Australia.

International and federal boundaries have many functions, while there may be different patterns of internal boundaries to serve separate functions. The combination of these two differences generally results in the international and federal boundaries being more deeply intrenched into the landscape than internal boundaries. Internal boundaries are often not demarcated in contrast with the other two categories, where provision is generally made for demarcation, although it may not always be carried out.

The often ephemeral nature of internal boundaries makes it much more difficult to trace their evolution in function and position than that of international and federal boundaries, which are usually defined in some published treaty. Internal boundary changes are usually published in a government gazette, and can be very difficult to follow. Freedom of movement across federal and internal boundaries makes it easier to carry out fieldwork in respect of these two categories than is the case with most international boundaries.

The Evolution of Federal Boundaries

Geographers are concerned with the evolution of boundaries in respect of definition, function and position, and it is important to realise that evolution in these respects may be related or take place separately. For example, in 1917 the latitudinal boundary which had allocated territory between the Northern and Southern Provinces of the Colony and Protectorate of Lagos was delimited. This change in definition was accompanied by a change in position which transferred 6,650 square miles to the Northern Provinces, but the function of the boundary remained unchanged. On the other hand, in 1921 the international boundary between Eire and Northern Ireland was created from existing county boundaries without any changes in definition or position.

Studies are available dealing with the evolution of the federal boundaries of the United States, Canada, Australia, the Soviet Union and Nigeria. The development of Nigeria's federal boundaries is distinct from the other four cases: first, because the area which became Nigeria had a large settled indigenous population long before the boundaries were drawn by colonial administrators; second, because the boundaries reached their present form as the primary internal boundaries of a unitary state — the Colony and Protectorate of Nigeria; and third, because there was no attempt to colonise the area by large numbers of Europeans. In Australia and North America the boundaries were drawn in areas being colonised by Europeans, who were opposed by numerically small indigenous groups, lacking political hegemony. Nor did any of these federal states experience a period of unitary government involving the whole of their present territory.

Taking the example of Nigeria first, we find that the existing three federal states and their boundaries can be traced to the original threefold division of the Nigerian coast amongst the Lagos Colony and Protectorate, the Royal Niger Company (RNC) Treaty Area and the Niger Coast Protectorate from 1892-8. None of these boundaries was demarcated. The boundaries of the Lagos Colony and Protectorate were intended to coincide with the known limits of the Yoruba Confederation based on Ijebu, Abeokuta and Ibadan, which were clearly distinguished from the hostile Yoruba groups around Ilorin, and the Edo Kingdom of Benin to the east. The other boundaries between the Niger Coast Protectorates and the RNC Treaty Area were arbitrary and resulted in the division of the Niger Coast Protectorate into two sections east and west of the River Niger and its delta. In 1900 the charter of the Royal Niger Company was revoked, and three British Protectorates occupied the area of Nigeria. The Niger Coast

Protectorate became the Protectorate of Southern Nigeria and was
expanded to include the former Royal Niger Company Treaty Area
south of the latitude of Idah — seven degrees ten minutes North.

In 1906 the two southern Protectorates were united, and in 1914
they amalgamated with the Northern Protectorate to create a unitary
state with its capital at Lagos. The primary division into Northern and
Southern Provinces was retained.

In 1917 the boundaries of the Northern and Southern Provinces —
drawn when the territory had not yet been explored and depending
upon no geographical or ethnological features — were carefully
revised so as no longer to bisect tribal unity, except where by the
usage of seventeen years a fraction of a tribe had become
incorporated with its neighbours. (*Report on the Amalgamation*,
1920, p.11)

In 1939, the present boundary between the Eastern and Western
Regions was created from existing provincial boundaries. It reflected
the distinction between the mature political organisation of the Benin
and Yoruba groups west of the Niger, and the organisation of the Sobo,
Ibo and Ibibio groups east of the river, which had not advanced beyond
the clan or family level. These three Regions formed the Federation of
Nigeria in 1954, and although the boundaries acquired fresh functions
in respect of taxation, education and land ownership, there was no
change in position or definition. The federal boundaries have not been
satisfactorily demarcated and are difficult to trace except near main
roads and along the railways.

In the United States and Canada, the different federal boundary
evolutions between the eastern region and the remainder of the
continent has been recognised for many years by scholars who include
Whittlesey (1956). In the eastern margin of the continent the first
boundaries, which allocated territory, were antecedent to settlement,
but modification to the final boundary form was subsequent to the
expansion of farmlands and settlements from separate coastal locations.
These eastern colonies formed the nuclei of the present States. New
States were added by the division of western areas as the nuclei of
mining (British Columbia) and agricultural activity (Manitoba) became
established. Although Brice, writing of the western States of the United
States of America, claims that the federal boundaries are entirely
arbitrary, Deutsch, Ullman and Whittlesey have shown that the
boundaries represent the compromise between opposed local political

forces, often based on sectional economic interests, and the desire to admit slave and free territories in pairs between 1800-50. Further, once a State was admitted, its boundaries became inviolate, even if the subsequent appreciation of the environment and of settlement trends indicated the need for adjustment. Apart from the creation of Washington DC, only two States have yielded territory to new jurisdictions: part of Massachusetts was transferred to Maine, and Virgina was divided to create the two States of Virginia and West Virginia. In Canada also, the State areas could not be diminished once they had been established, and Nicholson has shown that the underlying principle was the desire to create States or Provinces with approximately equal areas. This situation was revealed by the extensions of Alberta and Saskatchewan in 1905 and the additions to Manitoba, Ontario and Quebec in 1912.

Nicholson (1968) has also prepared a very interesting account of the arguments in favour of a further division of Canada's Northwest Territory, and has described some of the boundaries which were considered by the Council of the Northwest Territory for this purpose. He noted that the attempts by the Council to discover a division which united the principles of geographical regionalism and the realities of boundary construction in a tundra environment, were an advance on the former methods of drawing Canada's earlier federal boundaries, and drew attention to the different requirements of hunters and mining engineers. Hunters, trappers and fishermen prefer boundaries related to physical features which they can recognise in the landscape, such as rivers and crests. Mining engineers, aware of possible legal difficulties associated with such boundaries, prefer astronomic boundaries which can be easily plotted on maps, and which enable the surveyor to determine quickly where he stands in relation to the boundary. In 1965 it was decided not to proceed with any division of the Territory because the new territory would be cut off from the most densely populated Arctic area; because once a boundary is established it is hard to change; because insufficient information was available to allow a precise line to be defined; and because the boundary would divide the traditional hunting and fishing areas of the indigenes, and compel them to cope with two sets of different laws on each side of the line.

The federal boundaries of Australia evolved between 1826 and 1862 as the boundaries of separate British colonies. With the exception of the Tasmanian limits, the State boundaries were arbitrarily drawn to enclose coastal concentrations of settlement at Perth, Sydney, Brisbane, Melbourne and Adelaide. When the Australian Commonwealth was formed, the change in boundary functions was not accompanied by any change in boundary position or definition.

Shabad (1956) and Morrison (1938), in studying the intra-national boundaries of the Soviet Union, have shown that both federal and internal boundaries have been frequently altered to conform with significant changes in population distribution and industrial development. The Soviet boundaries show a higher correlation with the geographical divisions of the cultural landscape than the equivalent boundaries in America and Australia.

Of the writers considered, only Nicholson and Prescott have treated the evolution of federal boundaries in respect of definition, recognising the stages of allocation, delimitation and demarcation proposed by Jones (1945). Apart from these studies, and papers by Thomas (1949) on the demarcation of the federal boundaries of Idaho, and Griswold (1939) on the demarcation of federal boundaries in the northeast United States, there is a lack of studies related to boundary definition which contrasts with the multitude of studies concerned with the definition of international boundaries in Africa, Asia and South America.

All the papers dealing with boundary evolution adopt an historical approach, and while this is logical and clear, it is regrettable that none of the writers has used two useful methods suggested by Hartshorne (1950) and Day (1949). In considering the Franco-German boundary of 1871 Hartshorne considered the relative importance of three factors – nationality, strategy and the distribution of iron ore resources – in determining the final position of the boundary. It is clearly demonstrated that different factors were paramount in determining different parts of the line, and that the distribution of iron ore reserves played a minor role. Although Hartshorne was concerned with one set of boundary negotiations which occupied only a short period, the present author has satisfied himself that this technique could be used to show how the factors influencing the evolution of the Anglo-French colonial boundaries in Africa changes over a much longer period, involving several sets of negotiations.

Writing on the boundaries of India during the Hindu and Mogul Empires, Day indicated the value of considering boundary permanence, and this technique was used by Spate (1957), who greatly improved the cartographic representation of boundary permanence. Day showed the various boundaries over a period of time as separate lines, and in fact displaced coincident boundaries to avoid confusion. Spate represented the various boundaries by lines which had a thickness proportional to their permanence. This has produced a very striking and stimulating map. There is, however, still room for improvement in this method. It would be valuable if those boundaries still in use could be distinguished on a map so as to reveal any anomalies. In addition it would be valuable to discover some way of distinguishing between various periods when the boundary served different functions. For example, it would be unsatisfactory to show a boundary which had existed for eighty years as an internal boundary and twenty years as a federal boundary by the same symbol as that representing a federal boundary which had existed for one hundred years. It is to be hoped that future studies of federal boundary evolution will make use of these neglected methods.

Federal Boundary Disputes

A considerable proportion of the studies of intra-national boundaries deals with federal boundary disputes. Their authors include lawyers, historians and geographers, and it is interesting to compare their various approaches. Lawyers are generally concerned with the manner in which each claimant prosecutes his case before the local and federal law courts, the legal arguments on precedent and the admissibility of evidence, the interpretation of the boundary definition, and the formal decision of the court. Historians are generally concerned with the evolution of the dispute and the economic and social factors which have encouraged it to assume greater or less significance at various times. There is also an attempt by historians to assess the role of the main personalities concerned in the dispute, and the extent to which they were influenced by contemporary events and philosophical concepts. The geographer finds some common ground with both lawyers and historians. Like the lawyer, the geographer is interested in interpreting the boundary definition in the light of contemporary maps and geographical knowledge. On the other hand, the geographer shares the evolution interest of the historian, by discovering the geographical factors which have contributed to the development of the dispute. Lastly, the geographer is concerned with understanding the significance of the dispute to the economic and political development of the landscape, and in following the changes which may ensue after the dispute has been settled.

The causes of federal boundary disputes may be classified into three categories. First, there are the disputes which arise through the ambiguous definition of the boundary or its incomplete evolution. Rivers have frequently been a source of trouble where they have been used to define federal boundaries in India and the United States. Since federal boundaries are often left undemarcated errors and ambiguities in the definition may remain undetected for a long time. Second, disputes sometimes arise between neighbouring federal states because the boundary has been superimposed on the landscape in a way which arbitrarily cuts across the pattern of physical and cultural elements in the borderland. In such cases the boundary may divide national or linguistic groups, and this may be a serious problem in countries such as India, where ethnic characteristics are politically important. The boundary may also be drawn in a way which hinders the development of resources or the circulation of goods. Third, significant changes in the political or economic circumstances of one or both neighbouring states may provide grounds for disagreement. Each of these categories is considered in turn.

The majority of papers concerned with federal boundary disputes deal with cases which have arisen through the ambiguous or incomplete definition of the boundary; examples are taken from the United States, Australia and Nigeria. The boundaries of Texas have provided several interesting disputes which have been studied mainly by historians. Bowman (1923), Carpenter (1925), and Billington (1959) have examined the dispute between Oklahoma and Texas, where they are divided by the Red River. This dispute arose because the northern boundary of Texas was stated to be the south bank of the Red River, while the southern boundary of Oklahoma was put along the middle of the main channel. In any case Oklahoma had no rights over the bed of the river, because it was not navigable when Oklahoma was admitted to the Union; these rights belonged to the Federal Government. For a time the non-coincidence of the two boundaries was merely an academic matter, but this was changed when oil was discovered along the south bank. Immediately there was a flood of prospectors, and licences were granted by Texas, Oklahoma and the Federal Government. The dispute was further complicated by the frequent accretionary changes of the Red River, and the presence of an Indian reservation in the Oklahoma border area.

Bowden's interesting study (1959) of the Texas-New Mexico boundary dispute explains why the present boundary follows the course of the Rio Grande as it was on 9 September 1850, although the final legal decision was not settled until 1913. Chapman's paper (1949) on the Texas claim to Greer County reviews the historical development of the dispute and considers in some detail the survey and demarcation of the resulting boundary. The dispute, related to the Sabine River where it divides Texas and Louisiana, has similar features to the Red

River dispute, since it arises because of the non-coincidence of the eastern Texas boundary and the western Louisiana boundary, leaving a neutral strip of territory 70 miles long by 150 feet wide (Andrew, 1949).

Six papers consider in detail the problems associated with the interpretation of boundary definitions. In 1930, Martin recorded in detail the arguments used in the Michigan-Wisconsin boundary dispute from 1923-36, and the final judgement. The dispute arose through claims by Michigan to territory administered by Wisconsin, and the matter turned on the interpretation of such terms as 'the most usual ship channel', and the identification of the Lake of the Desert with either Island Lake, claimed by Michigan, or Lac Vieux Desert, claimed by Wisconsin. As a result of an error made in defining the adjudicated boundary in 1926, a further case was brought between 1932 and 1936, and this was also described in detail by Martin.

Ogier examined the Victoria State claim to a boundary along the Murrumbidgee River instead of the Murray River, in three papers published between 1902 and 1912. The whole case turned on the interpretation of the phrase 'a straight line drawn from Cape Howe to the nearest source of the River Murray'. Ogier contends that the source of the Murrumbidgee is also a source of the River Murray, and closer to Cape Howe than the source of the Hume River, another Murray tributary. Although the argument seems geographically impeccable, the River Hume continues to mark the federal boundary.

Misra (1976) in an excellent, unpublished thesis, describes problems associated with the use of the Ganga and Ghaghara Rivers as boundaries between Bihar and Uttar Pradesh. These rivers were designated as boundaries in 1867 and 1888 respectively; in each case the deep stream of the river was nominated as the specific line. Unfortunately both these rivers change their courses during the periods of flood and thus land is effectively transferred from one side to the other. Such fluctuations in the course of the rivers were verified and recorded in February and March by the authorities on both sides. Unfortunately the sowing season started in December in some areas, and this meant that in some cases land sown by a citizen of Bihar was later established to lie within Uttar Pradesh. Such discoveries led to conflict between some communities at harvest time. The difficulties were related to the nature of the rivers and the patterns of settlement along both valleys. Misra (1976, p.199) records that the Ghaghara changed its course erratically and generally deposited infertile sandy areas. In contrast, the course of the

Ganga River changed in a more predictable fashion and the newly created fields generally had a high level of fertility. The villagers on the banks of the Ghaghara River tended to have long river frontages, while the Ganga villages had only short frontages; in other words the long axes of village lands were parallel to the Ghaghara River and transverse to the Ganga River. In consequence of these differences friction in the Ganga valley was often at a more serious level than in the Ghaghara plains. Commissions in 1952 and 1962 were faced with the responsibility of allocating 192 villagers affected by alterations in the courses of these two rivers; 119 villages were awarded to Uttar Pradesh and 73 to Bihar.

The second class of federal boundary dispute arises because the boundary does not accord with certain elements of the physical or cultural landscape. Such disputes are very closely related to the territorial disputes associated with international boundaries. India provides a wealth of disputes in this category and the official report on the reorganisation of states (*Lok Sabha Debates,* 1955) is a mine of information which Misra has successfully exploited.

Soon after the decision of the Indian authorities to redistribute land amongst Indian states twenty-one disputes developed involving 130,573 square miles. The final delimitation of state boundaries resulted in the transfer of forty-one areas measuring 48,833 square miles. Nearly half the disputed area was claimed on the linguistic grounds either that the population in the claimed area spoke the same language as the population in the claimant state, or that they spoke a language which was clearly affiliated more closely with the claimant state than the state from which the territory was claimed. For example, Andhra Pradesh claimed 996 square miles from Bombay, 6,212 square miles from Mysore, and 958 square miles from Orissa because those areas were occupied by Telugu-speaking people. Three claims, totalling nearly 10,000 square miles, were based on the argument that the claimed territory had strong historical associations with the claimant state. In some cases the historical connections were rather tenuous. For example, Rajasthan claimed the Mandsaur District, measuring 4,160 square miles, from Madhya Pradesh, because it had belonged to Rajasthan in the period before 1803. Only two areas, measuring 6,724 square miles, were claimed exclusively on economic grounds. The larger claim of this nature was by West Bengal which sought to control 5,566 square miles of Bihar, because it would make it easier to administer the river flats along the Ajai and Kasai Rivers.

The remaining disputes between Indian states were justified on a variety of grounds. For example, Orissa claimed 5,077 square miles of Bihar on four grounds. Historically it was argued that the Saraikela-Kharsawan Feudatory States and Sadar were previously administered by Orissa; linguistically it was asserted that the population were mainly Oriya-speaking in common with the majority in Orissa; geographically it was maintained that the physiography separated the region from Bihar, while five roads gave easy access to Orissa; and economically it was declared that the area had close contacts with Orissa and that it contained parts of the catchments of some important rivers which flowed mainly through Orissa. This claim was successful and the region was transferred to Orissa in 1956.

Holdegel (1959) reviewed the problems resulting from the creation of the Federal State of Baden-Württemberg, with boundaries which divided areas of similar local and regional loyalties. He stresses the lasting importance of historical associations in these areas, and regrets the division between towns such as Hirsch (Essen) and Heidelberg (Baden-Württemberg), and between Ulm (Baden-Württemberg), and Neu-Ulm (Bavaria). It would have been interesting if Holdegel had been able to define more closely the regions of community consciousness, and indicate to what extent there were conflicts between the local and regional attachments. Holdegel calls for a *natürliche Grenze* along the crest of the Oldenwald but does not explain why such a boundary would be more satisfactory.

This brief review suggests that federal boundary disputes caused by ambiguous definition or incomplete evolution may occur in all federations. Disputes arising from the discordance between the boundary and the distribution of various elements of the borderland will occur in two different situations. First, this situation might result when new federations are created, as in Germany. Second, this problem might arise in federal states, such as Nigeria and India, where there are powerful national, tribal, religious or linguistic loyalties. Such a development is a real possibility when the boundaries which divide the federal state were drawn in the imperial period and are quite unrelated to the political and economic development which might have occurred in the post-colonial phase.

Internal Boundaries

An earlier study (Prescott, 1967, pp.178-9) suggested the need for a classification of internal boundaries; this seems less valuable than a classification of local government *areas*. It is doubtful, however, if elaborate and comprehensive classifications would repay the effort involved in their construction, due to the great complexity of local circumstances in the various states of the world. The most useful classification seems to be that between local government and special purpose administrative divisions described by Pounds (1963, chapter 8), which agrees with the distinction suggested by Fesler (1949) between governmental areas, possessing a measure of functional or fiscal autonomy, and field service areas designed for the convenient execution of individual government departments, such as gas board or road board areas.

It is therefore suggested that the most important division of internal boundaries is between local government boundaries and field service boundaries. They have some important differences. Local government boundaries are usually precisely described and represented on published maps. If they are changed the alterations must be published in government gazettes and often they will be justified in government statements. Local government boundaries encompass the whole territory of the state, and the authority which operates within them possesses several powers which usually enable them to levy and spend rates, and sometimes to regulate the use of land. Field service boundaries will sometimes be precisely described and represented on published maps; this is true for example of electoral boundaries and census district limits. However, many field service boundaries will be represented only by lines drawn with a coloured pencil on a map in some office concerned with a single activity such as fire-fighting or the enforcement of regulations dealing with the production and sale of livestock. In many cases the field service boundaries will not comprehend the entire country. For example, forestry boundaries and the bounds of conservation areas will only apply to very limited portions of the state. Apart from electoral and census district boundaries, field service boundaries are very easy to alter, and generally these alterations will not be announced. The other important distinction between these two categories is that there has been much more analysis of local government boundaries than of field service boundaries by administrators and scholars.

The literature describing the evolution of internal boundaries is much smaller than that dealing with international boundaries, but fortunately the available studies cover a range of administrative forms.

Fenelon (1956) deals with the geographical structure and boundaries of the *Départements* of France, and considers in broad outline the relationship between the modern boundaries and the former diocesan and county limits. He also refers to the relation between political boundaries and physical features.

Lipman (1949) includes a detailed note in his book on the way in which the division of France into *départements* was accomplished. The Commission of 1789 was apparently influenced by the egalitarian spirit of the day which demanded equality in size, the views of d'Argenson that the divisions should be as large as possible to secure efficiency without endangering the authority of the state, the scheme of Condorcet that each division should not exceed a maximum radius related to ease of transport and community of culture, customs and habit, and a map prepared by Robert de Hesseln, which for cartographical purposes was divided into eighty-one divisions measuring eighteen leagues square. The report of Thouret to the Assembly explained how the final decision to create eight *départments* was implemented. The basic geometric pattern was distorted to take account of the cultural and physical features of the landscape, including the existence of former historical boundaries.

Helin (1967) published a very detailed paper recording the changes in the administrative boundaries and system of Rumania between 1918 and 1960. He convincingly relates the system adopted at any particular time to the views of the government of the day; the excessive fragmentation created by the Averescu Government in 1919 was designed to keep the power centralised, and it contrasted with the seven regions of the National-Peasant Government (1928-30) which sought to give expression to the different cultures and aspirations of people in various parts of the state. This paper provides further evidence that administrative changes are a common feature of authoritarian governments, and it is interesting that in Rumania since 1945 there have been significant changes in administrative boundaries even though all the governments have been communist. Herlin attributes these changes partly to the changes in the leadership of the central government.

The only aspect of this subject not adequately considered by these papers is the effect on the landscape of the boundary changes; it is probable that this omission was enforced by limitations of space.

Sautter's study of the Republics of Congo (Brazzaville) and Gabon (1966) includes a chapter dealing with the evolution of the administrative map in both these areas. The information accumulated and mapped is very useful, but there is regrettably only slight reference to the reasons why boundary changes were made from time to time, and no discussion of the effects of these boundary changes. Figure 6.1 was prepared on the basis of Sautter's maps (vol.1, pp.180-3) and the 1966 changes, to show the length of time which present

Figure 6.1: Internal Boundaries of Congo

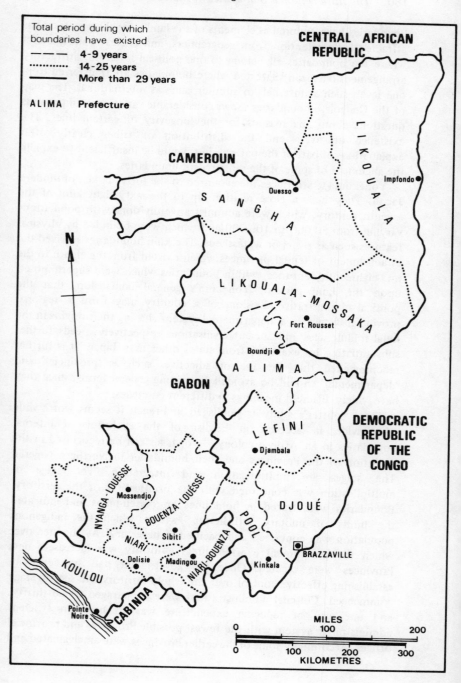

boundaries have endured as elements of the landscape. This method has attracted little attention from geographers, and is clearly most useful where the boundaries all belong to one political level; no satisfactory arrangement has been suggested where boundaries are transferred from one level, such as internal, to another, such as international. The map of the Congolese boundaries shows considerable variations and prompts questions about the reasons for the longevity of certain lines. The existence of rivers and the distribution of tribes clearly offer explanations of part of the pattern, but would be insufficient to explain the alignment of some of the more recent boundaries.

Yonekura (1956) traces the evolution of the forty-six ken of modern Japan. They bear a close relationship to the sixty-eight kuni of the seventh century, which were administrative divisions with populations varying from 50,000 to 100,000 and which were bounded by physical features such as rivers or watersheds. The kuni boundaries survived the establishment of feudal provinces which existed from the eighth to the mid-eighteenth centuries, within boundaries which were superimposed upon the kuni pattern. Yonekura's general conclusion, that the political-administrative divisions of a country may form a 'regional provincial system' or a 'departmental system', having their origins in the fedal middle ages and ancient civilisations respectively, needs further substantiating by examples from states other than Japan. It is further recommended that the use of adjectives such as 'provincial' and 'departmental' should be avoided in coining general terms, since they have widely different meanings in different countries.

Since Sautter's study is published in French it seems worthwhile to provide an account in English of the evolution of internal boundaries in an African colony. Two stages can be recognised in the evolution of the Provinces and their boundaries in Northern Nigeria. The stages are multiplication and integration. The stage of multiplication was concerned with the pacification of the territory. Boundaries were traced in bold lines on sketch-maps and indicated the limits of military jurisdiction, within which the indigenous population was contacted and pacified if necessary. As the area over which the government exerted direct authority was increased, new Provinces were created. Once the government had succeeded in establishing effective control over the whole territory the second stage commenced. Colonial administrations were encouraged to be thrifty, and one way of reducing expenditure was to have an efficient administrative system with the fewest possible Provinces and provincial offices. Accordingly some of the earlier Provinces were amalgamated and the boundaries were drawn with a view to assisting administrative efficiency and economy. By empirical methods a structure of Provinces was evolved. At first there were large-scale changes, but these gradually became smaller and fewer in number as a satisfactory condition was achieved. When this stage was reached closer delimitation of the boundaries was undertaken, and in some cases residents organised a simple kind of demarcation, mainly for their own references and to avoid inter-provincial disputes.

When the Protectorate of Northern Nigeria was created in 1900, the Government of that territory immediately organised the territory over which the Royal Niger Company (RNC) had exerted control, into nine Provinces – Borgu, Ilorin, Kabba, Nupe, Upper and Lower Benue, Kontagora, Zaria and the Middle Niger. The first aims of the new administration were to organise Bassa, which lay south of the Benue, and the Muri, Bauchi and Yola Emirates. There were three reasons given for this eastward advance. First, it was necessary to prevent any further depopulation of this area by slave raids; second, it seemed worthwhile to open up the trade routes in that area and counter French activities south of Lake Chad; and third, it was decided to exploit the reported 'salubrity and mineral wealth' of the area.

In 1901 the Middle Niger Province was absorbed by Kabba Province and five new Provinces were created – Bassa, Bauchi, Yola, and North and South Bornu. This brought the total number of Provinces to thirteen and it was increased to sixteen in the following year by the addition of Sokoto, Kano and Katagum. This meant that apart from Gando the entire area had been nominally placed under control. There were two reasons for this rapid northward drive. First, the government of the Protectorate could not feel secure while the strongest Fulani Emirates remained outside their control. Further, the continued independence of the northern Emirates created dual loyalties for the southern rulers, such as the Emirs of Bida and Kontagora, who had accepted British rule, and impaired their spirit of cooperation. Second, there was the need to occupy the Sokoto arc across which French columns were travelling between Niamey and Zinder. This occupation was designed to repair British prestige and make the French position at Zinder untenable by denying access to the *route practicable*. The year 1904 marked the end of the period of multiplication when Gando Province was created, bringing the total to seventeen.

It will be seen that during the period of multiplication a number of Provinces had been created, covering the whole territory. Within these divisions the first need was for peace and the establishment of authority. The policy of indirect rule through the indigenous chiefs, particularly the Fulani Emirs, meant that the Provinces were closely identified with the former indigenous states. With the exception of Upper and Lowe Benue the Provinces were named after emirates such as Sokoto, or independent kingdoms such as Borgu and Bornu.

The fact that 1904 marked the beginning of the period of integration demonstrates how quickly the government faced the problems of administrative convenience and economy. It was hoped to reorganise the seventeen Provinces into eight. Seven would be formed by the amalgamation of two Provinces, and the eighth by the union of Ilorin, Kabba and Nupe Provinces. In 1904 three of the new double-Provinces were organised. Sokoto and Gando, Kano and Katagum and East and West Bornu were joined to former larger Provinces. Table 6.1 shows that there were marked variations in the area and population of the various Provinces, and serves to underline the extensive use of indigenous divisions in constructing the provincial framework.

However, while government reports continued to discuss the need to reduce further the number of Provinces, no progress was made until 1908, when Borgu Province was added to Kontagora. This was the last major reorganisation before the amalgamation of the Northern and Southern Protectorates in 1914 to form the Colony and Protectorate of Nigeria. The period from 1908 to 1914 was characterised by boundary adjustments designed to avoid the division of ethnic groups and to exchange some of the geometric boundaries for lines related to the cultural and physical landscapes, which could be more easily recognised. There were twenty-one boundary changes between 1908 and 1914; sixteen were made on ethnic grounds and five were made on grounds of accessibility or easier boundary definition, usually by a river (Figure 6.2). Letters used in the following description refer to the ethnic boundary changes; numbers refer to changes connected with accessibility or easier definition.

The boundary of Kontagora was considerably altered on ethnic grounds. In the north-west (A) an area of 3,725 square miles was transferred to Sokoto Province. Most of this land lay west of Niger and was inhabited by Fulani and Dandowa groups who had little in common with the Bariba of Borgu District. The region in fact corresponds closely with the area around Gombe which was held by Gando against Borgu. The smaller area of Besse, east of the river, was also inhabited mainly by Fulani. In the north-east (B) the area of Kwiambana which had formerly been part of the Emirate was added to Sokoto Province. In the south of Kontagora two small regions (C and D) around Bajibo and Takum, both occupied by members of the Nupe

Table 6.1: The Provinces of Northern Nigeria 1905

Province	Area (sq. miles)	Population (000s)
Bornu East and West	33,000	1,105
Kano	31,000	2,192
Sokoto	35,000	521
Zaria	22,000	230
Bauchi	23,200	920
Yola	16,000	290
Muri	25,800	825
Nassarawa	18,000	1,500
Nupe	6,400	150
Ilorin	6,300	255
Kabba	7,800	68
Kontagora	14,500	79
Borgu	12,000	25
Bassa	7,000	100

Source: Colonial Reports, Northern Nigeria, 1905, Cmd. 3285, 1907, No.516.

tribe, were transferred to Niger Province (formerly Bida or Nupe). Niger Province received 19,025 square miles of the Gwari District of Zaria Province (E); this was the largest transfer made during this period of adjustment. There is no doubt that the southern portions of the transferred area were inhabited by Nupe people and that other parts were occupied by the Bassa and Ungwe groups who are more closely related, historically and culturally, to the Nupe than to the Zaria Emirate. However, there was little justification for including the Gwari people, who live in the north of the area, within Niger Province. These people are oriented towards the north, especially Katsina. It may be that this area was included to fix the boundary along the River Kara. The Koton Karifi District of Nassarawa was added to Niger Province by causing the boundary to diverge from the River Gwara (F). The Igbirra people of this valley had formerly been divided by the boundary.

From eastern Sokoto (G), 3,880 square miles were transferred to Kano Province on the dual grounds of historical association and easier administration. The new boundary lay within the former

Figure 6.2: Nigeria's Provincial Boundaries 1908-14

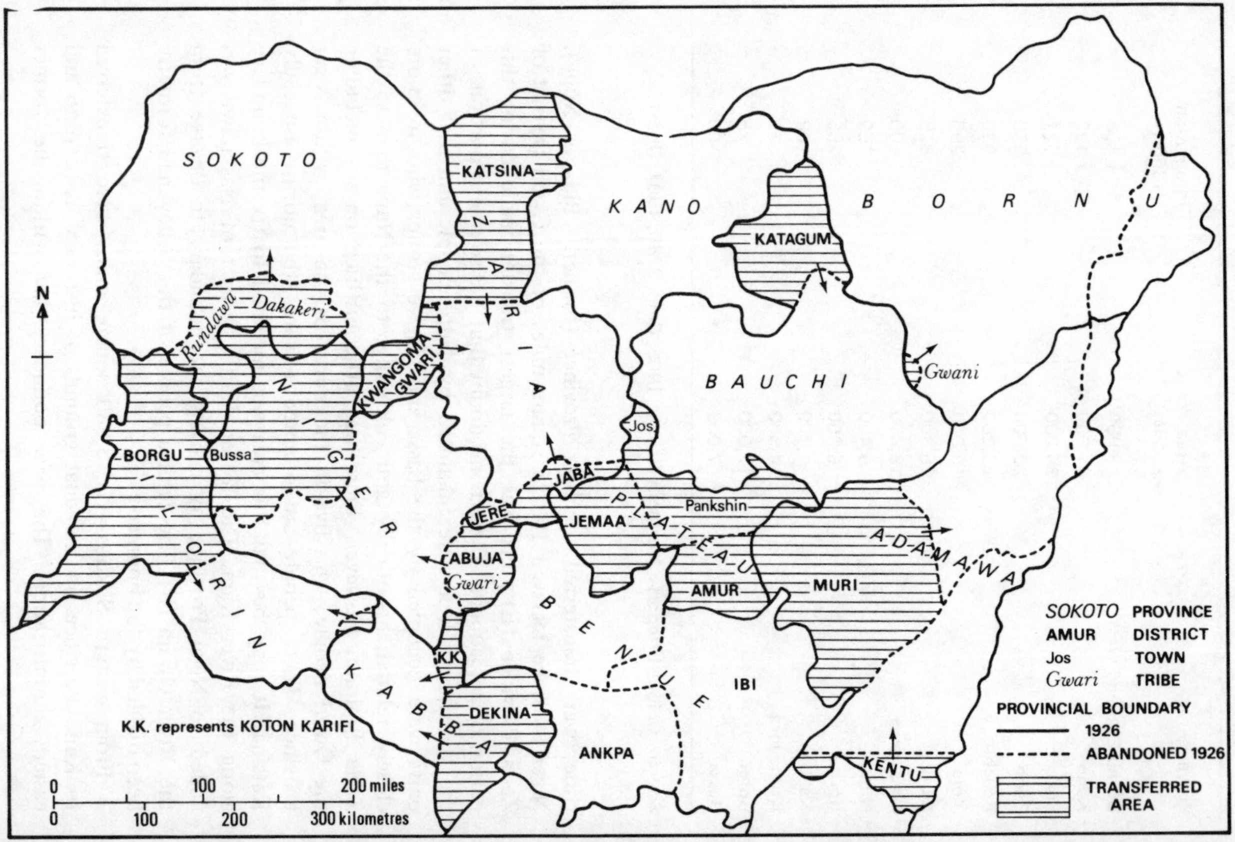

SOKOTO PROVINCE
AMUR DISTRICT
Jos TOWN
Gwari TRIBE
——— PROVINCIAL BOUNDARY
1926
----- ABANDONED 1926
▥ TRANSFERRED AREA

K.K. represents KOTON KARIFI

BORNU

KANO

BAUCHI

ADAMAWA

KATAGUM

KATSINA

ZARIA

MURI

AMUR

IBI

PLATEAU

Pankshin

JEMAA

Jos

JABA

JERE

ABUJA

Gwari

BENUE

ANKPA

KWANGOMI
GWARI

DEKINA

KK

KABBA

SOKOTO

N I G E R

ILORIN

BORGU

Bussa

—Dakakeri

Oli

KOTON KARIFI

KENTU

Gwari

N

0   100   200 miles
0   100   200   300 kilometres

uninhabited frontier between the Katsina and Sokoto Emirates. In the east Kano also received 495 square miles of Bornu Province around Kakuri (H), which had traditionally been part of the Hadeija kingdom. This gain was offset by the transfer of 1,675 square miles of Kano Province to Bornu east of Katagum (J). By fixing the provincial boundary along the River Katagum it was ensured that the Bedde pagans were all reunited in Bornu Province.

Four areas were transferred to Bauchi Province for ethnic reasons. In the Bukuru area (Q and R) the boundary was moved westwards to reunite the Rukaba, Kibyen and Surawa groups. The Burranawa and Angassawa groups which had formerly been divided by the boundary between Bauchi and Muri were reunited in Bauchi Province (M). In the east of Bauchi 5,280 square miles of Yola Province were added. This area contained groups of Jerawa and Waje who were closely related to other tribes in Bauchi Province, and groups of Tula, Balawa and Terewa who had formerly been split by the provincial boundary (L).

Muri Province was increased by transfers from Bauchi (N) and Yola (P) which reunited the Wirkum and Mumuye groups respectively. Yola was further reduced by the transfer of 6,000 square miles to Bornu Province (K). Tera, Bahur and Birra pagans occupied this area, which was marshy and which had formed part of the former frontier between Bornu and Yola.

The five changes made for reasons of accessibility or clearer boundary definition were much smaller than most of the ethnic transfers. The area of Kontagora Province was slightly increased by a northward extension to the Gulbin Ka (1) and a southward extension to the River Eba (3). Instead of just adding the Kwiambana District to Sokoto (B) the boundary was moved further south to the River Gulbi (2). There was a minor extension of Nassarawa Province at the expense of Muri when the boundary was moved eastwards to follow a short section of the Ankwe River (4). Finally, 2,625 square miles of Kano Province were transferred to Bauchi, by fixing the boundary along the River Wilka, because the transferred section could be more easily administered from Bauchi (5).

By 1914, when the Northern and Southern Protectorates were amalgamated, the number of Provinces had been reduced from seventeen to thirteen and extensive adjustments had been made to avoid dividing tribal groups, or groups having a common history or culture. The opportunity was taken in 1914 to make a further reduction in the number of Northern Provinces and to change some of the boundaries. Ilorin and Kabba Provinces were merged and Bassa,

Muri and Nassarawa Provinces were reorganised. The meridional boundary between Bassa and Muri was moved eastwards to nine degrees East, transferring the Marchaba and Kararaba Tiv groups to Bassa Province, which was renamed Munshi Province, the capital of which was Ankpa. There is no clear reason why this change occurred since the new boundary passed through a heavily populated Tiv region. In all, about 1,400 square miles, including the important Benue station of Abinsi, were transferred to Munshi Province. North of the Benue, Muri Province was extended by the addition of Munshi District of Nassarawa Province which comprised 810 square miles. This transfer was made because the area was more accessible from the capital of Muri Province, but it is difficult to understand why the Tiv on both sides of the River Benue were not included within one Province. Formerly they were split between Muri and Nassarawa Provinces; after the reorganisation they were divided between Munshi and Muri Provinces. Finally, Koton Karifi was transferred back to Nassarawa Province from Niger, re-establishing the boundary along the River Garara.

No boundary changes were made during World War I, although Yola and Bornu Provinces were increased by the inclusion of portions of the Northern Cameroons Mandated Territory. The next revision of the provincial boundaries was undertaken in 1926, and this revision provides the basis of the present provincial structure of Northern Nigeria. As a result of the reorganisation the number of Provinces was reduced to eleven by a series of boundary changes which are recorded in Figure 6.3.

Kontagora was absorbed by the surrounding Provinces. Borgu was transferred to Ilorin except for an area north of Bussa which was transferred to Sokoto Province on grounds of accessibility. Sokoto Province also absorbed 8,750 square miles of northern Kontagora, which was occupied by the Rundawa and Dakakeri tribes. The remainder of Kontagora was included as a District within Niger Province. Niger Province was further increased by the inclusion of Abuja District of Nassarawa, which was largely peopled by members of the Gwari tribe. The Kwangoma and Gwari Districts of Northern Niger Province were transferred to Zaria. Zaria Province was also increased by the addition of Katsina Emirate from Kano Province. It was noted in the 1932 Provincial Report that administrative convenience alone led to the inclusion of Katsina, Zaria and Gwari areas within one Province. While there were historical ties between Birnin Gwari and Katsina, there were no ties between these two areas and the

Figure 6.3: Nigeria's Provincial Boundaries 1926

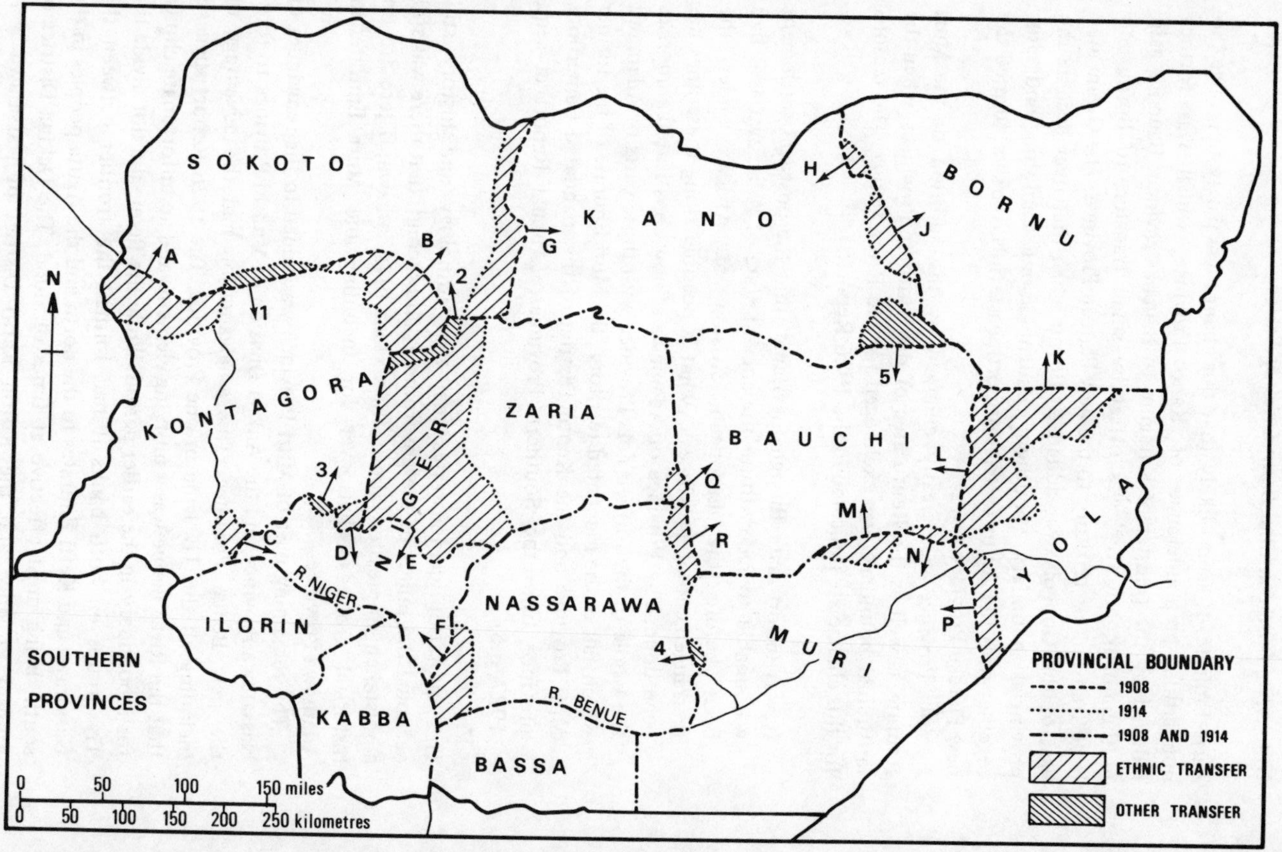

Zaria Emirate. It seems likely that this change was partly to reduce the population preponderance of Kano Province, which was further reduced by the transfer of Katagum to Bauchi Province. Bauchi's gain in the north, however, was offset by small transfers to Bornu and large transfers of territory to the new Plateau Province. The Gwani area east of the Gongola was added to Bornu when that river became the provincial boundary. Southern Bauchi about Pankshin and Jos, together with the Amur District of north eastern Nassarawa, formed the new Plateau Province.

Yola Province was greatly enlarged by the addition of the Muri Emirate as well as the Kentu area of the Southern Provinces, when the latitudinal boundary was exchanged for the River Donga. The reasons for this change are indicated in the 1926 Report:

> It was unfortunate though inevitable, that the post-war settlement was unable to reconstitute the ancient state of Adamawa as it had been before the European division of Africa. Under the rearrangement of Provinces...what is possible along these lines has been done. The Province of Adamawa as now constituted comprises the whole of the former Yola Province with those parts of Adamawa which fall in the mandated territory, the Muri Emirate of the former Muri Province and the Kentu District of the mandated Cameroons province from the Southern Provinces. (Annual Report et seq., 1927, p.6)

This quotation demonstrates first that ethnology and history still occupied the minds of the government, and second, that there was still a mistaken impression about the extent of Adamawa. There are no historical grounds whatsoever for including the Muri Emirate in Adamawa Province.

The remaining part of Muri Province was added to the remainder of Nassarawa Province and the Ankpa Division of Munshi Province to form the new Benue Province. This amalgamation had the advantage of including all the Tiv tribe in one Province. The 1926 Report suggests that the River Benue was a unifying element, and an unfortunate choice for a boundary in the earlier period. While the Benue did not divide the Tiv groups on both banks it had formed the frontier between the Nassarawa and Keffi Emirates to the north and the Aguta peoples in the south, being most effective at times of flood. The Dekina District of Munshi Province and the Koton Karifi District of Nassarawa were added to the reconstituted Kabba Province which now contained the

Niger-Benue confluence. The new boundary between Ilorin and Kabba Provinces was drawn further east so that all the Nupe on the south bank were included in Lafiagi Division of Ilorin Province.

The changes of 1926 represented the last major reorganisation of provincial boundaries during the colonial period, and the lines established by that date provided the administrative framework of Nigeria when it became independent in 1960.

Conclusion

If the chief aim of local government is considered to be the administration of public services for the benefit of all citizens, scholars can make a practical contribution to the establishment of a system of intra-national boundaries which will help to achieve that aim. First, by the compilation of historical accounts of boundary evolution scholars can demonstrate where boundaries existed in the past and the extent to which they were successful. Such information will be very useful in constructing new boundaries if the mistakes of the past are to be avoided. Second, geographers, historians and lawyers are trained to collect and assess evidence which would be necessary before any judgement could be made on the merits of federal boundary disputes. Third, historians and geographers understand the processes of change which might make boundaries constructed in a former period inappropriate. Steiner (1965, p.151) noted that the Japanese prefectures were drawn with the aim of enabling a man on horseback to reach the capital from any part in one day, and he observed that the present prefectures do not coincide with any areas that share common economic problems or needs. Fourth, geographers are capable of suggesting principles which should guide the selection of specific boundaries. The excellent work by Fawcett (1961), Gilbert (1948), and Taylor (1942) provided a useful initiative in this field which regrettably has not been satisfactorily developed by their successors, although that is not the fault of scholars such as Osborne (1967) who prepared some stimulating proposals for the reform of local government areas in the East Midlands of England. Perhaps the reason for this partial failure is the reluctance of administrations to seek the advice of academics in drawing intra-national boundaries.

References

Adejuyigbe, O., 1970, 'The problems of Unity and the Creation of States in Nigeria', *Nigerian Geographical Journal*, 11, pp.39-60

————., 1970, 'The Ife-Ijesa Boundary Problem', *Nigerian Geographical Journal*, 13, pp.23-38

Andrew, B.H., 1949, 'Some Queries Concerning the Texas-Louisiana Sabine Boundary', *Southwestern Historical Quart.*, 53, pp.1-18

Annual Report of the Northern Provinces 1926, 1927, Lagos

Billington, K., 1959, 'The Red River Boundary Controversy', *Southwestern Historical Quart.*, 62, pp.356-63

Bowden, J.J., 1959, 'The Texas-New Mexico Boundary Dispute along the Rio Grande', *Southwestern Historical Quart.*, 63, pp.221-37

Bowman, I., 1923, 'An American Boundary Dispute: Decision of the Supreme Court with Respect to the Texas-Oklahoma Boundary', *Geogr. Rev.*, 13, pp.161-81

Carpenter, W.C., 1925, 'The Red River Boundary Dispute', *American Journal of International Law*, 19, pp.517-29

Chapman, B.B., 1949, 'The Claims of Texas to Greer County', *Southwestern Historical Quart.*, 53, pp.401-24

Day, W.M., 1949, 'The Relative Permanence of Former Boundaries in India', *Scottish Geographical Magazine*, 65, pp.113-22

Fawcett, C.B., 1961, *Provinces of England: A Study of Some Geographical Aspects of Devolution*, revised by W.G. East and S.W. Wooldridge, London

Fenelon, P., 1956, 'Structure géographique et frontières des Départements français', *Abstract of Papers*, 18th International Geographical Congress, Rio de Janeiro, p.185

Fesler, J.W., 1949, *Area and Administration*, Alabama

Gilbert, W.E., 1948, 'The Boundaries of Local Government Areas', *Geogr. J.*, 111, pp.172-206

Griswold, E.N., 1939, 'Hunting Boundaries with Car and Camera, in the Northeastern United States', *Geogr. Rev.*, 22, pp.353-82

Hall, J.W., 1966, *Government and Local Power in Japan 500-1700: A Study Based on Bizen Province*, New Jersey

Hartshorne, R., 1950, 'The Franco-German Boundary of 1871', *World Politics*, 2, pp.209-50

Helin, R.A., 1967, 'The Volatile Administrative Map of Rumania', *Annals*, Association of American Geographers, 57, pp.481-502

Holdegel, H., 1959, 'Grenzproblem des Sudwest Staates', *Zeitschrift für Geopolitik*, 30, pp.9-19

Jones, S.B., 1945, *Boundary Making: A Handbook for Statesmen*, Washington

Lipman, V.D., 1949, *Local Government Areas 1834-45*, Oxford

Lok Sabha Debates, 1955, Part 11, 10, New Delhi

Martin, L., 1930, 'The Michigan-Wisconsin Boundary Case in the Supreme Court of the United States', *Annals*, Association of American Geographers, 20, pp.105-63

Martin, L., 1938, 'The Second Wisconsin-Michigan Boundary Case in the Supreme Court of the United States', *Annals*, Association of American Geographers, 28, pp.77-126

McColl, R.W., 1963, 'Development of Supra-provincial Administrative Regions in Communist China 1949-1960', *Pacific Viewpoint*, 4, pp.53-64

Misra, N., 1976, *Inter-State Boundary Disputes in India — a Study in Political Geography*, unpublished doctoral thesis, University of Allahabad

Morrison, J.A., 1938, 'The Evolution of the territorial-administrative system of the U.S.S.R.', *Amer. Quart. on the Soviet Union*, 1, pp.25-46

Nicholson, N.L., 1968, 'The Further Partition of the Northwest Territories of Canada: An Aspect of Decolonization in Northernwest North America', in Fisher, C.A., *Essays in Political Geography*, pp.311-24, London

Ogier, J.C.H., 1902, 'The Question of the Original Official Boundary between the States of New South Wales and Victoria', *Victoria Geographical Journ.*, 20 (New series), pp.71-84

————., 1905, 'The Victorian State Boundary', *Victorian Geographical Journ.*, 23, pp.78-106

————., 1912, 'The Riverina', *Victoria Geographical Journ.*, 29, pp.49-85

Osborne, R.H., 1967, 'New Countries for Old in the East Midlands: An Outline Scheme for the Reform of Local Government Areas', *The East Midland Geographer*, 4, pp.207-23

Pounds, N.J.G., 1963, *Political Geography*, New York

Prescott, J.R.V., 1959, 'Nigeria's Regional Boundary Problems', *Geogr. Rev.*, 49, pp.485-505

————., 1967, *The Geography of Frontiers and Boundaries*, London

Report on the Amalgamation of Northern and Southern Nigeria and their Administration, Cmd., 468, HMSO, 1920

Sautter, G., 1966, *De l'Atlantique au fleuve Congo: une géographie du sous-peuplement*, Paris

Shabad, T., 1956, 'The Administrative-Territorial Patterns of the Soviet Union', Chapter 15 in East, W.G. and Moodie, A.E. (eds.), *The Changing World*, London

Spate, O.H.K., 1957, *India and Pakistan*, London

Taylor, E.G.R., 1942, 'Discussion of the Geographical Aspects of Regional Planning', *Geogr. J.*, 99, pp.61-80

Thomas, B.E., 1949, 'Demarcation of the Boundaries of Idaho', *Pacific Northwest Quart.*, 40, pp.24-34

Whittlesey, D., 1956, chapter 9 in East, W.G. and Moodie, E.A., *The Changing World*, London

Yonekura, J., 1956, 'Historical Development of the Political Administrative Divisions of Japan', *Abstract of Papers*, 18th International Geographical Congress, Rio de Janeiro

7 BORDER LANDSCAPES

In the first chapter, it was stated that one of the principal interests in boundaries of any political geographer relates to the way in which a boundary or frontier influences both the landscape of which it is a part and the development of the policies of the states on either side. This view resulted from acceptance of the dictum, repeated by nearly all the authors reviewed, that it was meaningless to consider the boundary outside the context of the flanking state areas. Lapradelle termed this zone *le voisinage*, and 'border landscape' is suggested as an equivalent term. Political geographers are interested in boundaries because they mark the limits of political organisation which varies over the earth's surface. Variations in political systems are often accompanied by variations in regulations concerning economic activity and the movement of people, goods and ideas. The results of these variations are likely to be most clearly seen in the neighbourhood of the boundary, whether state functions are rigidly applied at the boundary, or whether the states combine to minimise the adverse effects of the boundary upon the border inhabitants. Few workers have selected this subject as the focus of their study, but many have included important references to it. Minghi (1963) did not suggest a separate group of such studies in his proposed classification of case studies, but included important papers by House (1959), Ullman (1939) and Nelson (1952) in categories dealing with the effects of boundary change and the characteristics of internal boundaries.

This chapter has been written because the author believes that students of political geography must concern themselves increasingly with the identification and description of political regions and the influence of political factors upon the cultural landscape. This is not to make any new conceptual suggestions, but rather to advocate a change of emphasis, and echoes Minghi's call for 'more attention to the normal situation in boundary research'.

There seem to be four aspects of this subject which fall within the province of the political geographer. First, there is the consideration of the boundary as an element of the cultural landscape. A boundary's physical existence results from the demarcation of the boundary and the construction of building, defences and systems of communications to give effect to state functions applied at it. The physical difference between an internal and international boundary is usually outstanding, but there are also important differences between different international boundaries. The suggestion has already been made that the appearance of any boundary in the landscape is a guide to the functions applied there, and the stringency with which they are applied.

Second, a geographer may wish to examine the extent to which variations in landscape and land-use on either side of a boundary can be explained by the proximity of two different political systems, and the regulations which they have developed. In this connexion it is important to distinguish such cases from those where variations in landscape and land-use result from the coincidence of the boundary with some linear physical feature such as a watershed which is also a climatic divide. Population distribution is one phenomenon related to land-use which may be partially explained by the nearness of the boundary. There are also cases where the existence of a boundary results in the duplication of transport, administrative and retail services.

The remaining two aspects are not directly concerned with the cultural landscape, but they may be conveniently considered here, since they may be the medium through which the boundary influences the cultural landscape. Third, there is the influence of the boundary's presence and operation upon the attitudes of the border inhabitants. Fourth, there is the influence which the boundary has upon the policies of the state, and in this connection it may often be difficult to separate the effects of the nature of the boundary from those of the nature of the state beyond the boundary. Each of these aspects is considered in greater detail.

A boundary is usually demarcated only when the separated authorities believe this to be necessary. Some of the most important internal boundaries, which decide where persons may vote, at what level rates will be levied and the schools which children must attend, are never marked on the ground, but are shown on maps hanging in municipal and local government offices. In some cases, for reasons of pride local authorities in major cities will indicate when travellers along main routes are entering or leaving them. On the other hand nearly all international boundaries are marked on the ground in some way, simply because most states feel it is desirable that their limits should be understood by their neighbours.

The boundary may be identified in the landscape by two sets of features. First, there is the indication of the boundary by means of markers, cut lines, fences and notices. Second, there are various constructions designed to allow the smooth application of state functions at or near the boundary. Many travellers will be familiar with customs posts located near barriers across main roads, and stations built on the boundary to allow passengers to be subjected to customs and immigration regulations. It should also be noted that international airports and seaports and coastal defences are types of border landscape.

Since nearly all international boundaries are demarcated in some way, it is possible to draw certain inferences from the nature of the demarcation about the nature of state functions and the relationship between the separated states. The following paragraphs indicate the type of conclusion which may be reached in the three most common situations, although the reader is reminded that boundaries tend to be unique.

If an international boundary is not demarcated there are three probable explanations. First, the states concerned may not feel that demarcation is necessary, or of high financial priority. Many of the international colonial boundaries were not demarcated because of the expense involved and the improved relations between the colonial powers. Second, boundaries may not be demarcated because the exact position of the boundary is disputed, due to some ambiguity in the definition of the boundary. This cause retarded the demarcation of many South American boundaries and currently continues to prevent any demarcation of the boundary between Somalia and Ethiopia. When a boundary is disputed, however, it will often be found that military and police installations are located in the border area in order to preserve rival claims. One obvious reason for not demarcating an international boundary may be found in the unfavourable nature of some environments. Where international boundaries lie within hot deserts or high mountain ranges demarcation is often regarded as unnecessary on the grounds of security and impossible on the grounds of finance. However, such views may change as mineral exploration raises the possibility of discovering worthwhile deposits in deserts, and improved military techniques and changed military power reduce the defensive value of mountain ranges. It seems likely that India will insist on boundary demarcation when its dispute with China is settled. Where a boundary is drawn within an unfavourable environment it will often be found that both the states establish their police and customs posts on the edge of the area. This means that the intervening area is not under direct and continuous control.

If the boundary is demarcated, two general situations can be distinguished. The first occurs when the demarcation is maintained, and the second when it is neglected.

Looking first at the case where the demarcation is maintained, two extreme conditions can be described which will limit a host of variations and combinations between.

At one end of the scale there are the boundaries between allies, such as Canada and the United States of America. Here the boundary vistas are carefully cut and the boundary monuments kept in good repair even on the more remote western borders. This is largely for reasons of administrative convenience, and not to restrict circulation. Structures to allow the application of state functions are located at the important recognised crossing points. Along such boundaries there is often an absence of permanent fortifications. At the opposite end of the scale there are those boundaries between unfriendly states where the boundary demarcation is maintained in order to prevent circulation and to simplify defence. The boundary in such cases is often marked by an obstacle such as a fence or a wall, and guard posts are located at regular intervals along the entire length. A strip of land adjacent to the boundary may be cleared to make observation easier and illegal boundary crossing more difficult. The civilian population is often evacuated from such a border. The crossing points on these boundaries are few and heavily guarded. These features may all be seen on some sections of the boundary between East and West Germany, especially in Berlin, and the land boundaries of Israel with its Arab neighbours.

Between these two extremes may be found a wide variety of boundary forms, and there may be significant variations along any boundary. Boundary form is also likely to vary with changing circumstances. The steady deterioration of relations between Ghana and Togoland in the 1960s resulted in clearer boundary demarcation and increased boundary supervision.

When a boundary has been demarcated and that demarcation has not been maintained, the political geographer may find this a useful pointer to changed political situations. In some cases colonial powers at the height of their competition carefully marked their boundaries, but once the period of competition gave way to a period of development, with its attendant concentration on internal affairs, the border areas were often neglected either for reasons of priority or to avoid incidents. Boundary vistas became overgrown, and people, animals and vegetation destroyed boundary pillars. The re-establishment of these boundaries by the independent successors to the colonial states often causes friction and gives rise to territorial disputes.

Both international and internal boundaries may mark changes in the landscape and economic activity which result from the separate areas being subject to different regulations. It follows, however, that the greatest variations occur between different countries, and will usually be more striking than the differences associated with internal boundaries. Since only a few studies have been made into this aspect of boundary research it seems worthwhile to record them, and to consider separately those related to internal and international boundaries.

Platt and Bucking-Spitta (1958) published an interesting descriptive account of the Dutch-German boundary, which passed through areas of agriculture, industry and mining. In examining agricultural landscapes and production in three different areas, Platt found no significant differences on opposite sides of the boundary. The three areas were the polder country near the North Sea, the moor-edge settlements of Bellingwolde and Wymeer, and the flood plain and diluvial terraces of the River Rhine. Not only were the areas used by farms of similar size, divided into similar field patterns producing approximately the same proportions of various crops, but the building styles were also similar on both sides. The textile industry north of the Rhine, including Enschede and Gronau, was originally established as an 'international industry' and its operation was unaffected before the First World War by the presence of the boundary. Since then the two areas have tended to become more national in character but there is still some movement of workers across the boundary. At the time of the study (1953) conditions were more satisfactory in Holland and there was accordingly a greater volume of movement of Germans into Holland than Dutch citizens into Germany. In the small coalfield around Kerkrade, Platt found no variations in distribution, method of production and output which could not be explained by the differing physical circumstances of the coal reserves on each side.

Platt then examined the political and economic organisation of the border areas, and again found that there were similar forms on both sides of the boundary. His conclusion was interesting, and seems to provide an important principle:

The preceding chapters have dealt with the characteristics of the border areas. Landscape and occupance have been found similar on opposite sides. The boundary is not natural and does not separate different uniform regions. It could be pushed east or west without changing the appearance of things in general on opposite sides. . . although the forms of areal organisation may be similar on opposite sides of the boundary the organisations themselves, the units of organisation, political, economic and social, as they have developed through years of human activity, are generally separate. A shift of the boundary in either direction disturbs the organisation in units small and large on both sides, and generally does damage which can only slowly if ever be repaired. (Platt and Bucking-Spitta, 1958, p.85)

Platt's conclusions indicate quite clearly that although the boundary separates areas with almost identical landscapes and systems of organisation there remain vital intangible differences of political attitude and social custom. These are aspects which a geographer finds difficult to measure, and about which only general ideas could be formulated even after a long residence in the borderlands.

This descriptive study was principally concerned with the present, unlike that made by Daveau (1959) which considered the Franco-Swiss borderland in the Jura over several centuries. This admirable study, which has not attracted the attention it deserves, shows clearly how the influence of the boundary on the borderlands will vary as political and geographical circumstances change. It would be surprising if this was not the case, but it is valuable to have such a clear demonstration. Daveau shows how the presence of the boundary has influenced the development of agriculture, forestry and industry since it was established.

The area considered lies west of Lake Neuchâtel, and the principal agricultural activity was the raising of stock and the preparation of dairy products, especially cheese. During the early eighteenth century there was a considerable measure of interpenetration of pasture lands, and Daveau calculated that Swiss farmers owned 400 hectares of French land while French farmers owned 1,000 hectares in Switzerland. The areas of greatest French colonisation were near les Verrieres and la Brevine, which carried a low density of Swiss. After the Reformation, many Swiss and French farmers sold their land across the boundary because of the rise of national consciousness, the complex regulations covering alien landownership, and the problem of maintaining the property when the countries were at war. During the nineteenth century further changes took place. There was a withdrawal of French population from the upper pastures of the French border and a concentration in the valleys. This coincided with a considerable increase in the Swiss herds, many of which were accommodated on leased French pastures. At the same time there was a greater concentration of beef and veal production at the expense of dairy products, which were now manufactured mainly in the valleys on both sides of the border.

The extension of Swiss control over French border areas was increased by the fall of the French franc compared with Swiss currency during the First World War. However, the threats of further falls in the value of the French franc encouraged Swiss farmers to lease land rather than buy it outright. They were in the fortunate position of being able to fatten the cattle cheaply in France and sell the meat at the higher Swiss rates in Switzerland. The French villages in the valleys do not benefit from the Swiss occupation of the uplands since the herdsmen generally bring all their provisions from Switzerland. Conventions of 1882 and 1938 allow free circulation of agricultural products within a zone ten kilometres wide on each side of the boundary. The actual wording of the relevant sections allows a number of interpretations, and variations are found between the arrangements in the Department of Doubs and the Canton of Vaud. Some landscape differences are noted where the boundary crosses a valley. One air photograph clearly shows the contrast at the boundary between the small strip fields of Amont in France and the summer pastures of Carroz in Switzerland, even though the physical character of the landscape on both sides is the same:

> In many forests of the mountains, the boundary between France and Switzerland is visibly marked by the misuse of our trees, and the traveller who remembers this fact will be able, without guide and without difficulty, to recognise the boundary in any place, and touch with certainty a Swiss fir tree with one hand and a French fir tree with the other. (Le Quinio, quoted in Daveau, 1959, p.386)

This quotation shows that even in the eighteenth century landscape differences could be noticed in respect of the exploitation of forests. Daveau shows that this situation exists today, although for different reasons. At first the forest was regarded as a useful buffer zone between the Swiss and French, and restrictions were imposed upon the cutting of wood. In the period before 1750 there were many cases of wood in French territory being illegally cut by Swiss citizens. In the post-1750 period the situation was reversed; French depredations in Swiss forests were the general rule and there were minor wars as the Swiss attempted to protect their territory. The conflicts eventually stopped as the areas became more densely populated and customs patrols became more active on each side. In 1882 under a boundary convention customs officers were given authority to pursue illegal wood-cutters across the boundary, and the duty-free transport of 15,000 tons of firewood was allowed within a zone ten kilometres wide on each side of the boundary. In 1938 this figure was reduced to about 9,000 tons.

Once, again as in the case of pasturage, the decline of the French franc in relation to the Swiss franc allowed Swiss citizens to gain an advantage. More and more forest in the French border has been bought by Swiss who have then realised quick profits by wholesale cutting and clearing, without any plans for reafforestation. The denuded lands are converted to pasture which is then sold or leased to Swiss cattle farmers. This practice produces striking landscape differences on opposite sides of the boundary. One air photograph, included by Daveau, shows how the forests on the French side of the boundary have been almost completely cleared while those on the Swiss side remain in a well-kept condition (Daveau, 1959, plate 11).

The analysis of farming and forestry in the borderland led Daveau to conclude that the economic boundary lies in Switzerland's favour, to the west of the political boundary. The reciprocity written into the border conventions is meaningless as long as the French franc stands at an unfavourable rate to the Swiss franc. This is a clear warning to geographers not to accept written guarantees in boundary treaties at face value; their application must be tested.

Daveau also examined the influence exerted by the boundary upon the watchmaking industry of the Franco-Swiss Jura. The industry began in Switzerland, and the first French factory was at Besançon. Before 1834 the French Government tried to protect the French industry from Swiss competition by high tariffs and the suppression of smuggling — which was a profitable occupation for French and Swiss citizens alike. In 1826 it was decreed that all French watchmakers must have their premises at least 7 kilometres from the boundary. The duty on Swiss watches was reduced after 1834 to 4 per cent *ad valorem* in 1836. This low rate did not make smuggling worthwhile and the activity declined rapidly, but by 1842 the smugglers realised that it was worthwhile to take French watches to Switzerland and then reimport them as Swiss watches. This flourishing trade continued for some time.

In the last years of the nineteenth century a tariff war between France and Switzerland resulted in a distinct rupture between the two industries. This helped certain sections of both industries. The Swiss apparently captured more of the market in small watches. In France certain workers who had specialised in making escapements could no longer export their product to Switzerland, and they turned to the manufacture of complete watches. Further, France began to deal directly with overseas markets which had previous been supplied by Swiss merchants who bought from French producers. We can see then that the regulations laid down by the governments affected the location of the industry on the French side and the traffic in watches, and caused variations in the type of production.

Kibulya (1967) studies the border landscape along the Congo-Uganda boundary between the Ruwenzori Mountains and Lake Albert. He describes sharp contrasts between the peripheral areas of the two countries which had their origin in colonial policies, and which have been maintained because the post-colonial governments have not significantly changed those colonial policies. The Ugandan side was characterised by a dispersed settlement pattern serviced by many adequate roads. There was a high population density resulting from a declining death rate consequent on improving medical services. Most of the land was farmed and coffee was the main cash crop. The Congolese borderland was characterised by a nucleated settlement pattern poorly serviced by badly-made roads. There was a comparatively low density of population resulting from a high rate of infant mortality off-setting the high birth rate. The Congolese farmers produced only subsistence crops from a small proportion of the area available. These differences are very interesting in view of the fact that the colonial boundary divided the Amba tribe when it was drawn through a uniform landscape. Kibulya found that Nyahuka in Uganda was the main trading centre for the whole borderland, and that while Ugandan currency circulated freely in the Congolese border, the Congolese franc had no currency in the Ugandan areas. When fieldwork is again possible along this border it will be interesting to discover whether the policies of President Amin's government have produced any changes in this borderland.

Reitsma (1971 and 1972) has shown how the agricultural policies of the United States and Canadian governments have encouraged the growth of distinct agricultural regions on opposite sides of the boundary as it passes through the plains west of the Great Lakes.

These studies by Platt, Daveau, Kibulya and Reitsma have shown that international boundaries may lie through identical cultural landscapes or mark significant changes in land-use and economic activity. However, they would all agree that even though the border landscape may be uniform, the two sides have a human distinctiveness which is difficult to measure, but which is nevertheless real to people living in the borderland. Daveau and Kibulya have shown how important it is for scholars to be aware of currency variations in explaining changes in the significance of the boundary over a long period. This view is confirmed by the experience of Sevrin (1949) who studies trans-boundary population movements on the Franco-Belgian borderland. In 1929 there were 10,219 Belgians working in the French borderland and this figure declined to 2,757 in 1946 as a result of the war and the attendant decline in the value of the franc. By 1947 the number had increased to 8,810 as there was an upsurge in textile production, and as measures were implemented to maintain the exchange value of the French franc.

It is possible that the recent study by Albrecht (1974) on the role of the Franco-German boundary in the evolution of the cultural landscape of the borderland centred on Strasbourg, will mark a major contribution and advance in boundary studies. It appears to be a meticulous piece of research which is well illustrated by maps, graphs, tables and photographs; unfortunately final assessment of this monograph will have to wait until a translation is available.

Ullman (1939), Nelson (1952), Rose (1955), Logan (1968) and Best (1971) have all written studies on the significance of internal boundaries as factors influencing the development of landscapes within a country.

Ullman's study of the eastern Rhode Island-Massachusetts boundary revealed that the boundary, which was accordant in situation but discordant in site, did influence the establishment of industries south of the Fall River. The industries were located in Rhode Island to gain tax concessions, but the tenements for the workers were located in Massachusetts, so that the workers could continue to enjoy the superior social and cultural amenities offered by that State. It was noticed that the boundary became zonal in some respects because water, gas and electricity services were common to sections of both States, and because some private properties spanned the boundary.

Nelson (1952) examined the boundaries of the Vernon area of California, to assess their contribution to an understanding 'of the areal distribution and functioning association' of various elements of the urban landscape. He plotted the distribution of residential, commercial, public, industrial and transport land-use, and found that the boundary of Vernon coincided with significant landscape differences. There was a remarkable concentration of land devoted to industry and transport within Vernon, almost to the complete exclusion of the other three categories. It also emerged that other boundaries in the Vernon area did not coincide with similar distinctions in land-use. This suggests that Nelson was fortunate in his selection of Vernon as a case study, and that the technique he used will be valuable only in a few instances. While it may be true that a simple land-use analysis will rarely show significant correlations with political boundaries, if Nelson's technique is carried a stage further and quality of land-use is studied, it should have much wider application. For example, instead of distinguishing residential and other types of land-use, it will be necessary to examine the residential category in greater detail, collecting information about house-types and rateable values. In a cosmopolitan city it may be of significance to record the nationality of house occupants or owners.

A further technique useful in such studies has been suggested by Mackay (1958), who has applied Dodd's interactance hypothesis to boundaries. By comparing the value of actual and computed interactance between cities or areas separated by a political boundary, Mackay suggests that it will be possible to obtain a measure of boundary interference. This would be useful in assessing the significance of individual boundaries, and in comparing the significance of two or more boundaries. These studies would be limited to areas for which detailed statistics are available, and Mackay warns that factors other than the boundary may produce differences between computed and actual interactance. It would also seem worthwhile to investigate the extent to which the model prepared by Dodd is applicable to boundary studies in areas dissimilar to North America in political, economic and social development.

Minghi (1963) has correctly drawn attention to the comparative neglect of Losch's work (1954) on the distortion which boundaries might produce in economic patterns. In view of the laudable desire of many geographers to introduce a greater measure of mathematical precision into political geography it is surprising that this subject has not attracted more attention.

The studies reviewed in this section suggest that internal boundaries do influence the development of the cultural landscapes in many ways, and that the analysis of these relationships is a worthwhile, though neglected, aspect of political geography, which could provide valuable information for those interested in economic and urban geography. The influence of the internal boundaries is less spectacular than that of international boundaries, and will be revealed only by careful research. Before leaving this subject it is necessary to counsel care in the use of statistics in demonstrating the influence of the boundary upon the cultural landscape. Federal boundaries always form the basic framework for statistical divisions, which may also coincide with some sections of internal boundaries. It is therefore not surprising that in many cases the political boundary will appear to separate areas with different population densities and *per capita* agricultural outputs. Such differences may only be apparent, and field examination may show the differences in population density and intensity of activity do not coincide with the political boundary.

It was suggested in the introduction to this chapter that a boundary may exert some influence upon the attitudes of persons living in the borderland and on the policies of states separated by the boundary. The studies have not yet been made which would justify or reject this concept, and accordingly the following views must be regarded as tentative.

If the influence of the boundary upon the attitudes of border dwellers is examined first, three points can be made. First, no one can doubt that 'frontiersman' denotes a person with a particular kind of philosophy and character: this point was most convincingly made by Turner and has been repeated by others such as Kristoff (1959). Since any international borderland bears some relationship to a frontier, we can expect the boundary to have some measure of influence. The influence is likely to be exerted through the opportunities which the presence of the boundary offers for economic gain, the inconveniences presented by the boundary to everyday living, and a greater awareness of the security needs of the state. One would expect the Belgians living on the German border to have a different awareness of the need for military preparedness from the Belgians living in the interior of the country and along the French border. The differences between the security viewpoints of the border and core dwellers is likely to be greater in countries larger than Belgium. The great difficulty is to measure the extent to which the attitude of borderland dwellers is distinctively influenced by the presence of the boundary. In some cases the borderland may give support to a specific political party which will express clear views on questions of tariffs, and boundary and security arrangements. In other cases referenda relating to the boundary may be informative. This is obviously true when the referenda concern the movement of a boundary, as some did in Europe after World War I, but is also true when they concern altering the functions of the boundary, as in the Australian referendum on the formation of a federation.

Logan (1968) examined the influence of the boundary on the attitude of border dwellers to the proposed federation. Two views are held by historians on this matter. Parker (1949) holds the opinion that most voters judged federation in terms of regional economic interest:

Federation by establishing a customs union, and perhaps by setting limits to railway competition and ensuring unhampered transport on the Murray system which flows through three colonies, is inevitably attractive to border residents and repulsive to the urban interests which rely on discriminatory legislation in order to participate in an otherwise uneconomic commerce. (Parker, 1949, p.1)

Blainey (1949) on the other hand believes that there is a considerable variation within the voting patterns of the borderlands, suggesting that this influence is not uniform. When the referendum statistics were plotted on a map the result tended to support Parker's concept. In southwestern Victoria the border constituencies of Lowan, Normanby and Portland recorded a higher proportion of affirmative votes than the state average (82 per cent) and the metropolitan vote (77 per cent). In the Victoria and Albert constituencies of southeastern South Australia 78 per cent of the voters were in favour of federation compared with the state average of 67 per cent and the metropolitan figure of 55 per cent. While proximity to the boundary is not the only factor involved, the figures are suggestive. Neglect of the more remote state areas by the metropolitan administrations may also have been responsible for the larger vote. There were variations within the border however, and Blainey's position can be understood. Some electorates which lay close to the boundary, but which had no trans-boundary contacts, returned lower percentages of affirmative votes. Port Macdonnell, which lies only fifteen miles within South Australia, is an example of this type of electorate.

It is difficult to establish beyond doubt that the nature of a particular boundary has influenced state policies, because it is neither easy, nor necessarily profitable, to distinguish the influence of the boundary from the influence of the state with which the boundary is drawn. For example, since 1967, farmers along Israel's borders have been discouraged from growing grain crops which can be burned, and fruit crops which will spoil if not harvested at exactly the right time, because of the damage and interference which enemy action might cause. Instead they cultivate crops, such as vegetables, which are not so easily destroyed by enemy action, and which can be harvested over a period of weeks. This policy is directly related to the hostility of some neighbouring states, but there are sections of the boundary where such enemy action is easier for attacks to be launched. It would not be very useful to attempt to separate these two intertwined strands in any analysis of the border.

There are two possible cases where policies may have been directly related to the nature of the boundary. In the second half of 1963 the Australian Government began to demarcate more clearly the boundary separating their New Guinea territories from West Irian. This policy probably resulted partly from the unsatisfactory condition of this longitudinal boundary, and also from the territorial friction between Indonesia and Malaysia. Had the Dutch remained in control of West Irian it is unlikely that it would have been considered worthwhile spending funds on boundary demarcation. Second, there is the example of India, which in the years following independence neglected her apparently secure Himalayan border in order to concentrate upon the development of the remainder of the country and the security of her Pakistan border. Even the re-establishment of Chinese influence in Tibet did not alter this policy, which was only ended when the Chinese allegedly invaded Indian territory in the Himalayas. Apart from examples of inferences of this kind, it seems likely that more concrete examples will have to be derived from historical studies in political geography using first-hand material in archives.

Conclusion

The range of examples provided in this chapter indicates that geographers are aware of the influence which boundaries may exert upon the development of cultural landscapes, and that this is a field which does not seem to attract the attention of other scholars, although economists may wish to pursue the ideas of Losch and it would be understandable if historians devote more attention to this subject. In most cases the studies of border landscapes were incidental to larger studies dealing with the evolution of the boundary and aimed at understanding its problems. This is to be commended rather than criticised, because students of boundary evolution and problems should always be aware of, and record, the changes which the presence of the boundary causes in the landscape.

References

Albrecht, V., 1974, *Der Einfluss der deutschen-französischen Grenze auf die Gestaltung der Kulturlandschaft im Südlichen Oberrheingebiet* (The Influence of the Franco-German Boundary on the Evolution of the Cultural Landscape of the Southern Upper-Rhine Region), Freiburger Geographische Hefte, 14, Freiburg

Best, A.C.G., 1971, 'South Africa's Border Industries: The Tswana Example', *Annals*, Association of American Geographers, 61, pp.329-43

Blainey, G., 1949, The role of Economic Interests in Australian Federation: A reply to Professor Parker', *Historical Studies of Australia and New Zealand*, 13, pp.224-37

Daveau, S., 1959, *Les régions frontalières de la montagne Jurassienne*, Paris

House, J.W., 1959, 'The Franco-Italian Boundary in the Alpes-Maritimes', *Transactions*, Institute of British Geographers, 26, pp.107-31

Kibulya, H.M., 1967, 'Geographic Contrasts on the Bwamba-Congo Border' in Kibulya, H.M. and Langlands, B.W., *The Political Geography of the Uganda-Congo Boundary*, Occasional Paper No.6, Makerere University, Kampala

Kristoff, L.A.D., 1959, 'The nature of Frontiers and Boundaries', *Annals*, Association of American Geographers, 49, pp.269-82

Logan, W.S., 1968, 'The Changing Landscape Significance of the Victoria-South Australia Boundary', *Annals*, Association of American Geographers, 58, pp.128-54

Losch, A., 1954, *The Economics of Location*, translated from 2nd revised edition by W.B. Woglom, with the assistance of W.F. Stolpter, New Haven

Mackay, J.R., 1958, 'The Interactance Hypothesis and Boundaries in Canada: A Preliminary Study', *Canadian Geographer, 11*, pp.1-8

Minghi, J.V., 1963, 'Boundary Studies in Political Geography', *Annals*, Association of American Geographers, 53, pp.407-28

Nelson, H.J., 1952, 'The Vernon Area of California – A Study of the Political Factor in Urban Geography', *Annals*, Association of American Geographers, 42, pp.177-91

Parker, R.S., 1949, 'Australian Federation: The Influence of Economic Interests and Political Pressures', *Historical Studies of Australia and New Zealand*, 13, pp.1-24

Platt, R.S. (assisted by Paula Bucking-Spitta), 1958, *A Geographical Study of the Dutch-German Border*, Munster Westfalen

Reitsma, H.J., 1971, 'Crop and Livestock Production in the Vicinity of the United States-Canada Border', *Professional Geographer*, 23, pp.216-23

————., 1972, 'Areal Differentiation along the United States-Canada Border', *Tijdschrift voor Economische en Sociale Geografie*, 63, pp.2-10

Rose, A.J., 1955, 'The Border Zone between Queensland and New South Wales', *Australian Geographer*, 6, pp.3-18

Sevrin, R., 1949, 'Les échanges de population à la frontière entre la France et la Tournaisis', *Annales de Géographie*, 58, pp.237-44

Ullman, E.L., 1939, 'The Eastern Rhode Island-Massachusetts Boundary Zone', *Annals*, Association of American Geographers, 29, pp.291-302

INDEX